Beyond Beliefs

A GUIDE to IMPROVING RELATIONSHIPS
and COMMUNICATION for VEGANS,
VEGETARIANS, and MEAT EATERS

MELANIE JOY, PhD

Foreword by KATHY FRESTON

Praise for *Beyond Beliefs*

"Melanie Joy thinks clearly, writes exquisitely, and persuades truthfully. *Beyond Beliefs* gently melts the bars of the cages which we erect around our beliefs. It deserves a place in every vegan library and on the reading list of every non-vegan."

—PHILIP WOLLEN, former vice president of Citibank and founder of Winsome Constance Kindness

"From the minute you meet Melanie Joy, it becomes clear that she is a catalyst for connecting you with your deepest levels of compassion and common sense. Instantly you wish you could be at least a fraction as articulate as she is. Luckily, you now have in your hands a guide to help you navigate distances between you and the others in your life, the world, and yourself. *Beyond Beliefs* will leave you feeling clearer, more connected, confident, and even—though many difficult issues are addressed—happier. Highly recommended for anyone who wants to be a more mindful agent for bringing the light of conscious living to everything from personal relationships to the predominant culture in which we live."

—LANI MUELRATH, author of *The Mindful Vegan: A 30-Day Plan for Finding Health, Balance, Peace, and Happiness*

"In this insightful and engaging book, Melanie Joy offers wisdom, comfort, and advice for any vegan or vegetarian who's ever felt misunderstood by meat eaters and for any meat eater who's ever felt confounded by vegans or vegetarians. This book can show you the way beyond your beliefs, so you can relate and communicate with clarity and compassion. I highly recommend it!"

—LISA BLOOM, civil rights attorney at The Bloom Firm

"Melanie Joy is fundamentally shifting the way we view our relationship with others and ourselves, making the world a better and more compassionate place in the process."

—NATHAN RUNKLE, Founder of Mercy For Animals

"Dr. Melanie Joy addresses an important subject with keen insight and lucid thought."

—GLEN MERZER, author of *Off the Reservation*

"Melanie Joy hit the nail on the head! This is the book all vegans need, to gain perspective, alleviate compassion fatigue, and live healthy lives with a purpose!"

—SHANNON KEITH, Esq., president and founder of ARME and Beagle Freedom Project

"As a member of a veg/non-veg marriage, I am grateful for Melanie Joy's wisdom about living with a partner's choices while honoring my own integrity. *Beyond Beliefs* is essential reading for anyone who wants mealtime to be a source of nourishment—physical, spiritual, and social."

—LINDA RIEBEL, PhD, licensed psychologist and faculty, Saybrook Graduate School

"Navigating relationships can be hard, particularly for new vegans trying to figure out how to relate to their non-vegan friends and family. Dr. Joy's book provides excellent guidance to help with these issues and provides vegans and others with the tools they need for social success."

—DAVE SIMON, Esq., author of *Meatonomics*

"Melanie Joy's work contains some of the very best thinking ever on the psychology of eating and provides the first really robust, consistent, deep analysis of some of our most critical food beliefs. In Beyond Beliefs, Joy has again made a major achievement. This book is, please excuse me, a joy to read. I cannot imagine anyone reading this without an "aha" moment, and one for the good."

—JEFFREY MOUSSAIEFF MASSON, PhD, author of *When Elephants Weep* and other books

"This book can help people with any food beliefs significantly improve their relationships and communication. And if you're vegan (or vegetarian), this book will also help you better understand yourself and be a much more effective ambassador for the cause."

—COLLEEN PATRICK-GOUDREAU, author of *The 30-Day Vegan Challenge* and other books

Printed in the United States of America
First Printing, 2017

ISBN 978-1-944903-30-5

10 9 8 7 6 5 4 3 2 1

Roundtree Press
149 Kentucky Street, Suite 7
Petaluma, CA 94952
www.roundtreepress.com

www.carnism.org

Contents

For the vegans and vegetarians whose caring and commitment is a gift to the planet; I hope this book gives back to you some of what you give to the world. And for those who stand with you as allies.

And for my husband, Sebastian Joy—my admired colleague, my dear friend, and the love of my life.

Acknowledgments

I am deeply grateful for the support of the many people who made writing this book possible. I want to thank Kathy Freston for getting me to even consider writing it in the first place, and then for her tireless support along the way. I thank my staff at Beyond Carnism, for holding down the fort so I could focus on writing. I am especially grateful to Nina Hengl, who was with me every step of the sometimes arduous process, sharing her wisdom and encouragement; Beth Redwood, who literally worked day and night to create graphics and create a unique cover image; Dawn Moncrief for her much-needed analysis that changed the course of my writing process; Brett Thompson for stepping in and making sure the book made it out into the world; Flavia D'Erasmo, for saving the day and formatting the manuscript; Helen Harwatt for taking the time to review the manuscript and for helping me come up with a much better subtitle; and Robin Flynn for the time and energy she invested in creating a support structure for my work. I also thank staff members Jeff Mannes and Jens Tuider for their impressive commitment and support. I thank Gero Schomaker, who—despite having a crazy busy schedule—made the time to meet with me over many months to discuss and help hone my ideas and to develop the concepts for graphics, and for being a good friend. I thank my editor, Joyce Hildebrand, who went above and beyond for this project; Jim Greenbaum, for helping provide the foundation from which much of my work has sprung; my former agent, Patti Breitman, for advocating for me yet again so I could have the rights to make this book as widely accessible as possible; Susan Solomon, for her steadfast wisdom and guidance and friendship; and Lucie Berreby, for helping me bring my work more fully into the world. I am incredibly grateful for Louise Pfeiffer and Markus Woltjer, who volunteered their time and energy to proofread and format the manuscript; and to Stefanie Sluschny, Carolyn Zaikowski, Nana Charléne Spiekermann, Tobias Leenaert, Wendy Aigner, Alex Higson, Jude Berman, and Teja Watson. Finally, this book would not have been possible without the support of my husband, Sebastian Joy, who was beside me every baby step of the way—helping hone my ideas, keeping me inspired, taking care of my practical needs, and making sure I kept laughing.

Foreword

BY KATHY FRESTON

It occurs to me as I write this foreword that I don't know what my life would be like had I not met Melanie Joy at a conference some six years ago and become close friends with her. I had known her brilliant work on the psychology of carnism and admired her strategic way of thinking about the culture of eating animals. She took a burgeoning social justice movement and packaged it into a psychologically compelling conversation. Why, she asked, do we love dogs, eat pigs, and wear cows? And with that question, Melanie set forth a map of critical thinking that connects the dots on why we cherish some animals but eat others. She made so much sense, taking the time to speak into the reader's rationale, all the while respecting their ability to find their way into a more conscientious way of eating. Melanie was clearly a formidable intellectual and had a thorough grasp on human psychology; that much I knew.

What I didn't realize when I met Melanie on that memorable day, was how much I would grow to lean on her keen ability to see inside my confused heart and help me put words to my struggles. At the time, I was married to a man I had deeply loved for many years, but had increasingly grown apart from. When my husband and I met, I ate steak and chicken with abandon, and proudly thought of myself as an All American Meat Eater, so when I began to see the world—animal foods—differently, we drifted. It wasn't anyone's fault, but we'd just lost the ability to see the world through each other's eyes.

For someone who found comfort in words and frank expression—I was a writer, after all—I suddenly didn't know what I had the right to feel or even how to articulate what was going on inside of me. It seemed that the more I realized my calling in life was about "conscious eating," the greater the gap was between periods of connectedness in my marriage. There were other issues, of course, as there are issues in every marriage. But the big one, the sadly insurmountable one, was that my husband and I had developed very different interests and philosophies, and too much disconnect over too many years had launched us into parallel lives. After a long while of anguish and arguing, we decided to divorce.

Toward the end of this period in my life, I met Melanie at that fateful conference, and she became my sage advisor. But more than that, she explained my heart to me. She gave me the words to help me express myself. And to be clear here, it was not only that she shepherded me to the realization that I deserved to have my feelings, whatever they were; she also gently led me to see where I needed to grow and mature. She never said this was her goal, of course, but this is what she did: she helped me evolve as a human being, skillfully guiding me to be more respectful and loving, more patient and humble, and more authentic in relationships of all kinds. Melanie has that rare gift of encouraging you to speak truth to power while at the same time helping you to course correct when you've missed the mark.

And this program of relentlessly examining the way you think and converse naturally leads to better relationships. More connection, more depth, more full-bodied love.

In the ensuing years since my divorce, I have made ever-stronger friendships and found love again. In case you were wondering, my partner is not vegan (although he's leaned in a lot and is "veganish") and only a handful of my friends are vegan. So, just because my veganism is foundational for me doesn't mean I can only be around other vegans. To the contrary, I think being closely involved with people who think differently than me is invigorating. It teaches me to be clear, to remain open, and to constantly stay curious. And it makes me love someone even more when one of us takes steps to better understand the other, to close the gap between "what I believe" and "what you believe." Love, it seems, is beyond "beliefs."

I have been the lucky recipient of Melanie's guidance throughout our friendship. And in that same spirit of illumination, this is Melanie's gift to you in the pages you're about to read: she will help you to understand yourself, to untangle the knotted emotions that come with believing in something fiercely while loving someone who doesn't think exactly like you do. You will come to know yourself more intimately and to speak more articulately; and in so doing, you will be better able to navigate your relationships—and your whole life, really—with more grace and wisdom. Be ready; this is not always an easy path. In a world where polarity seems to be calling out to us from every medium, and tribalism threatens to make us ever more separate from each other, this book will, instead, challenge you to build bridges.

As the poet Rumi eloquently wrote over 800 years ago,

Out beyond ideas of wrongdoing
and rightdoing there is a field.
I'll meet you there.

That field is love. That field is connection. And Melanie Joy is lighting the way to it.

—Kathy Freston, 2017

Chapter 1

VEGANS, VEGETARIANS, AND MEAT
EATERS IN RELATIONSHIPS: THE
PROBLEM AND THE PROMISE

By all accounts, it was a feast to be envied. The table was set with resplendent, festive wares—gold and silver cutlery, gleaming china, bouquets of winter boughs and berries—and it was dusted with glitter. The room was toasty from the heat of so many bodies and an oven that had been working overtime, and rich aromas hung in the air. Laughter and the clinking of silverware on porcelain filled the silence like the warmth and scents filled the space, creating a cozy, safe atmosphere.

But Maria was feeling anything but safe. She had that familiar tightness in her chest, like a vise grip around her heart, a feeling of dread. Up until two years ago, she looked forward to these family gatherings, to the comforting security and connection she always felt. She loved the constant joking that was a hallmark of her family's conversations and her parents' home-cooked meals, as well as seeing her young nieces and nephews. And she loved the fact that Jacob, her husband of nearly a decade, got along with everyone so well. Now, though, all that had changed.

Maria sat at the table feeling utterly alone. The conversation washed over her like waves against the shore, background noise. She had started tuning out after a brief exchange with her mother in the kitchen. Maria had asked if the butter in the mashed potatoes could be replaced with margarine, so that she, a vegan, could eat them, and her mother had retorted that she was being unfair by imposing her beliefs on everyone else who had come to enjoy a traditional meal.

Then, over dinner, the usual commentary about the food began—discussions of the best ways to cook the turkey, which part of the bird was most tender, how the sausage for the stuffing came from a new, local butchery that specialized in organic, humane meat. "So that means Maria can eat it, right?" chimed in her younger brother, ever the family clown. At the sound of her name, Maria's ears perked up. "Right, Sis? I mean, if the pig was happy to be turned into sausage, then it's only fair to eat it. It's what the pig would want—if *I* tasted so good, I'd sure want someone to eat *me*!" And at that, everyone burst into laughter, including Jacob, who had always been a fan of the family's indelicate humor.

Maria's dread turned to rage. The entire evening, she'd been fighting to keep the graphic videos of animal slaughter she'd witnessed out of her mind, and it took all her energy to keep those images at bay. When she looked at the turkey, stuffing, and buttery mashed potatoes on the table, she no longer saw food, as she once had. Instead, she saw carcasses, excretions, suffering. She saw what her family would have seen if the foods had been made from dogs and cats. And she saw the people she had once felt the most connected to, the safest with, putting these products of torment into their mouths as though nothing at all were wrong—and treating her like *she* was the crazy one. On top of all that, they knew she was vegan, that she was disturbed and disgusted by the food, and yet they still chatted about it as if she wasn't even there. Worse, they made jokes at her expense, laughing at comments that invalidated and ridiculed her deepest convictions.

But she bit her tongue, as always. She didn't know what to say that wouldn't make her look like the "hysteric," the "extremist," which was how her family saw her. If she pointed out that the jokes weren't funny, she'd be told that she had no sense of humor, that she needed to lighten up. If she forced herself to laugh along with the others, she'd be betraying her values, reinforcing the very attitudes that support eating animals. Maria felt she was being ridiculed with no chance to stand up for herself, and she felt humiliated.

Most of all, Maria didn't want to do anything to let the animals down. As their ambassador, as The Vegan at the table, she felt it was up to her to maintain a positive image so as not to reduce the chances that the others might one day consider becoming vegan, and she didn't want to reinforce the negative stereotypes of vegans as "overly emotional" or "radical." So although she was wilting inside, she hid her shame. And she sat in helpless silence, fighting back tears of frustration, confusion, and despair, forcing herself to accept that this was just the way her family was, the way the world was, when it came to veganism. She withdrew deeper inside herself, disconnecting further from those around her.

But although Maria had resigned herself to the fact that she'd lost her connection with her family, she simply couldn't tolerate feeling disconnected from Jacob. Yes, Jacob supported her veganism in many ways, agreeing to keep a vegan house and not ordering meat when it was only the two of them out to dinner. But he just didn't get it. He tolerated her veganism like someone might tolerate a hobby they didn't really understand or care about. And when he had chimed in on the dinner conversation, complimenting her father on the flavor of the meat and then laughing along with her brother, she felt betrayed, abandoned, and invisible to the most important person in her life.

Maria found herself wondering—not for the first time—if Jacob was the right person for her. If they had such different values, maybe she would never be able to feel truly connected with him. How could she respect someone who ate innocent animals simply because he liked the way they tasted? And how could she really be herself with someone who didn't see some of the deepest parts of her?

By the time they were in the car on the way home, Maria had become almost numb. Feeling exhausted and overwhelmed, and unable to articulate why she felt so betrayed, she simply shut down. Picking up on her coldness, Jacob asked her what was wrong. Maria answered with an icy "Nothing," shocked that he should have to ask.

Now it was Jacob's turn to feel distressed. He realized that Maria's withdrawal had something to do with having been around meat, but he wasn't sure exactly what part of the dinner had upset her so much. It wasn't like she hadn't known there would be meat on the table. And unlike previous family feasts, there had been plenty of vegan food for her, and he had even helped her prepare a vegan dish, which everyone had raved about. So it wasn't that she'd had nothing to eat. And he'd eaten mostly vegan this time, too, even though they had an agreement that he could eat non-vegan foods out of the house. So what was wrong?

Jacob felt oddly guilty, like he'd done something bad that he couldn't quite put his finger on. This feeling was familiar to him; he'd felt it often around Maria since she had become vegan. It seemed like no matter how far he stretched to accommodate her new lifestyle, it was never enough. Two years ago, he was eating meat for breakfast, lunch, and dinner. Now, he almost never ate any animal foods. And still, she was always on edge about the issue; even when she didn't say anything, he could tell she was disappointed in him for not being vegan like she was.

Jacob wondered if maybe Maria was no longer able to tolerate being around meat, if her growing sensitivity had led her to draw yet another ethical line. Each time he thought she'd gone as far down the vegan road as she was going to, she'd come up with a new need, a new issue she could no longer endure. First she stopped eating meat (and eggs and dairy). Then she refused to cook it. Now, no animal foods were even brought into the house. And through all the changes, Jacob had been a good sport. Despite some pushback on his part, he'd eventually gone along with Maria's requests. He wanted to keep her happy, and to some extent, he agreed that it was better to eat less animal foods.

But now Jacob found himself revisiting his fear of the slippery slope. Feeling the familiar knot in his stomach, he wondered just how far Maria's veganism would go—how far away from him it would take her. Would she grow into a person he was no longer compatible with? Would she eventually have a need, a lifestyle, that he wouldn't be able to live with? Or would *she* ultimately reject *him*, judging him as not ethical enough for her?

Jacob just wanted things to be the way they had been before Maria became vegan, when every meal wasn't a struggle. Sure, they'd had their problems, but don't all couples? They would sometimes get into heated debates over their different ideas about what now seemed like trivial issues, such as whether to live in the city or the suburbs, and how organized and prepared they should be when they made plans. And even though they would sometimes say hurtful things to each other, these arguments usually just faded away; eventually, one or both would tire of fighting and give up pushing for what they wanted. But the tension around Maria's veganism and Jacob's meat eating never seemed to wane. If anything, it was getting worse.

With a mix of anger, confusion, and worry, Jacob glanced over at his wife, who sat with tight lips looking out the window, staring at nothing, utterly withdrawn. Not knowing how to make things right and resenting Maria for putting her beliefs before their marriage, Jacob also withdrew. Sitting side by side, the couple drove home in stony silence, both feeling misunderstood, unappreciated, insecure, and disconnected. And both wondered if they'd ever find their way back to one another in the face of what seemed to be an irreconcilable difference between them.

THE HIDDEN COST OF VEGANISM: RELATIONSHIP BREAKDOWN

Maria and Jacob are not alone. For many vegans, the decision to stop consuming animals is one of the most empowering choices of their lives. And yet this decision often comes at a price—the disruption of relationships. This hidden cost of becoming vegan is often deeply painful, demoralizing, and shocking, as a vegan may suddenly find themselves having to deal with family and friends who react defensively to their new lifestyle, a lifestyle based on values that the vegan thought were shared by the others in their lives. And non-vegans, too, suffer from such disruptive dynamics.

Fortunately, relationship breakdown is not inevitable, nor is it irreversible. In fact, becoming vegan is an opportunity to strengthen connections and improve the health of relationships. Managing some of the challenges of "veg/non-veg" relationships requires us to do the hard, yet rewarding, work of becoming more self-aware, more emotionally mature—work we might not be motivated to do if our relationships were following a simpler course.

What Maria and Jacob don't realize is that Maria's veganism is not the cause of their unhappiness and distance. The problem is simply that they, like most people, have never learned the basic principles and skills for creating a secure, connected relationship, including how to communicate about their different beliefs and needs. And on top of not having a strong foundation from which to navigate the inevitable challenges that come with being in any relationship, Maria and Jacob are facing the special challenges that veg/non-veg relationships bring. Most notable among these is a mentality, or way of thinking, that causes each person to have inaccurate perceptions of themselves and each other.

The good news for Maria and Jacob and all people in veg/non-veg relationships—whether with family, friends, colleagues, or a romantic partner—is that there is a way out of these painful dynamics. Once you understand how to keep your relationships healthy and strong and you learn to spot the mentality that hijacks your perceptions, you can significantly improve your relationships, and your life.

THE RELATIONAL IMMUNE SYSTEM: KEEPING RELATIONSHIPS HEALTHY AND STRONG

Healthy relationships are like healthy bodies: they thrive when their immune system is stronger than the germs they are exposed to. The formula, then, for creating a healthy relationship is twofold: keep the relationship's immune system strong and know how to identify and treat the germs that threaten it.

Increasing Resilience and Recognizing Germs

A strong relational immune system is resilient. *Resilience* is the ability to withstand and bounce back from stress. In relationships, resilience is made up of two main features: *security* and *connection*. The more secure and connected a relationship is, the stronger—or more resilient—it is. When a relationship is resilient, it's better able to withstand the germs, or external stressors (intruders), it's exposed to, just as a resilient body is less likely to get sick when it's exposed to germs. If we're exposed to a germ, physical or relational, that's strong enough, our immune system can become depleted trying to fight it. We can end up weakened or sick, and we (or our relationship) may even die.

There are countless germs that can threaten the security and connection of a relationship, including financial problems, addiction, and the loss of a job. And one type of germ that we may be exposed to is especially dangerous. Not only does it target the vital organs of our relationship, affecting the very way we think of and relate to one another, but it is also extremely difficult to detect, and therefore to treat, because it's epidemic. Its symptoms are so widespread that we think of them as normal behaviors rather than as pathological ways of relating. Imagine if everyone in the world had chronic bronchitis. We would assume that coughing and fatigue were simply a normal part of the human condition and would fail to identify and treat the illness we all carried. And when certain people started to get well, their constant exposure to other sick people would make it difficult for them to stay healthy.

In veg/non-veg relationships, this germ is a psychological intruder, a way of thinking that causes us to disconnect from each other and also from ourselves and the world. This intruder is called *carnism*, and it is the invisible belief system, or ideology, that conditions us to think and feel certain ways about eating or not eating animals, as well as about vegans and non-vegans. Carnism can undermine the well-being of otherwise secure and connected relationships if it remains undetected.

Relationship DNA: The Building Blocks of Resilience

The principles and practices for creating a resilient relationship apply to all relationships, from those that last only a few moments to those that are closest and most intimate. They also apply to our relationship with ourselves. So our daily life, our minute-to-minute experience, is like a training ground on which we can learn to become more resilient, to grow and evolve.

Interactions are the building blocks of relationships. Every time we interact with someone, we are relating to that person: a relationship is essentially a series of *dynamic interactions*—living interactions—among the people in it. (Sometimes dynamic interactions are referred to simply as "dynamics.") And we are interacting pretty much all the time—with the cashier at the grocery store, with the woman sitting beside us on the bus, with our life partner, and even with ourselves. We are always in a relationship, in one way or another.

Because a relationship is a series of interactions, each interaction offers us the opportunity to interrupt a pattern of insecure, disconnecting relating (a *dysfunction*) and to practice secure, connecting relating. In other words, at any moment we can choose to change the way we relate and improve the direction in which our relationship is heading.

Once we have learned to recognize the elements of an insecure, disconnecting interaction and have developed the skills to create a resilient one, we can better prevent problems in our relationships and can quickly identify and effectively manage problems when they do arise. And the more we practice resilient interactions, the better we get at doing so and the more secure and connected our relationships, and our lives, become. With a secure, connected foundation beneath us, we can approach our ideological differences in a way that deepens, rather than weakens, our relationship.

THE RELATIONSHIP BENEATH THE BELIEFS

When we commit to developing relational resilience, we naturally shift our focus from debating our differences to deepening our connection. One of the reasons so many people in relationships get stuck in ongoing conflict is because they focus on the *content* rather than the *process* of whatever it is that's causing disagreement. In other words, they focus on the "what," on the subject of, for example, different beliefs or needs, rather than the "how," the way they approach and communicate about such differences.

Many people in veg/non-veg relationships end up debating the ethics of eating animals or arguing about the kinds of compromises each person is expected to make. Such an approach is likely to only cause more problems if the process of the relationship—the way people are relating to one another—is not attended to first. Beneath each person's beliefs is a relationship between people, and it is this deeper level, the level of relationship, that holds the key to navigating differences.

Sometimes, veg/non-veg interactions become toxic not because of the differences in beliefs about eating or not eating animals but because of the underlying dysfunction in the relationship. Veganism can act as a lightning rod for other problems that are already present, becoming an excuse to argue about, for example, whose way of life is more appropriate, what kind of image the family presents to the outside world, how partners should prioritize each of their personal needs, and so on.

Attending to the relationship beneath our beliefs can transform our experience, whether we are a vegan or a non-vegan. Attending to our relationship does not mean we choose our relationship *over* our beliefs. It means that we create a relationship that has space for our beliefs, so that our different beliefs don't lead to decreased security and connection. It means that, despite our differences, we become allies.

Becoming Allies

An ally is a supporter of another (or others) who is in some way different from themselves. When we are an ally, we understand and appreciate the other's world—their perspectives, values, and beliefs. We respect and stand by the other, especially in the face of adversity, when they need us most.

Developing an understanding of and appreciation for one another is central to navigating all kinds of differences. And it is only possible to have a secure, connected relationship when each person is committed to allyship.

Ideally, the only time we would not commit to allyship is when being an ally means violating our integrity—when we would have to support a way of thinking or behaving that is against our core values or that causes us to feel unsafe. For example, allyship would not work between a member of a white supremacist group and his sister, who believes racism is unethical.

Allyship and Veg/Non-veg Relationships

When it comes to veg/non-veg relationships, allyship is key. It is especially important for the non-vegan to become an ally to the vegan, because vegans are members of a non-dominant (minority) social group, as are women, people of color, and so on. Of course, the experience of individuals in different non-dominant groups is unique: the experience of a person of color, for example, is in many ways very different from that of a white vegan, with the person of color facing far more serious forms of prejudice and discrimination. But there is at least one important similarity among members of non-dominant groups: they live in a world in which their experience is largely misunderstood, disrespected, and invalidated. So if veg/non-veg relationships are to be healthy and sustainable, it is essential for non-vegans to become supporters of the vegans in their lives, in large part because vegans' beliefs, feelings, and needs are not supported by the rest of the culture.

Vegans, too, can practice some degree of allyship toward the non-vegans in their lives, even though vegans see eating animals as a violation of vegan values and often feel emotionally unsafe when exposed to the consumption of animals. Although vegans are not supporters of the behavior of eating animals and shouldn't expose themselves to anything that makes them feel unsafe, they can nevertheless try to understand the non-vegans in their lives so that they are able to respect the person beneath the behavior. Because eating animals (rooted in the ideology of carnism) is such a widespread practice, a social norm, it requires a different degree of psychological distancing than do those behaviors that are widely regarded as unethical. With this understanding, vegans may be able to practice a degree of allyship toward the non-vegans in their lives.

An ally stands beside us and has our back even if our cause is not the same. If Jacob, for example, were a vegan ally, he would not have laughed along when his wife was being taunted. Instead, he might have taken her hand, showing her she's not alone, and presented a united front with her in requesting that her family not mock her values. This book is written to help those in veg/non-veg relationships stand alongside, rather than against or apart from, one another.

HOW TO READ THIS BOOK

This book is written for vegans, vegetarians, and meat eaters who want to improve the quality of their relationships and communication with their partners, friends, family, and acquaintances. But because the experience of vegans and vegetarians, who make up only a small minority of the population, has received virtually no attention and is underrepresented in relationship and self-help books, vegans and vegetarians are the most likely readers of this book. Therefore, much of the book is written from the vegan/vegetarian perspective. Yet this perspective in no way precludes other readers from benefiting equally.

Ideally, both members of a relationship would read the entire book. Changing relationship patterns takes insight and effort, and when both parties are invested in the process, change is quicker and easier. However, even if only one person decides to change the way they relate, the dynamic of the relationship can often be shifted. Meat eaters who don't feel up to reading the whole book can read Chapters 5 and 2, in order of importance.

In Chapter 2, we discuss the principles of resilient relationships, principles that apply to all relationships no matter what the differences between the individuals. Chapter 3 examines the nature of difference and the maintenance of connection and respect in the face of divergent belief systems. In Chapter 4, we look at the systems that shape our interpersonal dynamics and that can keep us stuck in unhealthy patterns of relating. With an understanding of how systems operate in our lives, we turn our attention, in Chapter 5, to the specific "germ," or "intruder," that can cause even the most resilient of relationships to weaken—the psychology of eating animals and the impact of this psychology on both those who do and those who don't eat animal products. In Chapter 6, we explore more deeply the impact of the psychology of eating animals on vegans and vegetarians, and we discuss the traumatization that those who have witnessed animal suffering tend to experience. We look into how this trauma affects vegans' and vegetarians' perceptions of themselves and of those with whom they are in relationship. In the final three chapters, we look at the tools for transformation: understanding and managing conflict in Chapter 7, effective communication strategies in Chapter 8, and creating change in Chapter 9.

All the concepts in this book are presented with the goal of providing straightforward, actionable advice for those who want to improve their relationships and communication. With an understanding of the principles and practices for creating resilient relationships and of how to navigate the special challenges of being in a veg/non-veg relationship, vegans, vegetarians, and meat eaters can create the secure, connected, and fulfilling relationships that we all want and deserve.

A NOTE ABOUT TERMINOLOGY

No term truly captures the identity of those whose beliefs lean one way or the other when it comes to eating animals. With an understanding of the limitations of contemporary language, I have chosen to use the term "vegans" to refer to vegetarians and vegans, and "non-vegans" to refer to vegetarians and meat eaters.

Vegetarians can be in either category because what matters most for the purposes of this book is the way a particular vegetarian identifies or experiences themselves in a relationship. For example, a vegetarian in a relationship with a meat eater will likely identify more with the vegan perspective, while a vegetarian in a relationship with a vegan may identify more with the non-vegan perspective. In a few places, when necessary, I've used the term "meat eater" to describe those who are neither vegetarian nor vegan.

Chapter 2

RELATIONSHIP RESILIENCE: THE FOUNDATION OF HEALTHY RELATIONSHIPS

Vegans and non-vegans in relationships can face special challenges. It is fully possible, though, to manage these challenges, and even to turn them into strengths, as long as the foundation of the relationship is resilient. When our relationship is resilient, we have a strong base from which to navigate any difficulties we may face—and when it's not, even small issues can cause major damage. Resilient relationships are built on *security* and *connection*. We feel secure when we trust the other to keep us safe, and we feel connected when we feel understood, valued, and nourished.

Unfortunately, however, most of us have learned to act in ways that cause our relationships to become *less* secure and connected. Many "normal" ways of relating are dysfunctional and toxic to security and connection. And because we typically don't realize that security and connection require constant nurturing and attention, we often end up neglecting these vital aspects of our relationships.

In veg/non-veg relationships, security and connection may seem especially difficult to cultivate. Both parties may automatically feel disconnected because they feel they have to hide parts of themselves for fear of being misunderstood and judged. And vegans can feel insecure, or unsafe, when exposed to attitudes and behaviors that trigger memories of the animal suffering they are all too aware of. Vegans may also worry that they won't be able to feel respect for those whose beliefs and practices run counter to core vegan values, and respect is essential for feeling connected.

In this chapter, we'll discuss the principles of and practices for creating greater security and connection in relationships. All these principles and practices point in the same direction: toward integrity.

INTEGRITY: THE NORTH STAR OF SECURITY AND CONNECTION

Integrity is the North Star of security and connection, the guiding principle underlying all other principles of building a resilient relationship. Essentially, we feel secure and connected in a relationship when we trust that the other will practice integrity toward us.

Putting Values into Practice

Integrity is the integration of our moral values and our behaviors. It is practicing what we preach. For example, if we value justice (being fair to others), we practice integrity when we treat others the way we want to be treated. If we treat others differently, then we violate our integrity. Integrity is therefore not simply something we *have*; it's something we *do*. Integrity is a practice, a road map for guiding our behaviors to ensure that they lead us to greater security and connection.

The moral values that guide a relationship (and life) of integrity are compassion, curiosity, justice, honesty, and courage. *Compassion* is having an open heart and truly caring about the well-being of others and of ourselves, and acting on that caring. *Curiosity* is having an open mind, genuinely seeking understanding. *Justice* is doing to others as we would have others do to us—and vice versa, for those of us who tend to treat others better than we treat ourselves. *Honesty* is not simply about telling the truth but about seeing the truth. Honesty is not denying or avoiding important truths, even if they are painful to face. *Courage* is the willingness to be, for example, honest and curious even when doing so feels frightening; it is the willingness to be vulnerable with others and with ourselves.

When we practice integrity, the situation is always win-win. What's good for my integrity is good for yours. What's good for the integrity of a relationship is good for the integrity of everyone in that relationship. And what's good for each individual's integrity is good for the integrity of the world. So a useful guiding question when making any kind of relational decision is "What is in the best interest of my integrity?" or "What is in the best interest of the integrity of the relationship?" For example, imagine you're at a restaurant with your non-vegan friend and, to your dismay, you're mistakenly served a salad with chicken on it. Your friend suggests that you "lighten up" and just pick off the chicken. When you act with integrity, stating your feelings and needs honestly and compassionately, you honor your friend's integrity (you aren't lying to her), you honor your own integrity, and you also honor the integrity of your relationship, maintaining its authenticity.

Transforming Shame to Pride

To more fully appreciate the value of integrity, consider what it feels like when integrity is lacking. Think about how you felt when someone who interacted with you acted against their integrity. Perhaps your mother called you an extremist because of your veganism. Or your boss rolled their eyes at a suggestion you made. Now think about how you've felt when you violated your own integrity. Perhaps, in anger, you called a loved one selfish and ignorant because they're not vegan. Or you lied to a friend because you didn't want to face the consequences of being honest. Chances are, the feeling in both situations—when others treated you without integrity and when you violated your own integrity—was identical: the feeling of shame. Shame is the feeling of being "less than," and more specifically, of being "less *worthy* than." Unlike guilt, which reflects how we feel about a behavior, shame reflects how we feel about ourselves, our character.

Shame both results from and causes violations of integrity, in a vicious cycle. When we feel shame, we are less likely to pay attention to or practice integrity. Our focus is on self-defense, on preventing ourselves from feeling further shamed. For example, imagine you've recently started dating another vegan, which you're thrilled about. You reveal that your feelings are growing and you want to make a more serious commitment, but the other person expresses some ambivalence, or uncertainty, and asks for more time to consider what direction the relationship should go in. You may feel rejected, and therefore ashamed. You may be tempted to avoid the other's phone calls or to make it clear that you're actively pursuing other potential love interests.

These actions are designed to protect your sense of self-worth and possibly even to make the other person question theirs so that you feel more worthy by comparison. Shame can make us feel like we're emotionally drowning, so we grab for anything that floats rather than extend a helping hand. And often, we push others under in the process.

Shame is arguably the foundation of human psychological dysfunction and the driving force of many, if not all, of the violent and problematic behaviors in our personal lives and in society. The essential human need to feel worthy is so powerful, and shame is so disruptive to our psychological security and well-being, that we often will do just about anything to avoid this feeling: we may accumulate millions of dollars, sculpt our physical image to fit a cultural ideal of beauty, or become a paragon of success in the areas that matter to us. (Of course, in and of themselves, these behaviors don't necessarily mean we are compensating for shame; the determining factor is our motivation for them.)

To feel shame is to feel that the core of who we are is flawed, not good enough, invalid. And because feeling shame is itself shameful (we actually feel ashamed of being ashamed), we tend to hide our shame from others and even from ourselves. We pretend it doesn't exist: we bury it under endless piles of work, wrap it inside our achievements, tuck it away beneath the layers of distractions that keep us continually focused outside ourselves. We act as if we feel good enough, perhaps even superior, when inside we are self-doubting and feel like an impostor. In our relationships, we may act as if we don't care and withhold words of affection, when what we really want is for the other to tell us how much they love us.

Beneath all our striving to feel powerful, in control, beautiful, successful, and so on, what each of us truly wants is to feel that we are enough, that we are worthy. We want to feel that regardless of what we *do*, it is who we *are* that matters. We want to feel pride. Healthy pride is not the expression of an inflated ego but the feeling of being worthy. Pride is the opposite of shame. It is the essence of personal and relational health, just as shame is the foundation of personal and relational dysfunction.

Healthy pride should not be confused with grandiosity. Healthy pride is feeling that we are fundamentally worthy, that we are just as worthy as everybody else. Grandiosity, on the other hand, is the feeling of being better than, or more worthy than, others. While shame is feeling inferior, grandiosity is feeling superior. Both shame and grandiosity are illusions: when it comes to essential worth, there is no hierarchy.

Grandiosity is often a mask for shame. Consider the boy who falls down on the playground and is teased (shamed) for crying over his scraped knee. He pulls himself up, puffs out his chest, and punches at his bullies in an "I'll show you" display of force. The shamed becomes the shamer, perpetuating a cycle that is, unfortunately, a hallmark of many relationships.

The opposite of grandiosity is humility. When we are both proud and humble, we recognize our own worth and appreciate the worth of others. We recognize the inherent worth of everyone with whom we share the planet. A relationship of integrity transforms shame into pride; shame is incompatible with integrity. Secure, connected relationships, which are based on integrity, help prevent and heal shame, while insecure, disconnected relationships create shame.

THE POWER OF SECURITY

Security is fundamental to a resilient relationship. While we need more than just security to feel fulfilled and connected with others, without security nothing else matters. And when we have security, almost anything else is manageable. Cutting-edge research in neuropsychology has shown that we are actually hardwired to need our primary attachment figure—as adults, this is usually our romantic partner—to protect our sense of emotional safety, of security.[1]

We feel secure in our relationships when we trust that the other genuinely has our best interests at heart and is willing and able to prioritize our safety. The other is then careful not to engage in behaviors that would hurt us emotionally and violate our trust. We all need to know that the person we

---

1 Two excellent resources on attachment are Amir Levine and Rachel Heller, *Attached: The New Science of Adult Attachment and How It Can Help You Find—and Keep—Love* (New York: Jeremy P. Tarcher/Penguin, 2010), and Stan Tatkin, *Wired for Love: How Understanding Your Partner's Brain and Attachment Style Can Help You Defuse Conflict and Build a Secure Relationship* (Oakland, CA: New Harbinger, 2011).

are in a relationship with has our back, that they genuinely want to keep us safe and secure, and that they value our well-being. In short, we need to feel that the other will treat us with integrity.

Security is important in all relationships, but it is particularly important in relationships where we are more vulnerable, such as those with close friends and family, and especially with our romantic partner. These are also the relationships where we may be the least likely to protect one another's security. When we are vulnerable, we are more likely to feel self-protective and therefore defensive, and we are also more likely to take the other's presence in our life for granted, assuming that their attachment to us will keep them by our side. But each time we fail to protect one another's safety, we damage trust and diminish the security of our relationship. As Gandhi wisely said, "As the means, so the ends." How we relate to one another will determine the kind of relationship we end up with.

When someone chooses to enter into a relationship with us, especially a romantic relationship, which requires a high degree of vulnerability, it is a sacred gift. We live in a world replete with abuses of power, widespread suffering, and rampant competition and addiction, a world where narcissism and selfishness are largely celebrated and rewarded. Many people have personal histories in which their safety was not protected, and they carry these relational wounds through their lives. It takes courage to choose to be vulnerable in such a world, to show up rather than hide. There is beauty and honor in being trusted with another's vulnerability, and the very least we can do to respect this gift is to commit to protecting their safety.

Committing to the Security of the Other

Committing to prioritizing the other's security is part of the contract we enter into when we agree to be in a relationship. This contract is usually not explicit; it's simply something we both expect. We wouldn't enter into a relationship if we believed that the other was not willing to act in ways that kept us safe.

So committing to the safety of the other is a relationship non-negotiable. It's the price of admission we pay to enter (or remain in) their life. A relationship takes effort—daily, committed effort to create the security necessary for it to thrive. Expecting to be in a relationship without putting in such effort is like expecting a free ride on someone else's back. Many of us resist and complain when we are asked to attend to our relationships, to do the basic work necessary to create security. But when we appreciate the vital role of security and understand that a secure relationship does not create itself, we can commit to engaging in the practices that will help us create the kind of relationship that we truly feel good about and that can carry us through the challenges we will inevitably face.

Of all the practices outlined in this book, committing to one another's security is the most important. It's helpful to be explicit about this commitment. State aloud your desire to keep each other safe, especially in times of conflict, when vulnerability and defenses are high. If, for example, you and your non-vegan partner disagree about whether to request that your families bring only vegan foods to the potluck dinner you're hosting, you can tell each other that your goal is to find a solution in which you both feel safe and that you're committed to continuing to explore options until you're able to achieve this end. When we each truly believe that the other prioritizes our security, no subject is too threatening to discuss.

Security and Relationship Supporters

One way to maintain security in our relationship is to ensure that those we talk to about it are *relationship supporters*. A relationship supporter is someone outside the relationship who is committed to its integrity—to communicating about it in a way that respects each party, as well as the relationship itself.

A relationship supporter doesn't take sides, because they realize that a relationship is not a win-lose battle. Even if the relationship supporter believes, for example, that your partner's behavior is unacceptable and fully backs your position, they communicate in a way that your partner would be comfortable hearing if they were listening to the conversation. They discuss your relationship, and your partner, with respect.

For instance, suppose you told a supporter that your partner had made a negative comment about veganism at a recent get-together. Rather than say, "What a jerk! I can't stand people who say things like that!" they might say,

"That sounds like a disrespectful comment. I can understand why you're feeling so hurt and angry." This response validates your concern without judging or criticizing your partner as a "bad person."

THE POWER OF CONNECTION

We feel connected—or "emotionally connected," as psychologists sometimes say—when the other says and does things that we experience as validating, when they communicate that we are worthy and that we matter. And connection is not an either-or phenomenon: it's not that either we are connected or we're not. Rather, connection (like security) exists in degrees: we can be more or less connected. We simply need to feel connected (and secure) *enough* with one another to enjoy a resilient relationship.

When we feel connected, we are mutually tuned in to and responsive to each other's emotional experience. We feel seen and valued, and secure in the knowledge that we can count on the other to be there when needed, especially in vulnerable moments. For example, even if you don't feel comfortable with your partner's brother, who is a chef at a steakhouse, if your partner is upset because of a conflict he and his brother had, you would ask him about his experience, listen openly to his explanation (as long as the explanation is respectful of your needs, such as not hearing descriptions of cooking animal products), and offer support as you are able. Your partner would get the message that he matters and that he can count on you to be there when he needs you.

Keeping Connection Alive

Many promising relationships end not because of one major incident but because of the many smaller incidents that subtly yet powerfully disconnect people over time. Even if a single incident triggers a breakup, chances are the connection had already been eroding, and the relationship was not able to withstand the stress of the final blow. Most of our relationships don't die sudden deaths but rather the death of a thousand cuts, the series of little disconnects that slowly chip away at us—the countless little put-downs, the forgotten promises, all the missed opportunities to take up an outstretched hand, the chronic failure to really listen.

Research by psychologist and relationship expert Dr. Sue Johnson and her colleagues has shown that relationships end when we cannot trust that the other is tuned in to our feelings and needs, and so we can't count on them to be emotionally responsive in times of stress.[2] Johnson's research suggests that most arguments are actually a reaction to disconnection and an attempt at reconnection. Underneath the content of the arguments are often the questions "Can I count on you? Will you respond to me when I call? Do I matter to you? Can I feel safe with you?"

To be emotionally connected with another, especially in a close relationship, we must have the courage to be vulnerable, to share our truth—our authentic thoughts and feelings—and be willing to hear the other's. Most of us—especially males—have been taught to believe that vulnerability is both a sign of weakness and a liability. On top of this, most of us have a lifetime of experiences in which our vulnerability was not respected or protected, so we've learned, understandably, to associate vulnerability with being hurt, sometimes badly.

Unfortunately, defending ourselves against vulnerability gets us into a lot of trouble, because this approach is fundamentally non-relational. One step to take toward allowing yourself to be more vulnerable is simply shifting your attitude, recognizing vulnerability as a sign of strength and as a necessary ingredient for secure, connected relationships.[3]

Illusory Connections

Sometimes, we can feel a strong bond with another that creates the illusion of deep connection even though it is not. If we are aware of these illusory connections, we are less likely to fall prey to them.

One illusory connection is what social scientists refer to as *limerence*, a state that most of us refer to as being "in love."[4] When we are in a state of

---

2 Sue Johnson, *Hold Me Tight: Seven Conversations for a Lifetime of Love* (New York: Little, Brown, 2008).

3 A great resource on the value of vulnerability is Brené Brown's *Daring Greatly: How the Courage to Be Vulnerable Transforms the Way We Live, Love, Parent, and Lead* (New York: Avery/Penguin, 2012). See also Brown's TEDx talk titled "The Power of Vulnerability" (https://www.ted.com/talks/brene_brown_on_vulnerability).

4 See Dorothy Tennov, *Love and Limerence: The Experience of Being in Love* (Lanham, MD: Rowman and Littlefield, 1998).

limerence, we feel an intense bond with the other. This bond is the result of chemicals in our brains that are triggered by a new union, and it can cause us to trust another too readily because we mistake it for a deeper emotional connection than it actually is. (Deep emotional connection grows only over time, from being authentic and compassionate with each other.) Limerence typically fades after a period of between 18 months and three years, which is healthy and adaptive for us as individuals and for our relationship.

A similar illusory connection is *relationship addiction*, a state of being addicted to a person or relationship. Relationship addiction can result from many factors, but one key cause is being on the receiving end of disrespectful interactions, such as when we are dating someone who is doing the "push-pull" dance or when we are in an emotionally abusive relationship.[5] Many people in such situations have an inaccurate understanding of the strong attachment they feel. They may believe they have a special connection with the other, perhaps a spiritual connection, and that the intensity of their attachment is somehow a sign that they are meant to be together. They may therefore ignore or minimize all the ways in which the relationship is toxic and create justifications for what is actually controlling (or otherwise problematic) behavior. We often stay stuck in relationship addiction when we have fallen in love with another's potential, with who (we believe) the other *could be* rather than who the other actually *is*.

Empathy: The Cornerstone of Connection

Empathy is the cornerstone of connection. We empathize when we look at the world through another's eyes and not only see what they see but, to the best of our ability, feel what they feel. When we are not empathizing with the other, we are much more likely to say or do something hurtful, even if we don't intend to, and to cause them to disconnect from us in self-defense.

Most of us don't empathize enough, especially when there's tension in

---

5 Abusive relationships go beyond the scope of this book. However, if you suspect you are in a relationship with someone who is manipulative, controlling, or otherwise abusive or simply want to learn more about the issue, see Beverly Engel, *The Emotionally Abusive Relationship: How to Stop Being Abused and How to Stop Abusing* (Hoboken, NJ: John Wiley and Sons, 2002) and Lundy Bancroft, *Why Does He Do That? Inside the Minds of Angry and Controlling Men* (New York: Berkley/Penguin, 2002).

our relationship. The simple act of taking the temperature of our empathy can do wonders for our connection. To do this, we can simply pause regularly when we're interacting and ask ourselves whether we're feeling empathy for the other. We are not empathizing if we simply "see that she's feeling frazzled" or "get his main arguments." We are empathizing when we genuinely try to imagine what the world looks like through the other's eyes, to understand their experience.

There are times, however, when empathizing is not in our best interest or in the best interest of others, most notably when we are on the receiving end of controlling or disrespectful behaviors. When we empathize too much with someone who is not treating us (or others) with respect, we can lose touch with our anger. Anger is the emotional response to injustice, and it is the feeling that motivates us to take action on behalf of ourselves and others.

COMPASSIONATE WITNESSING

Compassionate witnessing[6] is the key practice for creating connection. It entails paying attention and listening with empathy, compassion, and without judgment. When we compassionately witness another, our goal is not to be right, to win an argument, or even to fix a problem; it is simply to understand the truth of the other's experience.

When we compassionately witness another, we are saying, "I see you: I empathize and I care." To be truly seen is a great gift, one that is sorely lacking in most of our lives and in the culture at large. Many of us go through our lives feeling largely invisible, feeling that in order to be accepted we have to stuff away parts of who we are—to swallow our words when we're hurting or ashamed or afraid, and to play the game of "let's pretend," often even with ourselves. To be a witness is also a great gift: when another chooses to share vulnerable parts of themselves with us, it is an honor. It is a statement of trust in our integrity, and in some ways there can be no greater compliment.

---

6 Kaethe Weingarten, *Common Shock: Witnessing Violence Every Day* (New York: NAL Trade, Brown, 2004).

The Healing Potential of Compassionate Witnessing

Compassionate witnessing promotes healing because it is validating. We feel validated when we feel accepted for who we are, when we don't feel judged for what we think and feel. And when we feel validated, we feel unashamed and worthy—we feel that we matter. Compassionate witnessing is therefore the antidote to shame. Every time we're told that our feelings or experience are "wrong," we get the message that we don't matter. Every time we're not responded to when we reach out to another, we get the message that we don't matter. And every time we're met with compassion and empathy, a part of us is healed. We're treated lovingly, and through the other's eyes we see ourselves as lovable, especially when they love the parts of us around which we have felt shame.

Many vegans in relationships with non-vegans suffer the pain of disconnection that results from feeling they cannot share a fundamental part of themselves with those they are closest to.[7] Because the mainstream culture is not vegan, and is in some ways even anti-vegan, vegans often feel invisible, misunderstood, and compelled to hide the parts of themselves that won't be accepted. Some of vegans' deepest and most important beliefs and experiences—which they may be most proud of and impassioned about—remain unseen and unappreciated. When this experience of being unseen (and often judged) is repeated in close relationships, it can feel like having salt poured on a wound. And although non-vegans are witnessed by the culture at large, to some degree they can feel unwitnessed in their relationships with vegans; they may hide parts of themselves for fear of being judged or causing conflict.

To have one's inner world known and understood is a basic relationship need, and everyone has not only a right to request this but a responsibility to do so. The exception is when our need to be understood causes the other to feel unsafe, and herein lies a core challenge in veg/non-veg relationships: sometimes what we need from the other is precisely what can make them feel less secure. Learning to understand and compassionately witness each other

---

7 See Appendix 7 for an example of how you can ask non-vegans to witness you, and Appendix 9 for a letter you can share with non-vegans to help them understand your experience as a vegan.

is key to overcoming this challenge, and we will discuss ways to facilitate this process in upcoming chapters.

Compassionate witnessing can transform not only our relationships, but also our lives and our world, because it is not simply an interpersonal practice. We can practice compassionate witnessing toward ourselves as well as collectively, toward our world. When we compassionately witness ourselves, we deepen our connection with ourselves and we increase our integrity and decrease our shame. When we practice compassionate witnessing toward the world, we empathize with those who are suffering and help create a more just and humane planet. Consider that virtually every atrocity was made possible by a populace that turned away from a reality they felt was too painful to face. And virtually every social transformation was made possible because a group of people chose to bear witness and encouraged others to bear witness as well.

Defining Reality: The Antithesis of Compassionate Witnessing

Compassionate witnessing prevents us from defining reality, a common yet toxic practice that can seriously undermine the security and connection of our relationships. *Defining reality* is dictating the truth of another's experience: we appoint ourselves the expert on what the other is thinking or feeling, even when they tell us otherwise. For instance, perhaps you tell your non-vegan sister that you feel healthier than ever since becoming vegan, but she replies that you're just saying that because you want to "win converts." Or a non-vegan says to his vegan girlfriend that he doesn't like veggie burgers, and she replies that of course he does; he eats them all the time.

Defining reality is fundamentally disrespectful, and it is the foundation of psychological abuse. Defining reality shames the other because it invalidates their experience, and it erodes their self-confidence because it causes them to distrust their own thoughts and feelings. In its extreme, defining reality is "gaslighting"—intentionally getting others to distrust their perceptions, thereby replacing their sense of self-control, confidence, and worth with self-doubt, insecurity, and shame. Whether slight or extreme, defining reality is always a disrespectful and harmful behavior.

We can also define our own reality and the collective reality. For example, you define your own reality when you tell yourself you "shouldn't" be feeling depressed because others are so much worse off than you, and the dominant white culture defines reality when it argues that racism no longer exists, despite the commentary of people of color whose personal experience directly contradicts such a claim. Humans define animals' reality when, for example, they insist that lobsters who struggle to climb out of a pot of boiling water are simply exhibiting an "instinctive response" rather than trying to escape pain.

BIDS FOR CONNECTION

Psychologist John Gottman conducted groundbreaking research on connection that has transformed the way we understand relationships.[8] Gottman suggests that we are always making "bids" for emotional connection in our relationships. A bid is an attempt to elicit attention, affection, validation, affirmation, or any positive connection from another, such as asking if they noticed our new haircut or reaching out to hold their hand. Whether our bids are productive depends on two factors: how the other responds to our bids and how we express our bids.

Responding to Bids

There are three ways of responding to bids: turning toward, turning against, and turning away.

When we turn toward another, we engage with them; we witness them and respond to their request for emotional connection. For example, even if your brother is not vegan, when you share with him how upset you are that your parents won't come to your house for Thanksgiving if you don't serve animal products, he can still turn toward you: he can listen openly and share his feedback so you know you've been heard and understood.

When we turn against another, we respond to their bid with aggression. For example, suppose your sister tells you she feels hurt because you've been too busy with your volunteer work to visit her, and she worries that she's

---

8 See John M. Gottman, *The Relationship Cure: A 5 Step Guide to Strengthening Your Marriage, Family, and Friendships* (New York: Harmony Books, 2001).

not a priority in your life. Feeling misunderstood and unappreciated, you turn against her: you lash out, saying, "I'm working my butt off to make the world a better place. And now you have to guilt me? Can't you think of anyone but yourself?"

When we turn away, we miss the bid—meaning we don't respond at all. For example, suppose your partner shares a concern that she may be at risk of getting demoted at work. You think that compared with what's happening to animals around the world, your partner's worries about demotion are trivial. So you turn away from her: you tune her out and keep going about your business as usual. When an opportunity to connect is missed, all the other really knows is what they can observe: we didn't respond when they reached out. So they will be less likely to reach out again.

Both turning against and turning away can damage the security and connection of a relationship. And while turning against is clearly problematic and can even be abusive, turning away can be even more devastating because it's often difficult or impossible to detect and therefore to address. Turning away is a form of neglect, and when chronic, it can also be a form of abuse.

Expressing Bids

Sometimes the problem in getting our bids for emotional connection met is that we haven't expressed our bids directly, respectfully, or at the right time. For example, suppose you feel hurt because your non-vegan friend didn't want to attend a vegan get-together with you. Instead of directly communicating your feelings and needs, you criticize them for being selfish. Or, suppose you feel rejected because your partner hasn't been romantic, so you withdraw and withhold affection in an attempt to make them feel less secure. Or perhaps you make a bid right before bed, when the other is too tired to respond. The problem with such bids is that they can bring about the opposite of what we hope for, creating defensiveness, damaging trust, and disconnecting us further.

CONNECTION AND NEEDS

In many ways, connection is all about needs. We tend to feel connected (and satisfied) when our needs are being met, and we feel disconnected (and dissatisfied) when they are not. The more of our needs that are met, and the more fully they are met, the better we feel in our relationship. And the needs that help us feel connected vary to some degree from person to person, so it's essential to become aware of our own and the other's needs.

All of us have bottom-line, non-negotiable needs, as well as less vital yet still important ones. Some bottom-line needs are shared by virtually all people in relationships: we all need to feel accepted, valued, appreciated, needed, respected, and, of course, secure. We all need to feel that we matter and that we can count on the other. When these core needs are not met, we feel disconnected. For example, if your partner repeatedly fails to follow through on promises, you will begin to feel distrustful and angry, which in turn will diminish your connection.[9]

When a need we have is not being met, we can feel chronic frustration, a low-grade anger that simmers and intensifies over time, until we blow up over seemingly trivial things and wonder why we're reacting so strongly. Or we may become depressed. Often, we're both angry and depressed. And we will inevitably feel deprived, so we may end up feeling the need even more strongly, like feeling ravenous after not eating for too long.

Despite how vital meeting needs is to feeling connected, many of us do not act in ways that genuinely attend to the needs of the other. For example, we may rarely, if ever, express appreciation, causing the other to feel taken for granted and resentful. When we don't say a simple "thank you" and acknowledge the other's efforts, no matter how small, they can feel taken advantage of and will likely protect themselves by withholding their generosity. Even if we *feel* appreciation, the other knows only what we communicate.

Simply recognizing and attending to each other's needs can transform a relationship from insecure and disconnected to secure and connected.

Distinguishing Wants from Needs

Many of us have a list of needs for our relationship that includes everything from how the other should dress to what kinds of friendships they should

---

9 See Appendix 1 for a list of other potential needs.

have. Of course, it would be problematic if, for example, the other dressed inappropriately and such behavior reflected a disrespect for professional or social customs, or if their friends were abusive or engaged in criminal activities. But we often end up with a long list of assumed needs, more accurately called "wants," that can prevent us from seeing our actual needs or that mask our needs. For example, if you want your partner to dress a certain way when accompanying you, it may be that what you really need is for them to be more respectful of the comfort and expectations of others in social situations, not simply that they have a certain style. Or a vegan may believe she can no longer stay in her relationship with her non-vegan partner because she needs to be with another vegan. However, it may be that she doesn't need another vegan, that what she really needs is a more attentive and supportive partner—one who does his best to see the world through her eyes, accommodates her needs, and makes sure she feels understood.

Recognizing and Attending to Our Needs

Apart from confusing wants and needs, a handful of other obstacles may get in the way of our ability to recognize (and therefore attend to) our needs. One such obstacle is the difficulty many of us have identifying and expressing the feelings that underlie our needs. For example, if your partner just had coffee with their ex, you may feel insecure and need reassurance. But if you don't recognize your feeling of insecurity, you won't know that what you need is reassurance.

Another reason we struggle to recognize and honor our needs is because we've been taught to think of needs as something to be ashamed of. We've been conditioned to overvalue qualities such as independence and self-sufficiency and to devalue interdependence and connection. The assumption that we can and should be islands unto ourselves has caused tremendous suffering, because it causes us to deny, ignore, and judge our normal, natural, and healthy relational needs as "wrong." There is such stigma around having needs that describing someone as "needy" is considered a shameful put-down. Interestingly, "needy" has no direct opposite equivalent: What do we call someone who doesn't have enough needs? Needs are like emotions: they are not inherently right or wrong. They just are. When we accept, rather than reject, our needs, we can begin to see and share them clearly and to evaluate how they affect us and our relationships.

If we devalue needs, we can second-guess and invalidate them even when we do become aware of them. For example, you may tell your partner that you need them to understand how anxious you are about going to their cousin's wedding, where there will be lots of meat and no other vegans. But when your partner says you're overreacting, you may suddenly second-guess whether your need is valid and feel ashamed. Compounding the problem, both vegans and non-vegans are more likely to see vegans' needs as less valid than non-vegans' needs, a phenomenon we will discuss in later chapters. In any case, invalidating our own and the other's needs—seeing them as wrong—is perhaps the best way to ensure that they are not met and to trigger the demise of a relationship.

Even if we recognize and accept our needs, we may not attend to them if we believe the common misconception that for one person to have their needs met, the other must sacrifice theirs—that one must lose for the other to win. When we understand how to negotiate needs, we can appreciate that in secure, connected relationships, the only viable solution to meeting needs is win-win. When one person's relationship needs are not being met, both people lose because the relationship becomes less resilient. Just think: Could someone truly enjoy a meal if a starving person with an empty plate were sitting at the same table?

When we are conscious of and able to articulate our needs, we empower not only ourselves and our relationship but also the other. We give the other the opportunity to give us what we want, thereby fulfilling *their* need to feel respected and competent. It is not respectful to withhold information that another needs in order not to displease us. For example, imagine that your dinner guest didn't inform you that she dislikes tomatoes until after she'd picked through your carefully prepared vegetable stew. Given that most of us need to feel like we are successful in our various roles, knowing another's needs enables us to reduce the likelihood that we will feel we have failed.

Vegans, Safety, and Needs

For a great number of vegans, being exposed to meat and other animal products is distressing. Most vegans have witnessed graphic imagery of animal suffering, and have had a shift of perspective so they no longer see meat, for example, as food but rather as a dead animal. So when vegans are exposed to animal products, it can cause a traumatic reaction: they can have flashbacks to the imagery they've witnessed and be unable to push such images out of their minds. The psychological term for thoughts or images of suffering we've witnessed that suddenly enter our mind is *intrusive thoughts*, and with such thoughts, all the related emotions emerge: horror, disgust, grief, anxiety, and often a sense of moral outrage.

The experience of many vegans when exposed to animal products is similar to what non-vegans (in a number of cultures) might experience if they were exposed to the flesh of a slaughtered golden retriever—especially if they had seen videos of the horrific butchering of dogs. The desensitization toward meat (and other animal products) that most of us grow up with blocks this natural reaction of horror, until something breaks through our conditioning, as it has for many vegans. Therefore, non-vegans often don't automatically empathize with vegans' reactions to seeing animal products.

Understanding the traumatic reaction often experienced by vegans who are exposed to animal products is essential to being able to negotiate needs in a veg/non-veg relationship. When we recognize that the vegan's need is not simply about personal preference but rather about emotional safety, we can begin to appreciate the weight of such a need.

Complicating things further is the fact that, vegan or non-vegan, our needs are always changing, because *we* are always changing. As individuals, we cannot help but change; every day we grow older and have new experiences. For instance, the financial security we need at fifty is probably a far cry from what we felt we needed at twenty.

Becoming vegan often brings about such a change in attitude and lifestyle that new vegans will inevitably have a whole new set of needs—and such needs will likely continue to change as the vegan continues to develop their awareness. For example, the assurance you may now need that your soup isn't made with chicken stock would not have been something you needed just last month before you stopped eating animals. Or you may find that you no longer feel comfortable eating at the steakhouse your family has always gone to; the lack of vegan options and the cattle skulls on the walls make the experience too distressing.

Complaining and Needs

Some needs are straightforward. We can easily identify and articulate them: "Can you please pick up after yourself so I don't have to?" But just because we communicate a need does not mean it will be met. And if it isn't met, we communicate it again: "Can you please pick up after yourself so I don't have to?" And again. And again. At which point, we may be perceived as complaining or as "never satisfied."

But here's the thing: complaining, by definition, is communicating dissatisfaction. And dissatisfaction is the feeling that arises when needs are not being met. Complaining is viewed as something negative and is typically referred to in an insulting way ("Will you stop complaining already?"). Complaining, however, is often not the problem; the problem is having to reiterate the original request because it was never adequately responded to. Framing the person who is requesting that a need be met as complaining is a way of shifting the blame for the problem, sort of like punching someone in the nose and then blaming them for getting blood on the rug.

And the expression of dissatisfaction is more likely to be seen as complaining if it's coming from a member of a non-dominant group who's directing it toward a member of a dominant group. For example, a woman who expresses dissatisfaction to her male partner about his behavior is likely to be seen as a "nag," while a man who expresses dissatisfaction to his female partner is likely to be seen as doing just that—expressing dissatisfaction. Similarly, vegans are more likely to be seen as "complainers" than are non-vegans.

SHAME, JUDGMENT, AND ANGER: TRIGGERS OF DISCONNECTION

Certain thoughts, feelings, and behaviors can trigger a sense of disconnection—in ourselves, the other, or both of us. The most important triggers to be aware of are shame, judgment, and anger.

When we think a disconnecting thought, it can trigger a disconnecting feeling, which leads to a disconnecting behavior, which triggers a disconnecting thought, feeling, and behavior in the other, and so on.

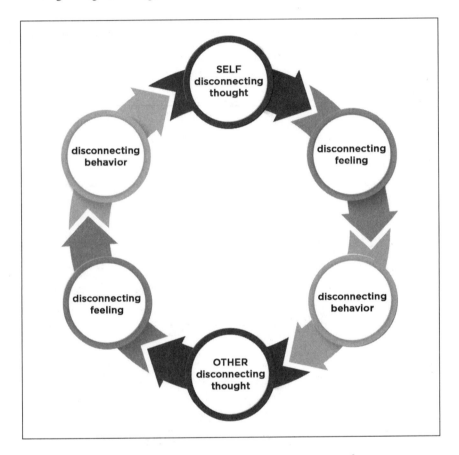

For example, suppose you discover that your partner forgot, again, to pick up soy milk from the grocery store while doing the weekly shopping, even though they remembered everything else. You think, "My partner is too immature to manage important responsibilities," and you feel judgmental and angry, and therefore disconnected. You tell your partner you're sick of their laziness, and then they feel judged, attacked, and ashamed, and therefore angry and defensive. They lash back at you, claiming that you're uptight and controlling. Feeling hurt, you disconnect further.

Shame is one of the most, if not the most, disconnecting feelings. When we feel ashamed, we put up protective barriers between ourselves and others to prevent further shaming. Shame is the emotional equivalent of having a scraped elbow that we instinctively protect from further harm. And the worse the wound, the more protective of it we are. Shamed people wrap themselves in the emotional armor necessary to feel safe; they withdraw or attack rather than connect. This armor may be necessary if the other is in fact unsafe, but it can limit potentially healthy relationships. And shamed people tend to shame others, creating a vicious cycle of shame-counter-shame.

Judgment is the mental counterpart of shame; it is the attitude that creates shaming thoughts and leads to the feeling of shame. When we judge someone (or ourselves), we perceive them as inferior. We look down on them. We feel less connected to them, in large part because judging limits our identification with and empathy toward them. And the less we empathize with another, the more likely we are to judge them. It's difficult to look down on someone when you are looking at the world through their eyes.

Judgment stems from an ego-based need to boost our own feeling of power and esteem through feeling separate from and superior to others. When we judge, we get to feel that we are right while the other is wrong, that we are better while the other is worse. But judging is ultimately a lose-lose strategy. While we may feel like a winner when we are standing in judgment of another, in the end we all lose—we lose the connection that is the lifeblood of our relationship and the true power and pride that come from knowing we are practicing integrity, and the other loses their sense of connection with us and, likely, some of their self-esteem.

Anger, the emotional response to injustice, helps protect us or others when necessary: it gives us the courage and drive to take action against unfair treatment. Anger enables us to act in protective ways, in large part because it disconnects us, psychologically and emotionally, from others; it disconnects us from our empathy.

Often, however, our anger is not a rational demand for fair treatment but a defensive reaction against incorrect perceptions. Anger creates (and is created by) a story in our minds about our rightness and another's wrongness. And even if we're angry because we've been treated unfairly, we can still choose to express our anger in a way that doesn't cause disconnection. Most people respond to another's anger defensively. So the more anger we direct toward others, subtly or overtly, the more they will push back or withdraw and disconnect from us.

When we feel disconnected but don't know why, we can ask ourselves if we're feeling ashamed, judgmental, and/or angry, and if so, why. Once we understand the source of our feelings, we will be better positioned to address the problem directly and heal the source of the disconnect.

CONNECTION AND RESPECT

Respect is vital to our sense of connection. But most of us have never learned what, exactly, respect is or is not. Although we often intuitively know when we are being disrespected, we are rarely aware of disrespecting another, because we have simply not learned to identify the specific attitudes and behaviors that either create or undermine respect.

Respect is having regard for the dignity and needs or rights of others (or ourselves). Respect is a belief, a feeling, and a behavior. Our feeling of respect is the result of our belief: if we feel respect for others, it's because we believe they are worthy of respect. And the behavior of respect is practicing the value of justice (fairness), doing to others what we would want done to ourselves.

Respect is therefore not something we earn. For example, we would expect the stranger sitting next to us on the train to treat us with respect even though we haven't done anything to earn their respect. However, once we have respect, we need to work to maintain it, and we do this by being respectful ourselves. We are respectful when we practice integrity—when, for example, we keep our agreements and act in ways that honor the dignity of others.

Acceptance and Respect

Respecting someone includes accepting them for who they are, accepting that their views, needs, feelings, and so on are valid, even if we don't agree with some of what they say or do and even as we may work to change society so that such behaviors are one day no longer common practice. Acceptance is understanding without judgment. Acceptance does not mean that we accept being on the receiving end of harmful behaviors or that we passively allow violence to unfold. It simply means that we accept the reality that the other is who they are, and we don't judge them as being less worthy. (In Chapter 9, we'll explore acceptance more fully.)

Vegans, Non-vegans, and Respect

But what if the other is acting in ways that violate our ethics and that we find impossible to respect? One of the most challenging experiences for vegans is trying to maintain respect for those whose behaviors run counter to some of their deepest values. And one of the most challenging experiences for non-vegans in relationships with vegans is feeling judged or disrespected for eating animals. So, what can be done?

First, vegans can appreciate that one reason they are struggling to respect the other may be that they are not separating the individual (non-vegan) from the behavior of eating animals or from the impact of that behavior—animal suffering. This blending of the person—or, more specifically, of their character—with their behavior is often magnified by the fact that the vegan has experienced some degree of trauma from witnessing animal suffering. Trauma blurs boundaries and magnifies emotions, issues we'll discuss in Chapter 6. Understanding the psychology of eating animals can help vegans separate the non-vegan's character from their behavior. Eating animals stems from massive social conditioning, which influences individuals in powerful, complex, and varying ways. Some people are able to step out of this conditioning fairly quickly after learning the truth of what it is and how it harms animals. Most people, though, are not able to do so, for a variety of reasons. It is helpful as well to understand the nature of differences—especially of moral value differences, an issue we will discuss in the next chapter. Separating character from behavior is a generosity we all deserve. We can respect the basic dignity of another even if we don't respect what they do.

Next, vegans can do their best to understand the reasons for and experience of the behavior. Is the other continuing to eat animals because they truly don't care about harming animals? Or are they worried about what becoming vegan might entail, such as the disruption of family relationships or a loss of social identity? Are they supportive of veganism in other ways?

In general, when we have a deep understanding of another's inner world, it is difficult to stand in judgment of them and to not respect them. Empathy is often the antidote to disrespect.

It's also important to make sure that our basic needs are being met, so that we feel secure and connected enough to explore the issue. When we truly understand each other's experience, attend to each other's needs, and are genuinely able to engage in open and compassionate dialogue about our experiences as vegan and non-vegan, we are likely to find that the problem of respect is, in fact, not a problem at all.

RELATIONSHIP RESILIENCE AND LOVE

In his seminal book, *The Road Less Traveled*, psychiatrist M. Scott Peck[10] contends that love is not merely a feeling; it is also an action. Love is (also) a verb. Someone can feel love for us all they want, but the only way we can know they love us is through what they say and do, how they treat us. For example, no matter how much your partner feels love for you, if they don't tell you that they love you or don't listen to you when you're speaking, or if they continually disregard important requests you've made of them, you simply won't feel loved; you won't feel that you matter to them. Peck says that the behavior of love is acting in the best interest of another, which is essentially practicing integrity toward them. Resilient relationships are loving relationships.

Love Brings Transformation

Love transforms us, in large part because love transforms shame. Shame maintains its power by staying hidden away in the dark recesses of our hearts and minds. The darkness of shame cannot exist under the bright light of love. Consider how you've felt when you've shared a shameful secret or shown a shameful part of yourself to someone who responded with compassion and acceptance, with love. Suddenly, what felt so debilitating and burdensome can feel like it's been released, freed.

---

10 M. Scott Peck, *The Road Less Traveled: A New Psychology of Love, Traditional Values and Spiritual Growth*, special edition with new introduction (New York: Touchstone, 2003; first published 1978).

Love is spacious. When we are spacious, we have room in our minds and hearts for a variety of ideas and feelings, some of which may seem contradictory. For example, you may believe that your father is a compassionate person but also believe that his meat eating is insensitive. Or you may desire greater intimacy with your partner and, at the same time, fear more closeness. Love allows these seeming inconsistencies to coexist. Love is flexible rather than rigid.

Love Is Imperfection

Many of us are taught to believe that people are either perfect or flawed, good or bad, heroes or villains, worthy or unworthy of love. This one-dimensional view inevitably influences how we think of people in general, including, of course, those with whom we are in relationship. We automatically assume that "good" partners, for example, don't engage in problematic behaviors, and so we can struggle to feel and practice love toward them. And while it's important to address disrespectful behaviors, it's also important that we not allow the illusion of perfection to limit our love.

Healthy relationships have wiggle room—space for each individual to make mistakes, to be their fallible human selves. When we can accept that we—and others—will inevitably mess up, we feel safer in bringing our authentic selves into our relationships, and we can therefore create deeper connections. And our relationships can recover more quickly from conflict, because we don't have to resolve the added problem of having disappointed each other, of having been less than perfect—and we don't have to deal with the righteous anger that accompanies perfectionistic thinking ("How could you do such a thing!"). Being a relationship perfectionist doesn't serve any of us.

Love enables us to accept and even value the messiness of ourselves and others. When we appreciate our imperfections, we can feel safer in our relationships, because we don't feel that in order to be loved, we must live up to an impossible ideal. Few things enhance loving connection and emotional healing more than knowing that the other has space in their mind and heart for us to be our authentic selves, warts and all. Love is the antidote to the deepest of wounds—in ourselves, and in our world.

When we commit to building resilient relationships, we commit to practicing love, which helps us evolve toward our highest, and deepest, selves. Love brings us into a state of *presence*. When we are present, we are in the moment, in the here and now.[11] We are not distracted by thoughts about the future or memories of the past. Buddhists refer to this state as *mindfulness*. And presence is our ideal state. When we are present, our minds and hearts are open and we feel secure and fully connected—with ourselves, others, and the world.

---

11 For excellent resources on presence, see the works of Eckhart Tolle.

Chapter 3

BECOMING ALLIES: UNDERSTANDING AND BRIDGING DIFFERENCES

One of the most common assumptions of those in veg/non-veg relationships is that they are too different to ever be able to see eye to eye, and therefore to feel secure and connected. However, while it is possible that the veg/non-veg difference is truly problematic, this is not necessarily the case.

Differences between people in all relationships are normal, natural, and inevitable. Everyone is unique, and so everyone brings different perspectives and needs to their relationships. Even what seem like similarities may actually be differences. For instance, even if you prefer a well-organized living space, your roommate may be more of an organizer than you are and may find you messy by comparison. And even if both partners in a relationship don't eat meat, one may be vegan and the other vegetarian.

Many differences are actually beneficial, encouraging us to grow. For example, we may not have valued taking care of our bodies before we met our health-conscious friend who helped us experience the benefits of regular exercise and wholesome nutrition. Or we may only realize that we're emotionally sensitive after starting a relationship with someone who's comfortable and in touch with their feelings. So differences can enrich us and our relationships in important ways.

Many of us, though, fear differences in our relationships, largely because of the romantic myth that differences drive people apart. That's one reason why, in the early stages of romantic relationships, people tend to selectively notice and exaggerate all they have in common. We have learned to overvalue being similar and devalue being different, and we worry that our differences will cause conflict and will ultimately disconnect us.

While some differences may indeed be irreconcilable, many are in fact bridgeable, including those between vegans and non-vegans. Determining which differences we can bridge and how we can bridge them requires an understanding of the nature of difference and of the various forces affecting relationships. It also requires that we develop the skills necessary to navigate our differences effectively.

THE NATURE OF DIFFERENCE

Differences between ourselves and others are typically the result of our differing personal traits, beliefs, or preferences. Each of these aspects of ourselves can be more or less central to who we are, and so the differences between the individuals in a relationship tend to be more or less fundamental. It's helpful to think of these differences in concentric circles. In the center are our core differences, which include differences in our hardwiring and in the socially ingrained attitudes that shape aspects of our personalities. Toward the outside are our peripheral differences, our more superficial preferences that may differ. A peripheral difference might be reflected in a desire to live in the city rather than the country, or an inclination to go to bed and arise early rather than late.

In general, peripheral differences are the easiest differences to manage, since they are more adaptable and often less emotionally charged than core differences. So although the principles discussed in this chapter apply to managing all kinds of differences, the focus is on those which are core.

Traits

The most central differences are those that are hardwired. The hardwired aspects of ourselves include our traits, which are our inborn characteristics, and, to some degree, our attachment style, how we attach to those we are closest to. Recent research suggests that much of what we used to think of as purely psychological characteristics—such as optimism and pessimism, extraversion and introversion—actually have a biological basis.[1] How much

---

1 See Colin G. DeYoung, Jacob B. Hirsh, Matthew S. Shane, Xenophon Papademetris, Nallakkandi Rajeevan, and Jeremy R. Gray, "Testing Predictions from Personality Neuroscience: Brain Structure and the Big Five," *Psychological Science* 21, 6 (2010): 820–28, and J. Patrick Sharpe, Nicholas R. Martin, and Kelly A. Roth, "Optimism and the Big Five Factors of Personality: Beyond Neuroticism and Extraversion," *Personality and Individual Differences* 51, 8 (2011): 946–51.

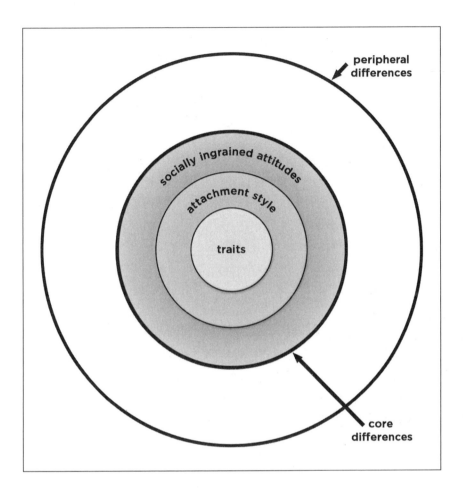

of a role genes play in shaping our personalities is still unanswered, but it is clear that some, perhaps even much, of our personality is in fact hardwired. This does not mean we cannot grow and mature, but it does suggest that our core personality traits are largely unchangeable. A few other examples of common personality traits that likely have a biological basis are our tendencies toward rationality or emotionality, spontaneity or planning, and philosophical or practical thinking.

It can be extremely useful to learn about personality types in order to better understand ourselves and those with whom we are relating. There are a number of systems that explain personality types, but the two that may be most beneficial are the Myers-Briggs Type Indicator (MBTI) and the Enneagram. The MBTI is supported by a number of empirical studies and is widely accepted around the world. It is used by many of the most influential institutions in the United States, as well as by countless psychologists and organizational consultants. The Enneagram has only recently begun to be studied scientifically, but it is a worthwhile system used by many well-respected psychotherapists and coaches. The MBTI and Enneagram are complementary systems that describe different dimensions of personality; they can illuminate some of the main areas where differences and conflicts arise in relationships and help explain some of the drivers beneath disagreements in veg/non-veg relationships.[2] (Though it's not focused on personality types per se, another system that can be helpful for addressing certain relational differences is based on "love languages."[3])

Because most of us aren't aware that many traits are biologically based, we tend to assume that they can (and often should) be changed. However, attempting to change such aspects of our personality is like trying to change our eye color. And if we do try to change these aspects of ourselves, we diminish the fullness of who we are. We truncate ourselves, like cutting limbs off a tree. It can be draining and depressing to deny or otherwise stuff down essential features of our personality. It takes effort to live against our nature, and we end up feeling, and being, inauthentic. Of course, we may choose to modify the behavior that accompanies some of our personality traits, but only to the degree that doing so is healthy for us. For example, if we're a strong extravert, we may learn to talk less and listen more, developing our "inner introvert." We will still always be extraverted, thinking as we speak and requiring a higher degree of social stimulation, but we can temper our tendency to be highly expressive and enjoy more balanced and productive interactions with others.

Attachment Styles

One core aspect of ourselves is our *attachment style*—the way we attach to others with whom we are in close relationship. Research suggests that while

---

2 See www.enneagraminstitute.com and www.16personalities.com to learn more about the Enneagram and the MBTI.
3 See Gary Chapman, *The Five Love Languages: The Secret to Love That Lasts* (Chicago: Northfield, 1992).

we may have a biological predisposition to develop a certain attachment style, our attachment style is largely the result of our earliest life experiences with our caregiver.[4] These first attachment experiences actually caused our brains to become wired in a particular way, because our brains were still developing when we had such experiences. So our attachment style is at least partly hardwired.

More than any other factor, our attachment style determines how we relate to the person we are closest to, which is usually our romantic partner. It determines how we view relationships in general—how much we value them and whether we see them as a source of comfort or danger or both. Our attachment style also determines what we notice or fail to notice in our primary relationship (and to a lesser degree, in our other relationships), and how we think and feel about what we do notice. In short, our attachment style determines, to a very large extent, how we perceive, feel about, and relate to the other.

There are three basic attachment styles, and the combination of our style with the other's determines, to a significant degree, how compatible we are, as well as how effectively we can manage the other differences in our relationship. In general, if our attachment styles are compatible, we can manage many of our other differences with relative ease, and if they are not, even small differences can pose serious challenges. But having incompatible attachment styles is not a death sentence for a relationship. With effort, attachment styles can be changed to create greater compatibility and security.

Two of the three attachment styles are categorized as "insecure," and the third style is referred to as "secure." We develop an insecure attachment style when our early experiences of attachment teach us that attachment to others is unsafe, that we cannot count on the other to be there for us when we need them. Perhaps we didn't have a primary attachment figure or caregiver in the first place, or perhaps the one we did have was unable to meet our basic needs for attention, soothing, and empathy. So we didn't develop the capacity to feel secure in our relationships or to trust or allow ourselves to rely on

---

4 See works by Stan Atkin, accessed through his website, *Psychobiological Approach to Couple Therapy*, 2003–17, stantatkin.com.

another. We develop a secure attachment style when our earliest experiences taught us that we can trust others to be a secure base for us; we learned that we can depend not only on those we love but also on ourselves. Each of the three basic attachment styles exists on a spectrum, so we will experience the style to a greater or lesser degree.

The two types of insecure attachment styles are *avoidant* and *anxious*. Individuals who have an avoidant attachment style value independence and personal freedom over interdependence and togetherness. They don't feel comfortable with the level of intimacy that's usually required for a close personal relationship, and they often feel highly protective of their personal space and can become defensive when they feel they have to compromise to meet another's needs for emotional connection. These individuals are not terribly tuned in to the emotional experiences of others; they tend to miss social cues that suggest their partner is distressed, and they often feel burdened by and resentful of the other's basic needs. Their core belief is that individuals should be able to take care of themselves and that depending on others is both dangerous and a sign of weakness.

Those who have an anxious attachment style are in some ways the opposite of those with avoidant attachment. The anxiously attached crave intimacy and are highly relational. They seek relationships and closeness and are exceptionally attuned to their partner's moods and needs. They want to please their partner and are generally happy to learn how to do so. However, they are insecure in the relationship: because of their early attachment experiences, they believe they are not worthy of love. They struggle with their self-worth and often need a lot of reassurance from their partner that they are loved and accepted. They also tend to have a strong fear of rejection and abandonment. They can come across as needy, because their attachment system—the part of the brain that is triggered by a perceived threat to the relationship—is easily activated, and they need soothing from their partner in order to decrease their anxiety. Though anxiously attached individuals can seem emotionally high-strung, it usually doesn't take much for their partner to reassure them. As long as their partner is empathic, compassionate, and reliable, trust builds over time and their anxiety can decrease significantly.

Those with a secure attachment style are balanced: they neither avoid intimacy, nor do they need extra reassurance that intimacy won't be lost. These individuals feel secure in themselves and their relationship. They don't expect the worst: they don't fear engulfment, as do the avoidant, or abandonment, as do the anxious. They are optimistic yet realistic, assuming that things will be okay but being open to seeing problems that are present. They don't play games, and they are not easily distressed. They are tuned in to their partner and are caring, attentive, and receptive to feedback. They are like rocks in the stormy seas of the insecurely attached.

The reason our attachment styles are so critical to determining our compatibility and our ability to feel secure and connected is because our attachment style determines our most fundamental relationship needs, as well as our ability to meet some of the other's most fundamental relationship needs. For example, if someone with avoidant attachment is partnered with someone with anxious attachment, there will probably be a major clash of needs: the avoidant partner may constantly feel that his freedom is threatened and the anxious partner may constantly feel the threat of abandonment as the avoidant partner defends his space. Accommodating one partner could mean that the other must give up needs they cannot securely or happily live without.

For veg/non-veg couples, attachment needs and fears may underlie the tension around their ideological difference. For example, if you are an anxiously attached vegan, naturally seeking to share your authentic self with your partner, you may experience your partner's disinterest in or resistance to veganism as rejection and abandonment. Or if you are an avoidant non-vegan, you may experience your vegan partner's requests not to be around animal products as controlling. It is therefore important that couples in veg/non-veg relationships explore how their attachment styles may be affecting their experience of their ideological difference.

What, then, is the solution to such differences in attachment styles? Understanding attachment is an important first step.[5] In addition, it can

---

5 For further reading on attachment, see Amir Levine and Rachel Heller, *Attached: The New Science of Adult Attachment and How It Can Help You Find—and Keep—Love* (New York: Jeremy P. Tarcher/Penguin, 2010), and Stan Tatkin, *Wired for Love: How Understanding Your Partner's Brain and Attachment Style Can Help You Defuse Conflict and Build a Secure Relationship* (Oakland, CA: New Harbinger, 2011).

help to be aware that some styles are naturally more compatible than others. Two securely attached individuals are an ideal match, as can be a pairing between anxiously and securely attached partners. All combinations are certainly possible, but for the relationship to work, partners need to understand each other's attachment style and be willing and able to attend to each other's attachment needs. And attachment styles can change, for better or for worse, over time. In a secure relationship (where partners are attending to each other's need for security), those who are anxious or avoidant can learn to be more securely attached, and even secure individuals can become less secure if they are in an insecure relationship.

Socially Ingrained Attitudes

Less extreme yet also essential are those aspects of ourselves that are socially ingrained—not hardwired, but deeply instilled in us by our society, culture, and family. These aspects include (but are not limited to) our gendered preferences, religious beliefs, and emotional sensitivities. For example, people of all genders tend to base female attractiveness largely on youth and physical appearance, and male attractiveness on the ability to provide and protect. Changing what attracts us to a male or female after such extensive socialization can be extremely difficult. Likewise, while some people change their religious beliefs during the course of their lives, many find such transformation unthinkable. And our families of origin impact us in such a way that we are automatically sensitized to certain emotions or situations. If, for example, an abusive parent used to scream at us in a rage, we may be so sensitive to verbal outbursts that we simply cannot feel secure in a relationship with someone who expresses anger strongly.

MYTHS ABOUT DIFFERENCE

We have inherited a handful of problematic myths when it comes to differences in relationships. The two primary myths are (1) that differences are negative and (2) that differences are the main cause of problems in relationships. Of course, differences *can* lead to conflict, and ongoing conflict *can* lead to relationship problems. For instance, consider the conflicting needs that might emerge when one person is an adventurer and the other is a homebody or, as we've been discussing, when one is vegan and the other is not. However, the true cause of relationship problems is rarely our differences; it is how we *relate* to those differences.

Most of us don't relate to differences in a way that enhances our security and connection, because we have learned to believe in three related myths about differences in relationships: (1) that differences reflect deficiencies, (2) that differences disconnect us, and (3) that we must be similar in order to be compatible.

Myth #1: Difference Means Deficiency

When we view differences as deficiencies, we see the other as deficient in a particular area, generally an area in which we feel *we* are sufficient. For instance, the homebody is "not adventurous enough," and the non-vegan is "not compassionate enough." (These judgments could also be worded to communicate that the other is excessive in a particular area—too boring, too selfish, and so on—but the result of seeing the other's difference as a problem is the same.) Sometimes we see ourselves as the deficient ones—maybe we feel that we aren't, for example, smart enough—but the problem remains that we are disparaging rather than accepting our differences.

Myth #2: Difference Means Disconnection

How we define a problem determines how we define the solution. If we define the problem incorrectly, then our solution won't solve the problem, and it may even make the problem worse. For example, if we believe that the other's differences are the cause of conflict in our relationship, then we also believe that the way to solve our conflict is by eliminating such differences—usually by changing the other to be more like we are. We may try, for instance, to inspire the homebody to take more risks or to get the non-vegan to become vegan. If the other feels judged—not accepted for who they are and pressured to conform to our way of being—they will probably resent us and be more resistant to changing than they might otherwise be.

Of course, there are certain times when it is appropriate to request that the other change, such as when their behavior is disrespectful. However, before we can determine which changes are reasonable to request, we must understand both the nature of difference and how to relate to our differences in a way that supports, rather than harms, the integrity and security of ourselves and our relationships.

Myth #3: Similarity Equals Compatibility

Compatibility is the ability to coexist harmoniously. When we are compatible, we relate to one another in a way that reduces the likelihood that we will have conflicting needs and experience toxic or chronic conflict. Compatibility therefore enables us to feel more connected to one another. But what, exactly, makes people compatible?

Many of us think that compatibility is the same as similarity—having common interests and characteristics. It's generally true that the more we have in common with another, the easier it is for us to get along and feel connected, especially when the common ground includes qualities and interests that are important to us. When we have similar qualities and interests, we typically have similar needs and wants, so we are more likely to have such needs and wants satisfied. For example, two extraverts will probably have their needs for social stimulation met, and two vegans will probably not have to worry about meeting some of their important dietary and lifestyle needs.

Similarity, however, does not necessarily translate to compatibility. In fact, sometimes similarities can actually get in the way of compatibility. When we are too similar, we may compete with each other to get our too-similar needs met. For example, the extraverts may both want to be the center of attention and have trouble listening to each other. Being too similar can also limit our opportunities for growth, and we may become stagnant and unbalanced. For example, two activists who both have the tendency to overfocus on the cause and underfocus on their own needs can become increasingly frustrated and burned out, in both their work and their relationship.

What makes us compatible is the ability to meet each other's needs sufficiently enough to be connected. We are compatible when we coexist harmoniously and happily.

COMPATIBILITY, EATING, AND VEG/NON-VEG RELATIONSHIPS

Throughout history and across cultures, food and eating have been key ways in which people have bonded, creating community, strengthening family ties, and reinforcing social connections. However, when one person is vegan, this naturally social, connecting experience can become just the opposite. Family meals, romantic dinners, and holiday feasts may become sources of extreme stress for vegans and non-vegans alike—arenas for power struggles and conflict. And unlike holiday feasts that occur infrequently enough to be tolerated or avoided, mealtime interactions occur on a regular basis. Food and eating, rather than being natural sources of connection, become causes of disconnection.

Misunderstandings, Conflicts, and Mealtime Stress

One of the reasons food and eating can become strained is because of the mistaken assumption that vegans and non-vegans are not compatible in this area. Often, this assumption is based on a simple lack of awareness about vegan eating; many people don't realize that vegan foods can be tremendously diverse, flavorful, and enjoyable. And the assumption is often reinforced by conflicts that begin surfacing around veganism, such as arguments about what to serve for dinner or the ethics of eating animals.

Such stress around food and eating also occurs because when non-vegans don't understand veganism, they can interpret the vegan's choice not to consume certain foods as a rejection not simply of eating animals but of their connection. Feeding and sharing food with others is a connecting experience for many people, so a vegan's refusal to eat foods that, for example, they once enjoyed and shared with their family can be seen as rejecting the family connection.

Of course, the stress surrounding mealtimes also occurs because food represents the very issue that is the focus of the disconnection between vegans and non-vegans in relationships. Food and eating naturally bring veg/non-veg fears and frustrations to the surface.

Changing Focus: From Content to Process

When it comes to eating, all people—vegans and non-vegans alike—tend to focus on the content rather than the process. The content is *what* is being eaten, while the process is *how* people are relating to the whole experience of eating. For example, the content could be pasta with meat sauce, or it could be pasta with veggie sauce. The process is people coming together to enjoy a meal and talk about their day, exchange ideas, relax over food and drinks, and simply connect. The process can include preparing the food as well, which can also be a connecting experience.

The process is what actually matters most in the experience of connecting around food. Although the content does matter—vegans obviously wouldn't want to eat animals and nobody wants to eat food that doesn't taste good—it's usually easy to find foods that satisfy everyone. For example, your non-vegan mother could simply exchange the ground beef in her traditional Bolognese sauce with soy ground beef, which is virtually identical, or she could make a mushroom sauce instead. Most of the content of our eating isn't even what we've chosen; it's simply what we inherited from our family and culture, and we keep eating the same foods in the same ways because it's what we're used to.

When one person becomes vegan, even though some of the content of eating changes, in many ways the process does not. We can still use our mealtimes as opportunities to honor what they're meant for in the first place: to bond with those we care about. The purpose of rituals and traditions centered around eating is generally not to serve particular foods—fish or potatoes, for example—but to bring people together and create connection. Many families with one or more vegans honor their traditions and mealtimes without causing disconnections, because they realize that the security and connection of the people they love matters more than the one or two ingredients they swap out to create a vegan-friendly process. So, for example, they may serve a tofurkey rather than a turkey at Thanksgiving or make their favorite Tex-Mex dish with beans rather than beef.

RELATIONSHIP CATEGORIES

Not all relationships require the same degree of connection. Most of us have a wide variety of relationships that vary in degrees of connectedness. We may have acquaintances, colleagues, family members, close friends, and romantic partners. Think of relationships as existing in concentric circles of closeness, or connection—the further out the circle, the less the need for connection and therefore the higher the tolerance for differences.

One mistake we sometimes make is assuming that we need the same or a similar degree of compatibility and connection in our more distant relationships as we do in our closer ones. We may use the degree of connection in our closer relationships as a yardstick with which to measure the connection in all our relationships. For example, if you share core values and can talk openly about your thoughts and feelings with your brother, you may assume that you should have the same compatibility with other family members. You can end up trying to force closeness, or give up on having any relationship at all with those family members, rather than accepting that different people are naturally more or less compatible with you and that you'll therefore be more or less close to them.

Compatibility and Changing Platonic Relationship Categories

Relationships, like the individuals in them, are not static. They are constantly growing and evolving, and sometimes that evolution moves the individuals in different directions. Relationships may change categories, or they may end.

Many of us have learned to impose a value judgment on relationships that grow in distance rather than in closeness. This judgment can get in the way of us deciding what is in the best interest of ourselves and our relationship and can keep our relationships stuck in categories they no longer belong in.

Our tendency to devalue and therefore resist the sometimes natural progression of decreasing closeness applies to both romantic and platonic relationships. However, deciding to change the category of or end a romantic relationship is often a far more complex and sensitive process, since partners have typically developed vulnerable attachments and made significant emotional investments. Committed romantic relationships are therefore often best served when both partners consciously steer the relationship toward compatible growth—that is, when they make decisions that do not threaten their ongoing compatibility. As long as such decisions do not require compromising core needs or limiting personal development and are made in the interest of maintaining the integrity of the relationship, they can be considered healthy compromises.

Deciding to change the category of a platonic relationship to less close, or to end it altogether, is usually more straightforward. But we often assume that if a friendship or family relationship becomes less close, this change reflects a problem in the relationship or in one of its members. For instance, if you had a former best friend whom you now only rarely make the time to see, you may feel that it's "too bad" that you're no longer as close as you once were. You may feel guilty for not making more of an effort to stay in touch, and yet you resist making such an effort because you don't actually *want* to stay in such close contact. Or you may force yourself to maintain the norm, acting like you're closer than you actually feel, since you don't want to accept that the relationship is growing in distance or you want to avoid hurting the other person.

Of course, it's natural to feel some sadness when a relationship becomes less close, since such a change is a form of loss. However, even if the loss triggers sadness, declining closeness in many relationships—particularly platonic ones—is often a sign of health. It is usually only problematic when the desire to change categories is not shared by both individuals, or when it's the result of an unresolved conflict in the relationship and is therefore not an organic process of growth but a disconnection that hasn't been attended to.

Veganism and Changing Platonic Relationship Categories

Becoming vegan often leads to relationships feeling less close. The vegan's new worldview and lifestyle, combined with the defensive reaction of many non-vegans, can lead to misunderstandings that become conflicts, which can quickly create distance. Sometimes, becoming vegan sheds light on the fact that a friendship or family relationship has already outgrown its current category; other times, it causes a relationship to outgrow its category. The focus of this book is learning how to either bridge such distance or determine whether it's in everyone's best interest to change the category of the relationship.

In the case of platonic relationships, it can be helpful to ask yourself, "Does this friendship or family relationship meet my basic needs for the level of closeness of the category it is in?" For example, if your aunt, with whom you have been somewhat close, is simply unable to understand and accommodate your veganism, rather than struggle and push to maintain your current level of closeness—insisting that she "get" you—you may simply decide to accept that you will be less close. And you can appreciate that you can be close in some ways but not in others; closeness is not a black-or-white issue.

When we give ourselves permission to change the categories of our platonic relationships, we may find that we can live with fairly significant personality and value differences in many, perhaps most, of them. And accepting this fact can relieve vegans of the burden many of them feel of having to convert to veganism those with whom they are close—who are, perhaps ironically, sometimes the least likely to respond to their message.

DIFFERENCES AND DISCONNECTION

Just as we tend to assume that similarities make us compatible and connected, we also assume that dissimilarities make us incompatible and disconnected. Differences, then, can cause us to feel disconnected simply because we have learned to believe that they cause disconnection. Especially when it comes to romantic relationships, the association of difference with disconnection is so strong that we may automatically perceive differences as threats to the sustainability of the relationship. In an effort to reduce the level of threat, we may deny or minimize the difference and fail to address issues that may cause relationship problems down the line. For example, we may fail to tell our new political activist partner—whom we met at a rally we'd attended simply because it included an animal protection issue we feel strongly about—that we're actually not into politics. We don't want to admit to them or ourselves that there may be such a lifestyle difference between us.

Differences sometimes cause us to feel disconnected because we often don't easily understand and empathize with those who are different from us—and understanding and empathy are central to feeling connected. For example, while we may be able to easily understand and relate to someone who shares our desire to discuss thoughts and feelings immediately after an argument, we may struggle to understand a friend who needs time to themselves before talking about their experience. And our lack of understanding and empathy can compel us to push that friend to communicate with us before they are ready to do so, so we end up disregarding their needs and creating further disconnection.

One practical reason our differences may cause us to feel less connected is simply because we may have fewer shared experiences—fewer opportunities for bonding—with one another. For example, if you love hiking and your partner does not, or if you thrive on intellectual analysis while the other prefers discussing practical matters, you will probably not form a strong bond with them in these areas unless their tastes change to adapt to yours, or vice versa.

Accepting differences as normal and natural is an important practice in secure, connected relationships. We obviously shouldn't accept behaviors that are disrespectful, nor must we choose to remain in a relationship in which a difference feels intolerable. However, accepting another for who they are—not judging them because of how they may differ from ourselves—is an essential first step toward determining whether we can feel connected enough to be fulfilled in the relationship.

The best way to accept a difference is to understand it. To understand a difference requires approaching the other with curiosity and compassion, with a genuine desire to know what the world looks like through their eyes. In fact, acceptance itself can often resolve what may have previously seemed to be an irreconcilable difference. For example, a sociable extravert can stop thinking of their introverted partner as a "party pooper" and instead appreciate the depth, peace, and thoughtfulness that often comes from this more internally focused way of being. A trait that had once been a source of contempt is now a quality of attraction.

IDEOLOGY AND DIFFERENCES

Ideological differences are differences in core beliefs and philosophies, such as those that may exist between a Democrat and a Republican, or a vegan and a non-vegan. These differences bring special challenges and are often the greatest area of concern.

How, we wonder, can we manage a difference as significant as that of ideology, which generally impacts every aspect of our lives—emotional, physical, social, psychological, and perhaps even spiritual? How do we know whether this difference is reconcilable?

While ideological differences do present very real and unique challenges, whether they are reconcilable is determined in large part by two factors: how we relate to each other (that is, whether we are practicing the principles that enable us to have a secure, connected relationship) and how we relate to our ideologies. How we relate to our ideologies is determined largely by two factors: how dominant the ideology is in each of our lives, and how we relate to the values that inform, or underlie, our ideologies—that is, whether and how our values may be different. (See the chart toward the end of this section for a visual overview of reconciling ideological and value differences.)

The Dominance of the Ideology in Our Lives

In terms of our ideology's dominance in our lives, the more strongly we are identified with it, the harder it will be to relate to and therefore feel connected with those who don't share it. For example, if we are strongly identified as a vegan—that is, if we feel that being vegan is more important to who we are than other important aspects of our identity, such as being a partner, a teacher, an American, or a friend—it will be difficult to feel connected with those who are not vegan.

Being strongly identified with an ideology is not the same as feeling strongly about it, though often these factors go hand in hand. It is possible, for example, to feel strongly about veganism and to want to maintain this practice without feeling that veganism defines who we are. If we see veganism as simply an expression of our values of compassion and justice or one way in which we practice integrity, then we are less likely to b identified as vegan.

It's natural to define ourselves based on the groups we belong to—such as those that define our nationality, religion, or ideology—and sometimes it's important to do so, as when members of non-dominant groups work to raise awareness of certain social issues. However, especially when it comes to our interpersonal relationships, the less we identify with external labels, the less we limit ourselves and the more we are able to connect with the others in our lives.

Even if we are not strongly identified with our ideology, our lifestyle may be strongly influenced by it. For example, some vegans who work for vegan organizations are not strongly identified as vegan, but their lives are nevertheless very much organized around vegan-related activities. Of course, as consumers, all vegans will find that vegan ideology influences a good deal of their lifestyle—but even then, there is much variation among vegans in terms of how strong that influence is. The more our lifestyles are organized around our differing ideologies, the more challenging it will be to feel compatible with one another. We will need to determine how and whether we can each compromise so that our lifestyles are compatible enough for us to feel connected.

Ideologies and Value Differences

One reason we can feel threatened by ideological differences is because we may assume that ideological differences reflect value differences, since ideologies are based in large part on values. While this is sometimes the case, it is not always so: the same values may underlie different ideologies and simply be interpreted and expressed differently. And even when our values do differ, it doesn't necessarily have to cause problems.

Many of us may feel especially threatened by the thought that those we are close to have different values, for two reasons. First, our values influence much of our lives and are generally unchanging, so compatibility may seem difficult, if not impossible. Second, we need to respect others in order to feel connected to them, and we respect others based on whether they practice the values that matter to us. So we may worry that our value differences will mean that we can't maintain our respect for, and therefore our connection with, the other.

Just as we tend to equate difference with deficiency, we tend to equate value differences with value deficiencies—we judge others' values as inferior to ours. And because of the moral nature of values, the judgment we feel toward the other's value "deficiencies" tends to be even stronger, and therefore more disconnecting, than the judgment we feel toward other types of differences. We tend to see the other as less moral, or even immoral.

Our values are our beliefs about what is good or bad, or what is desirable or undesirable. They inform our attitudes and behaviors and provide guidelines for our choices. And while all values have a moral component, since they reflect what we consider valuable or worthy, some values are more morally focused than others. A number of these moral values—including compassion, justice, and honesty—are thought to be largely universal. Research in moral psychology has found that five moral values tend to underlie and drive our political orientation: care (compassion), fairness (justice), loyalty to one's own group, respect for authority, and sanctity (purity). Most people share all these moral values, but the first two values are more important than the others to left-leaning individuals, while all five are important to those who lean toward the right.[6] Values of a more personal nature span a wide range of preferences, including optimism, directness, sociability, skepticism, sensitivity, creativity, punctuality, and uniqueness.

Our values, both moral and personal, are shaped by our personalities and our life experiences. Our personalities are made up of our temperaments (our inborn traits and tendencies, or our nature) and our social conditioning (the influence of our environment, or how we are nurtured). For example, someone who is born with a natural tendency toward rational analysis and who is raised in a family that encourages rational thinking will likely have rationality as a core value. This person will need solid reasoning on which to base decisions and will probably be skeptical of subjective or anecdotal information.

There is no question that shared values are essential to secure, connected relationships. However, no two people will share all their values, nor will they place the same weight on the values they do share. For example, both

---

6 See Jonathan Haidt, *The Righteous Mind: Why Good People Are Divided by Politics and Religion* (New York: Vintage Books, 2012).

you and your partner may value dependability, but your partner may value it less so, leaning more toward spontaneity. So if an opportunity arises that requires you to cancel a visit to your family, you may argue about whether to honor your commitment or seize the opportunity.

Given that there will always be some value differences in a relationship, whether the value differences are truly a problem depends on three factors: which of our values differ; how important the differing values are to each of us; and whether the values that differ are competing—in conflict—with one another.

If the values that differ are core values to both of us, such as our core moral values (e.g., protecting others from harm versus protecting personal freedom) or our attachment values (e.g., valuing intimacy and togetherness versus valuing independence and freedom), then the value difference is more difficult to navigate.

If the differing value is important to one of us but not the other, it probably won't require a compromise of values for either and therefore won't pose a serious challenge. For instance, perhaps directness is an important value to you—you like to say and hear things without any sugarcoating—but your friend doesn't really care either way.

If we and the other have competing values—even if they are not core moral values—we will probably struggle with this difference, since our needs will be in conflict. Referring back to our previous example, if you value directness but your friend values social diplomacy and needs to "keep the peace" in social situations, then you may each struggle to get your needs met.

Sometimes, what appears to be a value difference is really a power struggle. Suppose both partners in a relationship share the same moral values, but only one decides to become vegan. There may be any number of reasons for the other not to become vegan at the same time; people do not make such a lifestyle change until they are ready to, and that readiness is made possible by a variety of factors that must be in place. Now, perhaps the new vegan wants his partner to change her diet, so he begins telling her about animal suffering and all the other reasons to stop eating meat, eggs, and dairy. His partner resists—not because she has different values but because she doesn't want to be changed by another, or she feels pressured and her anger makes her not want to give in, or she doesn't want to appear to be doing whatever her partner does. As time goes on, the power struggle becomes increasingly entrenched, and it looks like there's a difference of values when in fact there is not. The vegan—who himself may have eaten animals just months ago and who previously had no concerns about value differences—can begin to assume that his partner lacks the values needed for a secure, connected relationship with him.

Veg/Non-veg Relationships and Moral Values

Often, vegans worry that the non-vegans in their lives don't share their moral values—most notably, the values of compassion and justice. Vegans may also worry that non-vegans are lacking in empathy, believing that an empathic deficit underlies the non-vegans' seeming lack of support for vegan values. However, the vast majority of individuals share the values of compassion and justice, as well as a capacity for empathy.

In terms of moral values, the difference between vegans and non-vegans is often not an actual difference of values but either a difference in the degree to which these values are held or a difference in the way the values are interpreted, or both. For example, a vegan may value compassion above all other values. Her partner may also value compassion. He might not use the term "compassion," but if asked, he would say that he thinks kindness toward others, especially those who are vulnerable, is important. However, the non-vegan may value compassion less than he values loyalty, so his desire to remain loyal to his family—for whom eating animal-based foods is a long-standing tradition—trumps his desire to adopt a more compassionate diet. For the vegan to determine whether this difference is too much to tolerate, she needs to understand the inner experience of the non-vegan—the meaning and application of the non-vegan's values—and also to practice the principles of creating secure, connected relationships. If the vegan understands her partner's values around eating animals, and if the relationship is relatively resilient (including the fact that her partner is a vegan ally), then the vegan can determine whether the value differences are truly problematic.

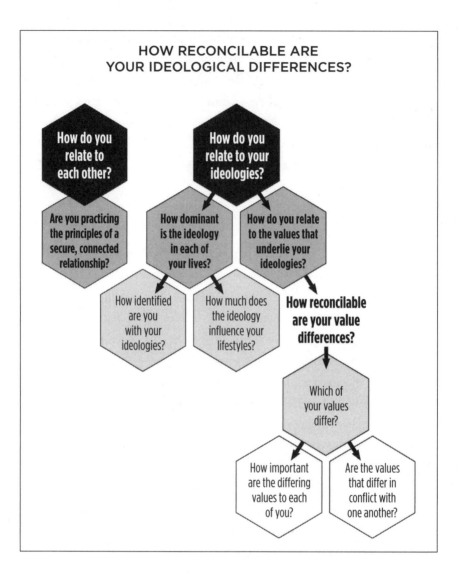

HOW RECONCILABLE ARE YOUR IDEOLOGICAL DIFFERENCES?

How do you relate to each other?

How do you relate to your ideologies?

Are you practicing the principles of a secure, connected relationship?

How dominant is the ideology in each of your lives?

How do you relate to the values that underlie your ideologies?

How identified are you with your ideologies?

How much does the ideology influence your lifestyles?

How reconcilable are your value differences?

Which of your values differ?

How important are the differing values to each of you?

Are the values that differ in conflict with one another?

In terms of empathy, most people are born with the ability to empathize and to increase their empathic capacity over time; people simply vary in the degree to which they naturally feel empathy. Also, some people may be naturally highly empathic but have had life experiences, such as certain types of trauma, that disconnect them from their empathy.

Of course, most of us need to trust that those we are close to share our moral convictions. In order to determine whether we are on the same moral page, we need to truly understand the other's inner world, which includes understanding what their values mean to them and how they practice such values. With this understanding, we can determine how morally similar or different we actually are. And if we find that there is a marked value difference between us, we can see if becoming allies is enough to make the difference manageable.

BRIDGING DIFFERENCES THROUGH BEING ALLIES

As we discussed in Chapter 1, developing a deep understanding of and appreciation for one another's inner worlds—values, ideologies, and general ways of being—is central to creating secure, connected relationships. This is the process of becoming an ally. When we are allies, we are supporters of one another, even when our beliefs differ. (The only exception to engaging in allyship is when doing so would cause us to violate our integrity or feel too emotionally unsafe.)

An ally stands beside you even if your paths are different. An ally has your back even if your cause is not the same. An ally may not share your views, but they fully understand and respect those views and they fully support and respect *you* for who you are and what you believe.

While it is obviously easier to be compatible with those who share our values, in many relationships, there is much room for difference—especially if we commit to allyship. The principles and practices discussed throughout this book are intended to lead us down the path of becoming allies, and we will expand on this issue in upcoming chapters. Many vegans may find that when the non-vegan in their life becomes a vegan ally—witnessing and respecting both them and their values—it becomes entirely possible to enjoy a secure, connected relationship.

Although the differences between vegans and non-vegans can pose serious challenges to relationships, they don't have to. When we understand the nature of difference, we can become allies rather than opponents. And when we stop judging our differences, we can see more clearly which differences may be getting in the way of our connection. We are then empowered to take positive action that is in the best interest of ourselves and our relationships.

Chapter 4

THE HIDDEN DANCES THAT SHAPE RELATIONSHIPS

All of us are members of multiple systems, each of which can have a profound impact on how we think and feel about ourselves and others. A system is a set of interconnected parts that form a whole. It can be helpful to think of a system as a dance.[1] The dance is an entity that is made up of dancers, music, and dance steps, and the way these parts interconnect, or come together, creates the whole dance. In each of the dances in which we are engaged, we may feel more or less secure and connected with our dance partner.

In human systems, which are the focus of this book (and which we will refer to simply as "systems"), the parts are the people (who play certain roles), as well as the rules, or expectations, of how we are supposed to interact. Some of our systems include just one other person, as with our couple system, while others include millions of others, as with social systems. When only two people are involved in a system, we refer to the system as simply a "relationship." Larger systems are, essentially, sets of relationships.

Like dances, each system has its own personality, or flavor. The personality of a system is made up of the personalities and behaviors of the people in it, as well as the way these individuals interact or come together. A family, for example, is more than just the composite of its members; how all those members interact creates the particular personality of the family as a whole. Consider the different families you know: some may be fun-loving and spontaneous, some may be reserved and not emotionally expressive, and so on.

---

1   This analogy was popularized by systems psychologist Dr. Harriet Lerner in *The Dance of Anger: A Woman's Guide to Changing the Patterns of Intimate Relationships* (New York: HarperCollins, 1985).

Systems can be healthy or unhealthy, increasing or decreasing the security and connection of everyone involved. Therefore, understanding the nature of systems and how they guide some of our most critical personal choices is essential for anybody who wants to improve their relationships or their lives. Such understanding is especially important for those in veg/non-veg relationships, where certain types of systems influence each person's perspectives, feelings, and behaviors in unique ways. With awareness, we can work to shift our systems so that they reflect and reinforce the security and connection we seek for ourselves and our relationships.

THE WORKINGS OF A SYSTEM: ROLES AND RULES

Systems are made up of roles and rules. *Roles* are the parts we play, and *rules* are the guidelines we follow.

Roles: The Parts We Play

Some roles we play in a system are explicit, meaning they are clearly stated, such as husband, mother, or boss. Other roles are implicit, or unstated. For example, we can be "pursuers" or "distancers" of intimacy, or we can be "underfunctioners" or "overfunctioners." The underfunctioner is someone who struggles to keep up with basic responsibilities, such as keeping the house clean and paying bills on time, and who takes on a more childlike role in a relationship, while the overfunctioner is the person who plays the role of parent and takes on the lion's share of responsibilities. In veg/non-veg relationships, sometimes the overfunctioner's role is—or includes—that of the *moral* overfunctioner, juxtaposed with the moral underfunctioner.

Family Systems and the Vegan Black Sheep Role

In some types of family systems, there is a so-called black sheep. The black sheep is the child who is a bit different from everybody else, perhaps eccentric, and who never really fits in. The black sheep is often (though certainly not always) the most sensitive child in the family and is frequently misunderstood and ostracized. This child is usually the family scapegoat, the son who is seen as causing the family's problems when, in fact, it is the dysfunction of the system itself that is causing the problems—the black sheep is just picking up on the underlying tension and acting out the problems. Family therapists refer to the black sheep as the "identified patient," the person who is identified as the patient, the problem ("If only Janie would get her act together, this family would be fine!"), but who is simply expressing the family's deeper problems. And being non-conformists, black sheep are naturally more open to issues such as veganism, so the black sheep is the most likely family member to eventually become vegan.

Our family roles tend to follow us into adulthood. So adult vegan black sheep can find that their veganism is seen by the family as another way they don't fit in, or as an attempt to "rebel" against the family norms. Such assumptions only reinforce the vegan's feeling of being misunderstood and unseen and can increase tensions around veganism. And even though the vegan's rational, adult mind may realize that becoming vegan was an empowering act of integrity, on another level, they can feel that their veganism is one more example of how they can't connect with their own family and are "less than." After a lifetime of hearing that they are flawed, adult black sheep often carry a good deal of shame, believing on some level that something is indeed wrong with them.

For vegans who experience tension in their families due to their veganism, it can be helpful to consider whether the family's reaction has more to do with unresolved interpersonal issues than with veganism itself. Discussing the ethics of eating animals or the benefits of vegan nutrition is unlikely to be productive as long as the deeper problematic dynamics remain unaddressed.

Rules: The Lines We Follow

Rules are the guidelines that dictate how we should feel and behave in our roles and in the system as a whole. For example, a rule might be that the father provides, or that the overfunctioner gets to control the majority of relationship decisions. And as with roles, rules may be explicit or implicit. An explicit rule, for instance, may be "no swearing in the house" or "no sexual relations outside the marriage." An implicit rule may be that nobody talks about Dad's drinking, or that the underfunctioner is not allowed to make important decisions for the couple, or that the black sheep's lifestyle choices, such as being vegan, shouldn't be taken seriously. Most rules—even some important ones—are implicit. Most of us therefore follow a set of invisible guidelines in our relationships that have never been stated aloud but that powerfully shape our experience with ourselves and each other.

"THE MORE, THE MORE": BECOMING POLARIZED

Roles can become extreme, especially if differences have not been managed effectively. We can become polarized, standing on opposite ends of a spectrum and inhabiting opposing poles. Consider, for example, a couple who began their relationship as a moderate Democrat and a moderate Republican. Each time a political issue came up, however, the Democrat argued for a more liberal approach while the Republican argued for a more conservative one. As time progressed and the partners asserted their own positions, they each increased their sense of being right, decreased their ability to see the potential rightness of the other's perspective, and became more extreme in their own views.

Any difference where one or both parties is unable or unwilling to truly appreciate the other's perspective will likely lead to the individuals becoming increasingly extreme in their positions. In many relationships, the same argument gets replayed over and over, and each time one person asserts their position, the other reacts by exaggerating their own. Psychologists refer to this dynamic as "the more, the more": the more one person expresses a difference, the more the other does the opposite. For instance, consider Jonas and William, a married couple. Jonas is the underfunctioner and William is the overfunctioner. The more Jonas forgets engagements, loses his keys, and so on, the more William takes charge of managing the couple's social calendar, finding lost items, and so on. And vice versa: the more William assumes extra responsibilities and sees Jonas as incompetent, the more Jonas feels incompetent and relinquishes responsibilities. Over time, both partners fully buy into the belief that Jonas is incompetent and incapable and that William has to take control.

The same dynamic can be seen in the moral over/underfunctioner dance. For example, a vegan can become increasingly morally focused when the non-vegan in her life doesn't express what the vegan sees as sufficient moral concern regarding ethical issues, issues that may extend even beyond veganism. Over time, the pair can become extreme in their views, with the vegan becoming morally perfectionistic and the non-vegan becoming morally apathetic.

As we become increasingly polarized in our relationship, we experience ourselves and the other as being either one way or the other, and we end up in rigid and unchanging roles. We are, for example, either "the responsible one" or "the child," "the pursuer of intimacy" or "the distancer," "the moral advocate" or "the selfish consumer." We fail to appreciate that each of us has the capacity to experience virtually all feelings and behaviors. We can be both responsible *and* childish, we need closeness *and* distance, and we can be moral *and* selfish. The real difference between people is usually a matter of degree.

CLOSED AND OPEN SYSTEMS

Psychologists and sociologists refer to two types of systems—closed and open. A *closed system* is closed, or resistant, to change, and an *open system* is open to change. Of course, like most phenomena, systems exist on a spectrum, so a system can be more or less closed or open.

In a closed system, roles and rules are rigid and unchanging. Closed systems seek to maintain the status quo—the way things are—even if everyone involved is miserable. Most of us have met couples who are spectacularly unhappy in their relationship and yet each partner has a long list of reasons why any change would be impossible. Closed systems force conformity: either we conform to the roles and rules of the system, or we are forced out. Imagine, for instance, that everyone at the animal protection organization you're employed by overworks compulsively. If you do the same, you'll be accepted and celebrated, and if not, chances are high that you will be seen as uncommitted and will end up either being fired or wanting to quit.

Closed systems also have a natural power imbalance among the people in them. Some people have more power to influence the attitudes, feelings, and behaviors of others. For example, in a traditionalist family system, the father's opinions, moods, and actions are more likely to impact the others than vice versa. ("Dad's spoken; end of discussion!" or "When Dad's in a mood, everyone needs to stay out of his way.")

Sometimes, closed systems appear to be changing when in fact they are not—they are just reconfiguring themselves. For example, consider a couple in which one person overfunctions and the other underfunctions. After years of the overfunctioner complaining about the underfunctioner not pulling their weight, when the underfunctioner finally starts becoming responsible, the overfunctioner may feel out of control and unneeded and start underfunctioning. This is not infrequently the case when an alcoholic begins recovery and the "caretaker" in the relationship suddenly becomes disoriented and depressed. So the overfunctioner-underfunctioner system doesn't really change at all: the partners simply swap roles, and the same dynamic stays in place.

Polarization is unlikely to occur in an open system, where roles and rules are modified as the relationship and its members evolve and grow. For example, in an open system, when one person decides to become vegan, the other—even if they are not ready or wanting to become vegan themselves—would be curious about and supportive of the vegan's new lifestyle.

OPPRESSIVE SYSTEMS

Our relationship system is actually a system within a system, a micro system of the broader macro, or social, systems of which we are all a part. Some of these broader systems are problematic closed systems, or "oppressive systems," which impose their implicit roles and rules on us to influence how we function in our personal relationships. These systems are germs, intruders in our relationships that can deplete our relational immune system without us realizing what's happening.

Because most of us have no idea that we're being influenced by such systems, we unknowingly bring these dysfunctional dynamics into our hearts and homes, where they can wreak havoc. We can end up acting against our integrity and decreasing the security and connection in our relationships—not because we're immoral or uncaring, but simply because we're unaware.

These oppressive systems are belief systems, or ideologies, such as racism, sexism, and carnism—the latter being the belief system that influences how we relate to one another as non-vegans and vegans. When it comes to veg/non-veg relationships, carnism is often the primary intruder, and we will discuss this system in depth in the next chapter. All oppressive systems, though, impact many of our deeply held beliefs, and they influence everything from whose opinions we take more seriously to whose needs we perceive as more valid and who has more permission to feel and express anger. They also determine whose version of history we teach to our children.

Oppressive Systems and Power Imbalances

A key way in which oppressive systems influence our relationships is by creating a power imbalance between us when we belong to different groups within a system. The system assigns us each a role, and one role comes with more power than the other. The role we play is determined by the social group we belong to—white/non-white, male/female, veg/non-veg, and so on. If we belong to the dominant group, sometimes referred to as the "majority," we have more power than we do if we belong to the non-dominant, or minority, group.

Of course, we belong to many groups, and each of our groups affects the amount of power we have in our relationship. For example, when you belong to one dominant and one non-dominant group, and so does the person with whom you're relating, power balances out a bit. Perhaps, for example, you are a male (dominant) and also a vegan (non-dominant), while your partner is female (non-dominant) and non-vegan (dominant). Still, this doesn't mean the power will be truly balanced, because some roles give us more power than others. Gender, for example, has far more influence on how much power we have than does veg/non-veg ideology. It's neither necessary nor possible to calculate the exact amount of power we bring to our relationships. It's simply important to understand the basic power dynamics in relationships that come with the roles assigned to us by social systems.

Perhaps the most important way in which oppressive systems cause problems in our relationships is by distorting our perceptions of reality. When we have more power in the system, we have more power to have our version of reality accepted and seen as true, even when it contradicts objective truth or the truth of the other's experience. None of us asked for this power, and most of us don't realize we have it. Nevertheless, it affects all of us, and unless we understand some of these power dynamics, we cannot loosen their grip on our lives and relationships.

Oppressive Systems and Narratives

Our *narrative* is the story we create based on our beliefs and perceptions; it is our version of reality. Narratives can be the result of our personal experience or of our social conditioning, inherited from our society. For example, if we have a personal history of being betrayed in our relationships, we may have a narrative that people cannot be trusted. If we grow up in a heterosexist society, our inherited narrative will be that heterosexuality is normal and natural and that other sexualities are abnormal and unnatural. And if we grow up in a meat-eating society, our inherited narrative is that eating animals is normal and natural and that not eating animals is abnormal and unnatural.

Not all narratives are created equal. Some narratives have more power than others, meaning they carry more weight and are automatically seen as more believable—even if they are not actually more valid. These narratives are *dominant narratives*, or *dominant social narratives*, the narratives of the person or social group with more power in a closed system.

Dominant social narratives are society's narratives, which members of all groups—dominant and non-dominant—grow up learning and believing. For example, both heterosexuals and non-heterosexuals learn to believe the dominant social narrative that heterosexuality is normal and natural and that other sexualities are *ab*normal and *un*natural, or deviant, which is one reason for the high rates of suicide among gay and lesbian teenagers. And non-vegans and vegans grow up learning and believing that eating animals is normal and natural; we are virtually never encouraged to think otherwise. When we impose our narrative on others, we are defining their reality, dictating what is true for them—and dominant social narratives are those that are imposed on everyone.

We all bring dominant social narratives home with us, to influence our personal relationships. As a result, many vegans and non-vegans can become ensnared in a struggle that has far less to do with their personal ways of than with the broader system of which they are a part. For example, the dominant social narrative that eating meat is necessary for health has more power than the vegan narrative that eating meat is not necessary for health—even though the data do not support the meat-eating narrative. So if a non-vegan and a vegan are discussing the issue, the non-vegan's narrative and experience, supported by the broader society, is automatically seen as more valid than the vegan's narrative and experience. Heated debates can break out— not only about the facts but also about the vegan feeling like their opinion isn't being given equal weight and the non-vegan feeling imposed upon by what they see as the vegan's "bias."

SHIFTING SYSTEMS

Given the power of the systems we are a part of, what are we to do if we wish to lead more balanced and authentic lives and create secure, connected relationships? Systems psychologist Harriet Lerner explains that in order to be a part of a system, we have to be dancing to the same song as the other, doing the same dance steps.[2] We simply cannot dance with a partner who is waltzing if we are doing the tango. The dance steps, of course, are the roles and rules of the system that we are operating in.

Lerner says that if we don't like the dance we're doing, we must change our own dance steps. In other words, we must change the role we play and the rules we follow. For example, if the person you're dating continues to order meat when you're at a restaurant even though you've made it clear that being exposed to meat is distressing, rather than continue to argue and get upset while eating out, you can say you'll no longer go on dinner dates as long as there is meat involved. If the relationship ends because of your decision to honor your own boundaries, you will likely have saved yourself future suffering. Your partner was either unable or unwilling to respect your needs, and in either case, this makes them not a good fit for you.

When we change our dance steps, the other is faced with three choices:

---

2 See Lerner's "Dance" series of books at www.harrietlerner.com.

they can change their dance steps with us, they can pull us back into the old dance, or they can stop dancing with us (i.e., leave the relationship). In a more open system, the other would accept and work toward healthy change; in a more closed system, they would push to revert back to the status quo or perhaps end the relationship.

How much influence we have when it comes to changing a system depends on the size of the system and the amount of power we hold in it. For example, in a system of two people, all things being equal, we have a 50 percent chance of influencing the system. When it comes to social systems, of which we make up only a tiny percentage, the shift we bring about will obviously be less impactful. But every time we refuse to play the roles and follow the rules of an unhealthy system, we are resisting rather than reinforcing that system. Generally, oppressive systems shift when enough people change their dance steps, which is the goal of a social justice movement, such as civil rights or veganism.[3]

As we grow and become healthier, we may influence our systems to grow with us, or we may find that we no longer fit into systems we were once a part of. Although it may seem that only the former is desirable, in both cases, the situation is win-win. Family systems expert Ernie Larsen uses the analogy of a watch to describe the experience of growing out of a dysfunctional system.[4] Imagine looking inside a watch and seeing that all the pieces are twisted and distorted. Yet they are all misshapen in such a way as to be able to fit together so the watch actually functions. If you remove one of the pieces and reshape it so that it's normal, it will no longer be able to fit into the distorted system it once conformed to. The same is true for the systems we are a part of. So just because we no longer fit into some of our systems, this is not necessarily a sign that something is wrong. It may well be that something is right.

---

3 Interestingly, because oppressive systems maintain themselves in part by creating narratives that shame those who challenge them, social justice movements often seek to cultivate pride in their proponents. For example, Black Pride was a movement that sought to transform the experience of black people so that they would feel empowered to transform the external power structures that kept them oppressed, and today, Veggie Pride seeks to validate the beliefs and experience of vegans who are working to transform the power structures that keep animals oppressed.

4 Ernie Larsen, *Stage II Recovery: Life Beyond Addiction* (New York: HarperCollins, 1986).

Chapter 5

CARNISM: THE INVISIBLE INTRUDER IN VEG/NON-VEG RELATIONSHIPS

In the cult classic movie *The Matrix*, the characters believe themselves to be living normal lives, when in fact they are hooked up to machines that have imprisoned their minds and the minds of almost all humans. All they see, feel, and perceive is a simulated reality, created in order to prevent them from rebelling against the machines that are using their body heat as an energy source. It's only when the characters are able to unplug themselves from the Matrix that they can free their minds and see reality as it truly is. And when they reclaim their freedom of thought, they also reclaim their freedom of choice. They no longer passively serve the violent interests of a more powerful group of others, but instead choose to act in accordance with their personal values and integrity. They refuse to support a system that is based on exploitation, and they fight for justice and freedom for all of humanity.

CARNISM: THE MENTALITY OF MEAT

When we are born into a meat-eating culture, we are born into a system that conditions our minds in a way that is strikingly similar to that of the Matrix. This system is a belief system, and it's invisible, so we don't realize how we have been conditioned to think, feel, and act in ways that are against our own interests and the interests of others. We are not aware that we have inherited a mentality that disconnects us from the truth of our experience and from the experience of others. What's more, this mentality has built-in defenses that make it especially difficult to illuminate or challenge.

This system is called *carnism*. Carnism is the invisible belief system, or ideology, that conditions us to eat certain animals. Carnism is a closed, or oppressive, system, like those we discussed in Chapter 4. And it is also a dominant system, meaning that it's so widespread that we don't even see it as a belief system at all: it's as though we're so immersed in the ocean of carnism that we don't realize we're under water.

Carnism is the opposite of veganism, but because carnism is invisible, we haven't labeled it, as we have veganism. We tend to think that only vegans (and vegetarians) bring their beliefs to the dinner table. But when eating animals is not a necessity, which is the case for many people in the world today, it is a choice—and choices always stem from beliefs.[1] Most of us eat pigs but not dogs precisely because we *do* have a belief system when it comes to eating animals. We simply aren't aware that we have a choice when we eat animals because we aren't aware of carnism.

Only with awareness of carnism can we reclaim our freedom of choice; without awareness, there *is* no free choice. And with awareness we can ultimately make choices that connect us, rather than disconnect us from others and from ourselves.

THE THIRD PARTY IN OUR RELATIONSHIPS

Of all the challenges to veg/non-veg relationships, carnism is perhaps the greatest. Carnism has a profound impact on both non-vegans and vegans, and it's often a cause of chronic confusion, frustration, and disconnection. Carnism distorts our perceptions, disconnects us from our feelings, and prevents us from thinking rationally or behaving compassionately.

Carnism is an invisible intruder in our relationships. It's a third party that disrupts our relationships and replaces our security and connection with tension and confusion. Carnism causes our relationships to become triangulated. *Triangulation* is the term psychologists use to describe the dynamic that results from adding a third, disruptive element to a relationship between two people. That element can be another person (as when one

---

1 The most notable exceptions to having a choice about eating animals are those who are economically or geographically unable to make their food choices freely, for whom eating animals is often a necessity.

partner in a couple has an affair), an addiction, or any force that changes the two-person dynamic in a negative way. Carnism is such a powerful force in our relationships that it turns a partnership into a triangle—a relationship between us, the other, and carnism.

THE PARADOX OF CARNISM

Most of us have never wondered why we eat certain animals but not others. We may go through our entire lives never asking why we find the flesh of a cow delicious but the flesh of a dog disgusting, or why we feel a connection with the cat in our home while we don't feel a connection with the pig or chicken who has become our dinner. And most of us know, on some level, that there really isn't such a difference between the dog and the cow, the cat and the pig. So what is it that makes our heart open up to one and shut down toward the other?

The reason is carnism. Carnism creates a paradoxical mentality. We would feel guilty eating certain animals, yet we take pleasure in consuming others. We cringe when faced with images of animals suffering, yet we may eat their bodies multiple times a day. We love dogs and eat pigs, yet we don't know why.

Because this paradoxical mentality is shared by virtually everyone in society, it's considered normal, so we rarely, if ever, stop to reflect on it. And we're not encouraged to reflect on it: when we're growing up, nobody asks us whether we *want* to eat animals, how we *feel* about eating animals, whether we *believe* in eating animals—even though this daily practice has profound ethical dimensions and personal implications. Eating animals is just "the way things are." In fact, if anything, we are *dis*couraged from reflecting on our food choices: when children make the connection that their meat is from an animal, they often become distressed, and the adults in their lives have to coax them back into unquestioning acceptance of carnism. When any attitude is so widespread, no matter how irrational, it's simply accepted as a given, and it remains unchallenged.

We're conditioned not to self-reflect when it comes to eating animals precisely because if we did, we would quite probably question the entire system on which animal agriculture is built. Most of us are rational people:

we want to make choices based on what makes sense, not simply on what we've been taught to believe. And most of us care about animals and would never want to cause them to suffer, especially when that suffering is intensive and completely unnecessary. So carnism requires rational, caring people to support irrational, harmful practices without realizing what they are doing and to become defensive whenever they *are* asked to reflect on their food choices.

CARNISTIC DEFENSE MECHANISMS

Because carnism runs counter to core human values—values such as compassion and justice—it needs to use psychological defense mechanisms, mental distortions, to disconnect us, psychologically and emotionally, from the truth of our experience when it comes to eating animals. These carnistic defenses cause us to, for example, see a hamburger as food rather than as a once-living animal and therefore to feel appetized rather than disgusted. If the hamburger were made of dog flesh, our perceptions and feelings would be dramatically different, because we haven't been conditioned to disconnect from our authentic thoughts and feelings when it comes to the idea of eating "non-edible" animals such as dogs. Carnistic defenses enable us to support unnecessary violence toward animals without the moral discomfort we would otherwise feel. In other words, because we naturally feel empathy toward animals and don't want them to suffer, carnism must provide us with a set of tools to override our conscience, our natural resistance, so that we support a system that we would otherwise likely find deeply offensive.

Denial: See No Evil, Hear No Evil, Speak No Evil

The primary defense of carnism is denial: if we deny that there's a problem, then we don't have to do anything about it. Denial is expressed largely through invisibility. One way carnism remains invisible is by remaining unnamed. If we don't name it, then eating animals appears simply as a given, a morally neutral behavior with no basis in a belief system. If we don't see the system, then we can't question or challenge it, and we don't realize that we have a choice when it comes to whether or not to eat animals.

Carnism also remains invisible by keeping its victims out of sight and therefore conveniently out of public consciousness. For example, in just one week, more farmed animals are killed than the total number of people killed in all wars throughout human history, and their body parts are literally everywhere we turn—yet we virtually never see any of these animals alive.[2] And farmed animals suffer an almost unimaginable fate. They are, for instance, forcibly impregnated and castrated, and their beaks, horns, and tails are cut off—all without any pain relief.[3] The vast majority of farmed animals spend their entire lives confined in windowless sheds, sometimes in crates so small they can barely move, and it's not uncommon for them to have their throats slit while conscious or to be boiled alive.[4]

Despite the fact that they are treated as commodities, the animals who become our food are not very different from the animals we consider our friends and family. For example, studies have shown that pigs are more intelligent than dogs (some people say they're even as intelligent as three-year-old humans) and they even empathize with others.[5] Chickens are often kept as pets: they can learn their names and bond closely with people, and recent research has shown them to be more cognitively and socially complex than previously believed.[6] Scientists have found that chickens are even altruistic—

2   For number of animals killed worldwide in 2011, see Christine Chemnitz and Stanka Becheva, eds., *Meat Atlas: Facts and Figures About the Animals We Eat* (Berlin, Germany: Heinrich Böll Foundation and Friends of the Earth Europe, 2014), 15. For number of people killed in wars, see Chris Hedges, *What Every Person Should Know About War* (New York: Free Press, 2003), 1.

3   See "Castration of Pigs: Livestock Update, January 2008," Virginia Cooperative Extension, Virginia State University, http://www.sites.ext.vt.edu/newsletter-archive/livestock/aps-08_01/aps-0111.html; Eleonora Nannoni, Tsampika Valsami, Luca Sardi, and Giovanna Martelli, "Tail Docking in Pigs: A Review on Its Short- and Long-Term Consequences in Preventing Tail Biting," *Italian Journal of Animal Science* 13, 1 (2014); Jacquie Jacob, "Beak Trimming in Poultry in Small and Backyard Poultry Flocks," May 5, 2015, http://articles.extension.org/pages/66245/beak-trimming-of-poultry-in-small-and-backyard-poultry-flocks; American Veterinary Medical Association, "Literature Review on the Welfare Implications of the Dehorning and Disbudding of Cattle," July 15, 2014, https://www.avma.org/KB/Resources/LiteratureReviews/Documents/dehorning_cattle_bgnd.pdf.

4   See Elaine Dockterman, "Nearly One Million Chickens and Turkeys Unintentionally Boiled Alive Each Year in U.S.," *Time*, October 29, 2013, http://nation.time.com/2013/10/29/nearly-one-million-chickens-and-turkeys-unintentionally-boiled-alive-each-year-in-u-s/, and Gail A. Eisnitz, *Slaughterhouse: The Shocking Story of Greed, Neglect, And Inhumane Treatment Inside the U.S. Meat Industry* (New York: Prometheus Books, 2007).

5   See, for example, Lori Marino and Christina M. Colvin, "Thinking Pigs: A Comparative Review of Cognition, Emotion, and Personality in *Sus domesticus*," *International Journal of Comparative Psychology* 28 (2015), http://animalstudiesrepository.org/cgi/viewcontent.cgi?article=1042&context=acwp_asie.

6   See J. L. Edgar, J. C. Lowe, E. S. Paul, and C. J. Nicol, "Avian Maternal Response to Chick Distress," *Proceedings of the Royal Society B* 278 (2011): 3129–34.

they will risk their own lives to protect others from harm. Cows develop "best friendships" and become stressed when separated from those individuals with whom they've bonded.[7] And recent studies have demonstrated that some fish and crustaceans have pain receptors and intelligence, so harming these animals is illegal in some places in the world.[8] Carnism depends on us denying the tremendous suffering of these individuals, because if we didn't, we would likely have a very hard time continuing to eat them.

Justification: Eating Animals Is Normal, Natural, and Necessary

Another carnistic defense is justification. Carnism teaches us to justify eating animals by teaching us to believe that the *myths* of meat, eggs, and dairy are the *facts* of meat, eggs, and dairy. There are many myths surrounding eating animals, but all of them fall under the "three Ns of justification": eating animals is *normal*, *natural*, and *necessary*. And of course, these same myths have been used to justify violent practices throughout human history, from slavery to male dominance.

Eating Animals Is Normal

Eating animals is a social norm—a behavior that is considered socially acceptable and legitimate. Social norms force conformity: when we go along with them, our lives are easier and we are considered "normal." For example, if we eat animals, we'll have no problem finding food wherever we travel and we'll be seen as just like everybody else, part of the dominant group, the majority. But what we call "normal" is simply the beliefs and behaviors of the dominant culture. Social norms change over time, as societies evolve. For example, it was once normal and acceptable to keep African slaves and to stone women who were suspected of infidelity.

Because carnism is a social norm, we don't see the irrationality of the system: when everybody is doing something, it can be difficult to see

---

7 K. M. McLennan, "Social Bonds in Dairy Cattle: The Effect of Dynamic Group Systems on Welfare and Productivity," PhD diss., University of Northampton, 2013.

8 See, for example, C. Brown, "Fish Intelligence, Sentience and Ethics," *Animal Cognition* 18, 1 (2015): 1–17, and Jonathan Balcombe, *What a Fish Knows: The Inner Lives of Our Underwater Cousins* (New York: Scientific American / Farrar, Straus and Giroux, 2016).

how that something may make very little sense. For example, many well-intentioned people support the concept of "humane" (sometimes referred to as "organic" or "bio") meat. These people are willing to spend more money in order not to support animal cruelty; they are voting with their dollar, hoping to make a positive difference in the system. But the idea of "humane" animal foods becomes irrational the moment we step outside the carnistic box: most of us would consider it cruel to slaughter a happy, healthy golden retriever simply because people like the way her legs taste, and yet when the very same thing is done to individuals of other species, we are told to consider it kind. Because carnism is so normal, we don't realize that "humane meat" is a contradiction in terms. The concept of "humane" animal products is actually a public relations strategy created by carnistic industries to maintain their profits; the vast majority of "humanely" manufactured animals suffer terribly, not only in their dying but also in their living.

And carnism is normalized worldwide. In meat-eating cultures around the world, people tend to feel comfortable eating only those species they have learned to classify as edible. All the rest, they perceive as inedible and disgusting (such as pigs in the Middle East) or even unethical (such as dogs and cats in the United States, or cows in India) to consume. And members of all cultures tend to see their own classification of edible animals as rational and judge the classifications of other cultures as disgusting and/or offensive. So, while the type of species consumed changes from culture to culture, people's experience of eating animals is similar across carnistic cultures.

Eating Animals Is Natural

What we learn to call "natural" is actually just the dominant culture's interpretation of history. In the case of carnism, "natural" does not reflect *human* history but rather *carnistic* history. In other words, we learn history from the carnistic perspective.

When we look at history through the lens of carnism, we learn to look only as far back as necessary to justify current carnistic practices. For example, rather than use our earliest ancestors, who were plant eaters, as the reference point for how we define what a natural diet is for humans, we look to their descendants, who were flesh eaters.[9] And although murder and rape are at least as long-standing, and therefore as natural, as eating animals, we would never use the longevity of these practices as a justification for them today.

In recent years, the justification that eating animals is natural has been reinforced by the notion that locally-sourced foods make up the most natural (and sustainable) diet—and that animal products are an important part of such a diet. However, studies on human nutrition have disproved this claim.[10]

Another way in which supporters of local-sustainable carnism often argue that eating animals is natural (or that *not* eating animals is *un*natural) is by pointing out that hunting is a widespread and long-standing practice and that modern food-production methods have removed us from the (natural) process of killing so that we have become overly sensitized to harming animals. The main problem with this argument is that it assumes that not wanting to harm others is a bad thing, that sensitivity to violence is unnatural and therefore negative. Vegans are seen as animal-loving sentimentalists who live in cities and are disconnected from the natural world. While it is true that most people—vegan and non-vegan—are no longer close to the process of raising and killing animals and are therefore more sensitized to such a process, it is also true that most of us are no longer witnesses to public hangings or gladiator killing games and we are therefore more sensitive to harming other humans.

Because we are hardwired to empathize with others, empathy is our natural state. So what has changed is not necessarily that we have become "sensitized" to animal suffering, but that we have stopped being "desensitized"

---

9 See, for example, Rob Dunn, "Human Ancestors Were Nearly All Vegetarians," *Scientific American Guest Blog*, July 23, 2012, https://blogs.scientificamerican.com/guest-blog/human-ancestors-were-nearly-all-vegetarians/.

10 See, for example, N. Wright, L. Wilson, M. Smith, B. Duncan, and P. McHugh, "The BROAD Study: A Randomised Controlled Trial Using a Whole Food Plant-Based Diet in the Community for Obesity, Ischaemic Heart Disease or Diabetes," *Nutrition and Diabetes* 7, 3 (2017): e256; Philip J. Tuso, Mohamed H. Ismail, Benjamin P. Ha, and Carole Bartolotto, "Nutritional Update for Physicians: Plant-Based Diets," *The Permanente Journal* 17, 2 (2013): 61–66; "Position of the Academy of Nutrition and Dietetics: Vegetarian Diets," *Journal of the Academy of Nutrition and Dietetics* 116, 12 (December 2016); the works of Dr. Michael Greger at nutritionfacts.org; and Winston J. Craig, "Health Effects of Vegan Diets," *American Journal of Clinical Nutrition* 89, 5 (May 2009): 1627S–33S.

to it. We are more likely to create the kind of world we all want to live in if we see empathy, compassion, and fairness as qualities to be cultivated rather than transcended.

Eating Animals Is Necessary

Often, what we learn to think of as necessary is simply what's necessary to maintain the dominant culture. It is indeed necessary to continue eating animals in order to maintain a culture of carnism. But for those of us who are geographically or economically able to make our food choices freely, it is not necessary to eat animals for survival or for health. Today, there is an overwhelming body of evidence demonstrating that diets without carnistic products can be very healthy. In many cases, they may be even healthier than carnistic diets.[11] And while nutritionists used to believe that animal protein was necessary for muscle strength, we now know that plant protein is in many ways superior.[12] In fact, more and more professional athletes are choosing to eat a plant-based, or vegan, diet to enhance athletic performance and optimize health. (And consider how some of the strongest animals on the planet, such as elephants and rhinos, are herbivores.)

SOCIETAL CARNISM

Carnism is institutionalized, meaning that it's supported and promoted by all major social institutions, including medicine, law, education, and business. In other words, carnism is built into the very structure of society, shaping norms, laws, traditions, and our very way of life. When a system is institutionalized, its beliefs and practices are promoted as facts rather than opinions and are accepted unquestioningly. For example, homosexuality used to be classified by the medical and psychiatric community as a mental

---

11 See the sources referred to in note 9 on the facing page.

12 See, for example, Chesney K. Richter, Ann C. Skulas-Ray, Catherine M. Champagne, and Penny M. Kris-Etherton, "Plant Protein and Animal Proteins: Do They Differentially Affect Cardiovascular Disease Risk?" *Advances in Nutrition* 6 (November 2015): 712–28; Mingyang Song et al., "Association of Animal and Plant Protein Intake with All-Cause and Cause-Specific Mortality," *JAMA Internal Medicine* 176, 10 (2016): 1453–63; and T. Colin Campbell and Thomas M. Campbell II, *The China Study: The Most Comprehensive Study of Nutrition Ever Conducted and the Startling Implications for Diet, Weight Loss and Long-Term Health*, rev. ed. (Dallas, TX: BenBella Books, 2016).

illness: same-sex couples were not allowed to get married, and heterosexuality was considered the normal, natural, necessary way of life for all people. Eating animals is similarly supported by social institutions: it is promoted by doctors and nutritionists even though the data show that these products are unnecessary for health and are often actually *bad* for health; farmed animals are legally classified as property, making it legally impossible to argue for their rights; and of course, eating animals is considered normal, natural, and necessary.

When we are born into an institutionalized system such as carnism, we simply don't see the bias of the system, so we don't realize that, for example, those who study nutrition actually study carnistic nutrition. We internalize the system's logic, absorbing it as our own. In other words, we learn to look at the world through the lens of carnism.

PSYCHOLOGICAL CARNISM

Carnism uses a set of defenses that distort our perceptions in such a way as to distance us, psychologically and emotionally, from the animals we learn to think of as food. For instance, carnism teaches us to see farmed animals as objects, so we learn to refer to the turkey on our Thanksgiving platter as some*thing* rather than some*one*. Carnism also teaches us to see farmed animals as abstractions, as lacking any individuality or personality of their own: we learn to believe, for example, that a pig is a pig and all pigs are the same. And carnism teaches us to place animals in categories in our minds so that we can harbor very different feelings and carry out very different behaviors toward different species: dogs and cats are family and chickens and cows are food.

FROM ABSURDITIES TO ATROCITIES

When we look at the world through the lens of carnism, we fail to see the absurdities of the system. We see, for instance, an advertisement of a pig holding a butcher knife and gleefully dancing over the fire pit in which she is to be cooked, and rather than take offense, we take no notice. We accept the claim of the companies who profit from killing animals that the animals in their hidden-away factories are free from harm, despite the fact that it is often illegal for civilians to obtain access to these buildings or even to photograph them from a distance.

As Voltaire wisely said, "If we believe absurdities, we shall commit atrocities." Carnism is but one of the many atrocities, one of the many violent ideologies, that are an unfortunate part of human history. And although the experience of each group of victims will always be somewhat unique, the systems themselves are similar, because *the mentality that enables such violence is the same*. We did not create this mentality; we inherited it. And when we recognize the carnistic mentality for what it is, we can appreciate that eating animals is not simply a matter of personal ethics: it is the inevitable end result of an oppressive system.

VEGANISM: THE COUNTER-SYSTEM TO CARNISM

Social progress happens when enough people step outside of the matrix created by an oppressive system and start to question and challenge it. Eventually, a counter-belief system is formed, which evolves into a social justice movement. Of course, oppressive systems fight back; such systems resist change. When we look back on history, we can see that many of the beliefs we accept today as rational, ethical, and essential to a functional society were dismissed, invalidated, ridiculed, and even met with violent hostility. For example, it was once considered ludicrous and offensive for people of color to patronize the same institutions as white people or for women to attend college.

Over the years, as more and more people began to question carnism, a new, counter-belief system, veganism, emerged and evolved into the social justice movement it is today. The vegan movement seeks to deactivate the carnistic matrix so that all members of society are able to make choices that are in their own best interest and in the best interest of the animals and the environment, and the movement will have succeeded when enough people have opened their hearts and minds to the truth behind carnism.

Despite the fact that most people's hearts and minds are in alignment with veganism—they care about animals and they want to lead healthier lives—most people are also resistant to hearing the truth about carnism. This is because *carnism causes us to resist the very information that would unplug us from the carnistic matrix.* And one of the ways it does this is by causing us to resist the people who bring us that information—vegans. Carnism teaches us to believe a whole host of myths and stereotypes about a group of people whose sole purpose is to raise awareness of an irrational and violent belief system so that we can reclaim our freedom of thought and choice. So we end up opposing the very people we might otherwise see as natural allies.

SECONDARY DEFENSES

To keep itself alive, carnism must ensure that it remains more powerful than the vegan movement, so that the scales of power don't tip. Carnism maintains this power imbalance in part by using the defenses we discussed, which are *primary defenses*. Primary defenses validate carnism: they encourage us to believe that eating animals is the right thing to do. Carnism also uses another set of defenses, *secondary defenses*, which invalidate veganism: they encourage us to believe that *not* eating animals is the wrong thing to do. Secondary defenses invalidate veganism by invalidating the vegan movement, vegans, and vegan ideology or beliefs.

Secondary defenses, like primary defenses, are internalized, meaning that they shape our perceptions without us realizing it. Often, even vegans have internalized at least some of these defenses, which can cause them to feel confused, frustrated, and despairing. Given the tremendous negative influence of carnism on some of our deepest attitudes and most frequent behaviors, and given that non-vegans and vegans alike are largely unaware of this influence, it's almost impossible to avoid misunderstandings, confrontations, and disconnection in our relationships when one of us is vegan and the other is not.

Secondary Denial

One secondary defense, *secondary denial*, teaches us to deny the facts that veganism is a valid belief system and that the vegan movement is a valid social justice movement. We learn to believe, for example, that veganism is a trend, or even a cult, and that the vegan movement is just a small group of radicals and hippies who want to impose their beliefs on others. Denial hides the fact that the vegan movement is based on the very same principles as other major social justice movements and that it is one of the fastest-growing social justice movements in the world today.

Secondary denial follows logically from primary denial—the denial of any dominant belief system in the first place. Secondary denial teaches us to believe that there is therefore neither a dominant group (non-vegans) nor a non-dominant group (vegans). In other words, the power imbalance between non-vegans and vegans is made invisible. (As we discussed in Chapter 4, members of dominant groups automatically have more power than members of non-dominant groups.)

The Carnistic Narrative

The carnistic power imbalance is due to the carnistic narrative. As we discussed in Chapter 4, a narrative is a story we learn to believe about ourselves, others, and/or the world. Dominant narratives are the stories we inherit from the dominant systems we are born into. These narratives reflect and reinforce the beliefs of the system, and they have more power than other narratives, meaning they are automatically seen as more believable, more valid—even if they are less accurate. So, for example, non-vegans who believe in the (dominant) carnistic narrative that eating animals is normal, natural, and necessary are automatically perceived as more credible than vegans who challenge that narrative.

Non-vegans did not ask for the power they have, nor do they (or vegans) even usually realize that they have it. However, this doesn't change the fact that such a power imbalance exists and that it has serious implications for relationships in which one person is vegan and the other is not.

The Carnistic Narrative and Perceptions of Needs

Although a variety of factors, such as our temperament and personal history, affect how we relate to needs, dominant narratives also play an important role. In oppressive systems, we learn to view our needs as either too important—when we have more power than the other—or not important enough—when we have less power than the other.

The carnistic narrative teaches us to give more weight to the needs of non-vegans than to those of vegans. For example, it is quite common for a vegan who suggests to their non-vegan dinner companion that they choose a vegetarian restaurant to be told by the non-vegan, "There's nothing I can eat there," as though non-vegans do not and cannot eat foods without meat. This same non-vegan might assume, however, that it would be appropriate for the vegan to dine in a restaurant with very limited (if any) vegan options and where the vegan would be exposed to animal foods they find disturbing. The non-vegan may even feel put upon and get angry at what they perceive as the vegan's unfairness.

When we view our needs as not important enough, we may have trouble recognizing them in the first place. And even if we do recognize our needs, we may have trouble articulating them, because we fear the other will respond with anger and perceive us as demanding. If we nevertheless express our needs, we can end up feeling guilty and ashamed, believing the other's narrative that what we are asking for is invalid and unfair. And we can feel resentful, since a part of us knows that there is an imbalance of power in our relationship, with us on the lower end.

Consider, for instance, the common experience of a vegan requesting that the Thanksgiving turkey be kept and carved in a different room than the dining room. Often, the vegan's need to not be exposed to an emotionally disturbing sight that would ruin the entire holiday for them is perceived not as a valid request but as an unfair demand. And the vegan's need to be emotionally safe is viewed as less important than the non-vegans' need to have a traditional table setting. Vegans often apologize for "inconveniencing" hosts with simple requests such as keeping the uncarved meat in a separate room, or having one or two dishes without animal products, or serving the salad with the cheese on the side so the vegan can also eat it.

The carnistic narrative also causes us to view vegans' requests to have their needs met not as neutral appeals but as controlling impositions. For example, when a vegan asks that there be no meat in the home, rather than consider that this may be an important need worth discussing in order to find a comfortable solution for both parties, the non-vegan often perceives it as an attempt to control them. And yet a non-vegan's insistence on having meat in the home is rarely perceived as controlling.

Similarly, parents who raise their children vegan are seen as imposing their veganism on their children, while non-vegans are never seen as imposing their carnism on their children. Of course, we usually appreciate the fact that parents naturally raise their children according to their own beliefs, which is why we don't expect Christians to raise their children as atheists, or Democrats to raise their children as Republicans. Also, no matter how vegans present their ideas, they often still end up being seen as controlling: either they are direct and are seen as overtly controlling, or they are indirect and are seen as manipulative.

The Carnistic Narrative and Perceptions of Anger

Because anger is the emotion that drives people to challenge injustice, it is a threat to systems that are based on injustice. If enough people are in touch with and able to express their anger about such systems, these systems become destabilized. So dominant narratives need to distort our perceptions of anger.

When someone who challenges an oppressive system expresses their anger, it is often perceived as far more intense than it actually is, because the system has such a low tolerance for anger directed against it. Furthermore, the person expressing anger is often framed as an "angry person" rather than as a person who is angry: the focus is on an internal problem with the individual rather than on the external circumstances they are angry about. For example, when women discuss sexism, the slightest hint of anger is often seen as an aggressive attack and the women are labeled "bitches" or worse, making their anger seem like it's a problematic aspect of their character rather than a legitimate emotional response to injustice. Similarly, when vegans express their anger at the mass exploitation of animals, they are often perceived as "hysterical" and their commentary is often perceived in a far more negative light than that of, for example, human rights activists expressing their anger about a form of socially unacceptable human exploitation.

The Carnistic Narrative and Perceptions of Opinions

The carnistic narrative causes us to assume that non-vegans' opinions hold more weight than those of vegans, and when there is a disagreement, the burden of proof is generally on the vegan. For example, vegans are often much better informed about veganism than are non-vegans—just as gay, lesbian, and transgender people are generally much more informed about issues of gender than are cisgender people. And yet, when the topic of veganism arises, non-vegans may argue passionately against vegans, claiming that the vegans are wrong about the main ideas and practices of their own belief system. In addition, when vegans share information about nutrition, food, and eating, they are often seen as biased, while the non-vegans' opinions are considered neutral. And it is the vegans who must prove that their understanding is correct, not the non-vegans.

The Carnistic Narrative and Prejudice

When we don't recognize that vegans are a non-dominant group, we can fail to see the ways in which they may suffer from carnistic prejudice—from negative, preconceived assumptions about them that can lead to unfair treatment. For example, teasing vegans by demeaning them is, unfortunately, epidemic. It is extremely common to hear derogatory jokes that attack the vegan's beliefs or character, often in front of others. Such jokes can be anything from making "moo" sounds when a steak is served to calling the vegan a "Bambi-lover." And if the vegan doesn't laugh, they are seen as not having a sense of humor, which reinforces the negative stereotype of the holier-than-thou, overly serious moral advocate. Such behavior would be unthinkable to carry out toward members of many other non-dominant groups. Yet the invisibility of carnism prevents vegans and non-vegans alike from seeing just how insensitive such prejudicial behavior is.

Projection: Shooting the (Vegan) Messenger

Perhaps the most common secondary defense is *projection*—projecting onto vegans negative and inaccurate ideas about them that invalidate their message.[13] Projection is a form of shooting the messenger: if we shoot the messenger, we don't have to take seriously the implications of their message.

---

13 Although carnistic projection sometimes involves projecting unconscious impulses or qualities onto another (or others), this section is not referring to projection in the strict Freudian sense of the term.

Projection is often expressed through the negative stereotyping of vegans. When we believe in these stereotypes, not only are we more resistant to the information vegans are sharing; we are also less likely to feel connected to the vegans in our lives. Stereotypes reduce people to one-dimensional caricatures; they make people less relatable and highlight points of negativity. If, for example, a non-vegan's partner becomes vegan and the non-vegan believes the stereotype that vegans are irrational animal lovers, he will judge his partner before she even has a chance to share her opinions with him. And in his judgment and perhaps resistance to what the vegan is trying to tell him about her experience and ideas, he may cause her to become even more emotional, since now she is hurt by feeling unheard and unwitnessed. Stereotypes also cause us to assume that all people in the stereotyped group are alike—that, for example, a vegan is a vegan and all vegans are the same—so that we fail to appreciate that members of the stereotyped group can be as diverse as members of the dominant group.

Vegans, too, have internalized some negative vegan stereotypes and can react to these stereotypes in a way that causes problems in their relationships. For example, many vegans believe the stereotype that they are hypersensitive. Vegans can feel ashamed of their sensitivity to animal suffering and therefore hide or downplay their emotions, failing to recognize that their sadness, grief, and outrage are actually normal, healthful, and appropriate responses to the atrocity that is carnism. The numbing and apathy that carnism conditions people to feel is far more problematic; when it comes to animal suffering, the world needs more emotion, not less. And when anyone—vegan or non-vegan—feels they have to hide their feelings and thoughts from those they are in relationship with, connection becomes impossible.

The stereotype of the hypersensitive vegan is also a powerful way for carnism to discredit the vegan message: overly emotional people are, by definition, not rational, and irrational people are not worth listening to. Perhaps not surprisingly, this same stereotype has been used to discredit those who have challenged other oppressive systems: African slavery abolitionists were called "sentimentalists" and suffragists who fought for women's right to vote were portrayed as hysterical.

Sometimes vegans are stereotyped as anti-human. This stereotype is based largely on the assumption that people can't be compassionate toward humans and animals at the same time, even though usually the opposite is true: compassion begets compassion. The more compassion we allow into our lives, the more compassion we are likely to feel overall. And since animal agriculture exploits not only animals but also humans and the environment, being vegan is a way to alleviate multiple forms of harm at once.[14] Framing vegans as anti-human is an effective way to reduce vegans' threat to carnism: if much of the population believes vegans are against them, then the vegan movement will surely not attract enough supporters to weaken the system.

Another projection is that of the all-powerful vegan, expressed through the expectation that vegans can and should live up to an impossible ideal. For example, vegans are expected to have all the answers to the problem of carnism whenever they discuss veganism, to be experts on agricultural economics ("What would we do if all the factories closed down?"), environmental bioethics ("How could we fertilize our crops without manure? What about the fossil fuels it takes to ship produce that you can't buy locally?"), animal ethics ("What if we kill animals humanely?"), history ("But didn't we develop our big brains from eating meat? We'll get stupid if we all stop eating animals."), and so on. And when vegans can't answer all the questions thrown their way, their entire ideology comes into question.

Similarly, vegans are expected never to get sick. For example, when a vegan catches a head cold, the first assumption is often that they are sick because of their diet, but when a non-vegan has a heart attack, the first assumption is often that they have bad genes. And vegans must also live up

---

14 See, for example, Human Rights Watch, *Blood, Sweat, and Fear: Workers' Rights in U.S. Meat and Poultry Plants* (New York: Human Rights Watch, 2004), https://www.hrw.org/sites/default/files/reports/usa0105.pdf; Lance Compa and Jamie Fellner, "Meatpacking's Human Toll," *Washington Post*, August 3, 2005; Timothy Pachirat, *Every Twelve Seconds: Industrialized Slaughter and the Politics of Sight* (New Haven: Yale University Press, 2011); Robert Goodland and Jeff Anhang, "Livestock and Climate Change," *World Watch Magazine*, November/December 2009, 10–19; Henning Steinfeld, Pierre Gerber, Tom Wassenaar, Vincent Castel, Mauricio Rosales, and Cees de Haan, *Livestock's Long Shadow: Environmental Issues and Options* (Rome: FAO, United Nations, 2006); David Pimentel et al., "Water Resources: Agricultural and Environmental Issues," *BioScience* 54, 10 (2004): 909–18; and R. Sansoucy, "Livestock: A Driving Force for Food Security and Sustainable Development," *World Animal Review* 84/85 (1995): 5–17.

to impossible moral ideals. Vegans may be seen as hypocrites, for instance, if they wear wool, and as extremists if they don't.

Sometimes, vegans are stereotyped as eating-disordered. For example, when a young woman chooses to become vegan, people often assume that she's using veganism as a cover for what's actually anorexia, when it's just as likely that she is making a healthy choice to live her values and practice integrity. Pathologizing those who challenge oppressive systems is not new. In the pre-abolition United States, for example, slaves who attempted to escape from slavery were diagnosed with the mental illness "drapetomania": it was considered crazy not to want to be enslaved.

Vegans may also be stereotyped as picky eaters when, for example, they won't eat pasta sauce that's had the meatballs taken out or they won't eat vegetable soup that's made with chicken stock. This stereotype has taken hold largely because carnism prevents us from recognizing that eating animals is a moral issue. So we don't realize that what seems like fussiness is actually a normal psychological reaction that psychologists refer to as *moral disgust*—the disgust that we feel when we are confronted with consuming something that we are morally opposed to. It is the same feeling a non-vegan might have if, for example, they had to pick dog meatballs out of a sauce or eat soup made with cat stock.

Secondary Justification

Primary justification teaches us to believe the myths that eating animals is normal, natural, and necessary. And secondary justification teaches us to believe that *not* eating animals is *ab*normal, *un*natural, and *un*necessary. Of course, these same myths have been used to discredit other counter-belief systems and social justice movements, such as civil rights and gay rights.

Secondary justification is, like other secondary defenses, part of a backlash against veganism. A *backlash* is a reaction of an oppressive, dominant system to its power being threatened; it is an attempt to regain lost power. New myths are created to prevent us from taking seriously the people who challenge the system, despite the fact that the system itself is based on a mythology.

BEYOND CARNISM

Carnism is a global phenomenon, so we are all participants in the system, for better or worse. Our choice is not *whether* we participate but *how* we participate. In order to be part of the solution rather than part of the problem, we must be committed to staying awake—to maintaining and growing our awareness—because oppressive systems such as carnism are structured to pull us back into the cocoon of unknowing. To stay awake, we must keep ourselves informed and connected with others who are also committed to awareness. When we stay awake, we stay present to ourselves—to our authentic experience—and to others. We become active witnesses rather than passive bystanders.

With awareness, we can choose whether and how we want to relate to eating animals. If we believe in the values of veganism and want to remove our support from carnism, then we can stop eating animals and become vegan. If we believe in veganism but are not yet ready to become fully vegan, we can commit to reducing our participation in carnism over time. Often, where we are on the spectrum of carnism-veganism is less important than where we are heading. Obviously, in a veg/non-veg relationship, the closer we are on the spectrum to each other, the less complicated our dynamic in this area will be.

BECOMING ALLIES IN THE TRANSFORMATION OF CARNISM

Even if we are not yet fully vegan, we can become a vegan ally, a supporter of veganism. Sometimes, vegan allies are advocates for veganism, using their personal or professional influence to further the vegan cause. For example, a patron may donate to a vegan organization, or a journalist may publish a story to raise awareness of carnism. Or vegan allies can simply support vegans. When we are an ally to the vegan in our life, we unite with the vegan against the intruder that is carnism to reduce its negative influence on our relationship. We do our best to understand the vegan's experience, and to appreciate their struggle. It is a unique struggle (as all struggles are), and it is a challenging one. If we don't learn what the world looks like through vegan eyes, we will never truly connect with the vegan with whom we are in relationship.

Being vegan can feel like waking up from the Matrix. For those who are not vegan, perhaps a useful way to understand the vegan perspective is through such a scenario. Imagine one morning you emerge from a deep sleep to find that you have been unplugged from the Matrix. Suddenly, you realize that all the meat, eggs, and dairy in the world around you are not, as you had believed, from pigs and chickens and cows but rather from dogs and cats. The person who unplugged you takes you on a tour of the "real world" and shows you the factories where the animals are raised and killed, and you see torment, hear yelps, hisses, and screams; you witness kittens being ground up alive, puppies being torn from their howling mother, animals being skinned and boiled while fully conscious. When you drive to work later that day, you see truckloads of these animals on their way to slaughter, their eyes and noses pushed through the slats in the sides of the vehicle, and you do everything possible to avert your eyes and harden your heart because you know you are helpless to save them.

Later, you return home to your family, all of whom are still plugged into the Matrix and who are serving steak for dinner. When you look at the steak, you are flooded with memories of the horrors you just witnessed and feel overcome with emotion. You do your best to keep your feelings in check as you try to explain to your family what you have learned. But they didn't see what you saw, and to them, you are just coming across as a little unhinged. You press harder, desperate to get them to see the world through your eyes, but your pushing, combined with the emotional charge around it and the fact that the Matrix they're still plugged into causes them to automatically feel defensive around this topic, leads to them feeling attacked. The conversation ends with them telling you to stop imposing your values on others: "You make your choices, I'll make mine."

Many vegans don't know what to do with the emotions that can naturally arise after they've stepped outside the carnistic matrix. Nor do they know how to make sense of the resistance they encounter when they try to help solve the problem of carnism. One important function you can perform as a vegan ally, then, is to appreciate that the vegan in your life is doing the best they can to cope with a psychologically devastating situation—a situation they have chosen to open their eyes and hearts to simply because they care, because they want to make the world a better place.

If you can be a witness to the vegan in your life, if you can really see them for who they are and appreciate what it means to them to be vegan, much of the tension in your relationship will likely dissipate. As a witness, you can appreciate the courage and commitment it takes to keep their chin up despite the grief they may carry and the frustration of feeling chronically invalidated and misunderstood. You can empathize with the constant pressure they are under to justify and defend doing the work that needs doing if we ever wish to live in a world we can feel good about.

When those who are non-vegan step outside the matrix of carnism, it can be transformational. Never underestimate the difference a single person can make when the other feels all alone. These are moments of healing, and the threads of connection that weave us most closely together.

Chapter 6

BEING VEGAN: LIVING AND RELATING SUSTAINABLY IN A NON-VEGAN WORLD

Being vegan is, in many ways, a tremendously empowering experience.[1] Vegans often say that becoming vegan shifted their whole way of thinking about and relating to the world, that they now feel more connected with their authentic thoughts and feelings and more engaged with life. And because veganism is centered around compassion and justice, vegans also say they feel a greater alignment with their core values, that being vegan is a powerful way for them to practice integrity.

However, being vegan also comes with challenges. Because the world is in carnism, there is a very limited understanding of what veganism actually is and of how vegans experience the world. In fact, misconceptions and negative assumptions about veganism and vegans are very common. So vegans have precious little guidance for understanding and managing the challenges they may face and for talking about veganism without triggering defensiveness,[2] which can lead to ongoing conflict. The exhilaration that many new vegans feel can quickly give way to confusion, frustration, and even despair. Vegans can feel like they stepped outside of the carnistic matrix only to find that their newfound freedom and clarity have landed them in another painful system, a system of human interactions that are difficult or impossible to navigate.

---

1 Much of the information in this chapter also applies to being vegetarian.
2 For excellent resources on the experience of being vegan, see the works of Carol J. Adams and Colleen Patrick-Goudreau.

Becoming vegan brings about a paradigm shift: vegans don't see different things; they see the same things, differently. This transformation is captured by a saying among soldiers: "Once you've been to war, you can never go home." It's impossible to ever see the world the same way again. Innocence is lost and is often replaced by trauma. Although vegans are not veterans of war, the paradigm shift that accompanies becoming vegan often includes a loss of innocence, and vegans experience a form of traumatization that can color their worldview in significant ways.[3]

Once we become aware of an atrocity—any atrocity—it can seem like our moral sense of the universe has been turned upside down, and we can feel spiritually or philosophically lost. When we witness an atrocity, we may begin to wonder about the meaning of life, of existence: How can we have faith in any sense of order in the universe when such horrors are happening? We can despair: How can we possibly feel hopeful about the future when we are surrounded by misery and there seems to be no sign of things ever changing? Our optimism can turn to pessimism, and our view of humanity can turn dark and misanthropic: How can we trust other human beings when they are capable of such brutality? And, burdened by the weight of our knowledge of the suffering, we can feel compelled to do everything in our power to lessen it. This means getting others to see what we've seen and to halt their participation in the problem.

But when it comes to the atrocity that is carnism, the automatic defensiveness that non-vegans feel around the issue—coupled with vegans' lack of training in how to communicate in a way that bypasses such defensiveness—makes it challenging, at best, for vegans to raise awareness. As a result, vegans can feel helpless as they try to bring about the change they need in order to feel like empowered agents of social transformation.

---

3 This statement is not meant to suggest that vegans and veterans of war have equivalent experiences, nor is it meant to minimize the serious trauma suffered by those who have experienced combat. It is simply used to highlight some of the common ways in which atrocities can impact the human psyche.

SECONDARY TRAUMATIC STRESS (STS): COLLATERAL DAMAGE OF CARNISM

As discussed in the previous chapter, carnism is an invisible intruder in veg/non-veg relationships. But the vegan paradigm shift often brings another invisible intruder, a byproduct of carnism, into relationships: the traumatization that results from being exposed to an atrocity. Some vegans have a classic traumatic response, while others have what could be considered a "subclinical," or less intense, response. However, virtually all vegans experience some degree of the distorted perceptions and dysregulated emotions that result from being exposed to an atrocity.

For vegans and non-vegans to create more secure, connected relationships and for vegans to have more sustainable, balanced lives, it's vital to recognize not only the intruder of carnism but also the collateral damage of carnism, vegan traumatization.

Many of us are aware of post-traumatic stress disorder (PTSD), which is the traumatization experienced by, for example, veterans of war or others who have been directly exposed to, or direct victims of, violence. PTSD includes symptoms such as flashbacks, sleep disturbances, anxiety, and depression. However, most of us are not aware of secondary traumatic stress (STS)—sometimes referred to as secondary traumatic stress disorder, or STSD—which is just like PTSD except that it impacts those who have been indirectly exposed to violence, including the witnesses of violence.[4]

STS is widespread among paramedics, police officers, and other first responders. It is also common among therapists who treat victims of trauma. And it affects many individuals involved in social justice movements who have witnessed atrocities. So STS is, perhaps not surprisingly, very common among vegans, the vast majority of whom have been exposed to traumatic material depicting animal suffering and slaughter and who are continually

---

4 There is some debate about how to differentiate PTSD from STS(D). Some clinicians suggest that even witnesses to violence suffer from PTSD, and that what we call STS is the result not of seeing violence, but of hearing stories, or second-hand information, about violence toward others. Here, I've chosen to use "STS" rather than "PTSD" because vegans are secondary, or indirect, victims of carnism and because I believe STS is a more intuitive and accessible term.

exposed to the aftermath of such trauma—the meat, eggs, and dairy products that are everywhere they turn.

While not all vegans have STS and not everyone who has STS is impacted in precisely the same way, many vegans have some degree of STS, and most people with STS have somewhat similar experiences. Common symptoms of STS include the PTSD symptoms mentioned above, as well as the following: intrusive thoughts (thoughts or images of the suffering we've witnessed that suddenly enter or "intrude" in our mind); a sense that we can never do enough; a minimizing of the suffering of other people (e.g., assuming that their suffering is minimal compared to that of the animals); dissociation (feeling disconnected from ourselves, others, and/or the world); self-neglect (seeing our own needs as unimportant and neglecting them); experiencing "too much" or "not enough" emotion, or swinging between these extremes; misanthropy (a dislike of humankind); grandiosity (feeling superior to others, feeling that we can and should fix all problems); workaholism; and an inability to let go of activism and/or feeling guilty for enjoying ourselves when others are suffering.[5]

Traumatization is an inevitable biological and psychological response to experiencing terror or horror, particularly when we feel helpless to control the situation. STS is not a sign of weakness; nobody is immune to trauma.

STS is not only a personal and relationship hazard; it is also a hazard for the vegan movement. STS is one of the primary reasons vegan activists burn out and quit the movement—and high turnover in the movement significantly decreases its effectiveness. Imagine a company where a high percentage of employees quit after just a short time on the job, compared to a company where most staff stayed on for long stretches.

The good news is that, with knowledge about the causes, symptoms, and treatments for STS, vegans can decrease the likelihood that they will be traumatized. In so doing, vegans can improve the quality of their own lives, their relationships, and the vegan movement.

---

5 For a more comprehensive list of symptoms, see Appendix 2.

THE DISCONNECTING TRAUMA NARRATIVE

Victims, Perpetrators, and Heroes

When we have been exposed to an atrocity, we can develop a worldview that is based on trauma, a *trauma narrative*, where we see the world as one giant traumatic system with only three roles to be played: victim, perpetrator, and hero.[6]

The vegan trauma narrative underlies some of the most painful conflicts between vegans and non-vegans in relationships, in large part because it is so disconnecting. What happens is that the vegan can automatically see the non-vegan as a perpetrator, since consuming animals is contributing to the very atrocity that the vegan is trying to transform and that has traumatized the vegan. When we view another in the role of perpetrator, no matter how much we wish we didn't or tried to feel otherwise, we simply cannot feel connected with them. For non-vegans, one way to understand this phenomenon is to imagine an issue that is near and dear to your heart—perhaps it's orphans of war or homeless people who are victims of street violence. Now imagine that someone you're close to is an executive at a company that's responsible for some of the suffering you care so deeply about. Even though you may *know* the other is a good person, part of you may struggle with knowing they are contributing to the violence. And if you have STS, your brain might make such a distinction impossible.

Traumatized vegans can feel further disconnected from the non-vegans in their lives if they also feel unwitnessed by them. When we are not witnessed, we get the message that our experience is not worth paying attention to, that our experience isn't valid. People who feel invalidated feel victimized; they feel the other has not treated them with respect or compassion. And when we feel victimized, we see the other as a perpetrator. Non-vegans might feel the same if, for example, they had been traumatized by witnessing dog slaughter and those they were in relationship with were regularly consuming dog meat and didn't understand why the situation was so distressing to them.

---

6 Somewhat similar roles are described in the Karpman Drama Triangle, a model established to describe destructive interactions that may emerge during interpersonal conflict.

And people who feel unwitnessed—especially in a vulnerable area such as their traumatization—will not feel emotionally connected, since they are unable to share essential parts of themselves. Imagine, for example, that you narrowly escaped being involved in a terrifying car crash on your way home from work, and you watched in horror as bloody and dying victims were rushed to the hospital. But when you get home, you feel you can't share what you saw—or how it's impacted you—with those you are closest to, so you just keep it to yourself and try to stay focused on the usual end-of-day conversation.

Many vegans suffer a great deal of pain because, despite how hard they may try, they're unable to see the non-vegans in their lives in a way that allows for their precious connection to be maintained. What a vegan may do, then, in an attempt to reconnect, is try to get the non-vegan to stop eating animals—to eliminate what appears to be the cause of the disconnection. However, this approach often leads to the non-vegan feeling pressured, which leads to greater disconnection. When people feel pushed—when they feel that they can't say no to a request and still be accepted for who they are—they feel controlled, and when people feel controlled, they typically resist doing what is asked of them. So the tension and pressure that many non-vegans feel from the vegans in their lives is frequently the result of more than just the strong moral convictions that vegans have about not eating animals. It may also be the vegan's reaction to the loss of security and connection that is the lifeblood of healthy relationships.

It's important for vegans to appreciate that although consuming animals *does* help maintain carnism, this does not mean that non-vegans are simply perpetrators. People are nuanced and complex, and they inhabit multiple roles at once. For example, the vegan protester holding a sign of tortured animals at a rally may be wearing sneakers that were made by child slaves in China. Is this person a perpetrator? Or are they a hero? How do we decide which category they belong in?

When we look at the world through the lens of trauma, our minds cannot tolerate the complexity of human behavior. Rather than appreciating that good people participate in harmful practices—that we are all guilty and innocent, perpetrators of some problems, victims of others, and heroes in various ways—we reduce individuals to one-dimensional roles in which they are all good or all bad; they are innocent or guilty. And we react to them accordingly: we rage at the perpetrator and celebrate the hero, not realizing that how we classify these individuals may have more to do with our own projections than with who they are and what they do.

Reductive Thinking

The trauma narrative is organized around *reductive thinking*, reducing an individual to a behavior or a set of behaviors whose impact we tend to exaggerate in our mind, assuming that they have a much greater impact on the problem than they actually do. For example, if you're vegan and your partner eats meat, you may perceive your partner's meat eating as a major driving force of the meat industry: when seeing them eat meat, you may flash back to a slaughter video you saw and think, "*He's* the reason those very animals were killed!" Even if you know, statistically, that the impact of one person's occasional meat eating is extremely low, you may experience the behavior quite differently.

Similarly, the trauma narrative may cause us to assume that vegans have more of an impact than they actually do. We may celebrate someone for being vegan while criticizing a vegan ally whose impact is far greater than that of the vegan: consider, for instance, how many animals are spared by the meat-eating journalist who publishes articles raising awareness of carnism that reach millions of readers, or by the pescatarian philanthropist whose donations to vegan organizations allow activists to do concerted vegan outreach. We might also have exaggerated perceptions of vegans' power so that we become terrified that the problematic actions of a single vegan, especially if they are in a position of leadership, might cause the downfall of the whole movement.

Reductive thinking robs us of our appreciation of others' individuality. Vegans might, for example, assume that non-vegans are all alike and not realize that they have more in common with some non-vegans than they do with other vegans. Reductive thinking traps all of us—vegans and non-vegans—in roles that ultimately limit our ability to create positive change in our lives and in the world.

Perfectionism

The trauma narrative also reinforces the myth that if someone is not a hero, they must be a perpetrator. This kind of perfectionism is both irrational and counterproductive. It's irrational because being perfectly vegan, all the time, is impossible; if we wish to be functional human beings we will, unfortunately, harm animals in the process (simply walking on the sidewalk crushes insects). It's counterproductive because it presents an impossible ideal to others (for example, how many non-vegans will be attracted to a lifestyle in which they have to scrutinize the trace materials in the tires of their bicycle?) and because it makes vegans' lives unsustainable: perfectionism is a leading cause of burnout and it reflects a mentality that intensifies, rather than alleviates, trauma. The trauma narrative can also cause vegans to feel overwhelming guilt when they are not practicing "perfect" veganism, and guilt can be a major contributor to STS.

Survivor Guilt

Survivor guilt is the guilt we feel when we have experienced a trauma where others were harmed but we were not. For example, those who survive an earthquake, boating accident, or war can develop a profound guilt simply for having survived when others perished. Witnesses to atrocities can also develop survivor guilt—especially if they were, at one time, contributors to the atrocity (i.e., if they were "perpetrators").

Also, because the trauma narrative can cause us to conflate our behaviors with our self-worth (to believe that if we do something "bad," we are a "bad person"), our guilt easily grows into shame. And when we feel shame, we are less likely to act in ways that keep us resilient and help maintain a secure, connected relationship.

When we are not aware of our survivor guilt, rather than addressing the true source of our pain, we can end up using problematic coping mechanisms to manage it. Guilt is the feeling we have when we have done something bad, when we have been what we see as a perpetrator. So we can become obsessed with being "good," doing whatever we can to prove to ourselves (and often to others) that we are *not* perpetrators. We can become hypersensitive to any suggestion that we may not be good, since we can interpret that suggestion as confirming our view of ourselves as bad, grating against the raw guilt we feel.

Survivor guilt may also drive us to become so preoccupied with trying to save the victims of the atrocity that we neglect our own basic needs in the process. While it's noble and important to be active in the transformation of atrocities, when we are driven by survivor guilt rather than by our own internal moral compass, we can carry our trauma into the important work we do. Trauma-driven behaviors can create a toxicity in our interactions with others and ourselves, making us less effective in our activism and less secure in our lives and relationships. Survivor guilt is likely one of the reasons workaholism is near-epidemic among vegan activists, who feel guilty (like a perpetrator) as soon as they take time away from their activism.

We may also try to alleviate our survival guilt by focusing on others who are "more guilty" than we are, so that we feel less so by comparison. But such activities only feed the trauma narrative and reinforce traumatic symptoms. For example, vegans who attend conferences or rallies where non-vegans are portrayed as selfish and uncaring often end up feeling more judgmental of, and therefore more disconnected from, the non-vegans in their lives, who have been cast in the role of perpetrators. And when vegans accuse other vegans of not being vegan enough, the accused can find that their survivor guilt is triggered and the associated counterproductive behaviors kick in.

Any communication that reduces others—non-vegans or vegans—to perpetrators or heroes, any communication that is shaming and fails to appreciate the complexity of being human and the dynamics of trauma, feeds the trauma narrative and creates divisions between vegans and non-vegans, as well as among vegans.

The Trauma Narrative and Objectivity

The trauma narrative makes it harder for us to think objectively and to let the facts guide our choices. We can end up doing what feels right in the moment, what temporarily alleviates our pain, rather than what is in the best interest of ourselves, our relationships, and the cause we believe in. For example, vegans may spend tremendous amounts of time and energy trying to get those closest to them to become vegan, even though influencing family and friends is often more difficult than influencing strangers, since existing power dynamics and other long-standing relationship issues may get in the way of constructive communication. That energy would be better used in reaching out to many others who would probably be more receptive to the vegans' message.

One way to shift toward a more rational mindset is by asking what actions will have the greatest impact on our own well-being, our relationships, and the cause. Generally, what is good for one of these things is good for the others. And then we can appreciate that our own sustainability—our ability to maintain our veganism and be an effective ambassador for the cause—is far more important than getting a handful of the non-vegans in our lives to stop eating animals.

TRAUMA, SAFETY, AND CONNECTION

The difference between a traumatic experience and one that is painful has to do with our sense of safety, or security, and connection. When we experience trauma, we feel fundamentally unsafe and disconnected. Even in times of great grief, in the absence of trauma a part of us still knows we're going to be okay, and we still feel some connection with ourselves and others. It is no coincidence that the most fundamental relationship need is the need for safety and that without this, we cannot feel truly connected.

Individuals with STS feel unsafe, and they bring this sense of unsafety to their relationships. One reason people with STS feel unsafe is because they worry about not being able to avoid exposure to traumatic triggers, to anything that reminds them of the trauma and triggers the emotions associated with it. For example, refugees of war are often triggered by sudden loud noises; for this reason, some cities in Germany with a high refugee population are no longer holding fireworks displays.

For vegans, triggers often include the very products that surround them out in the world and even in their own homes—meat, eggs, and dairy. Triggers can also be comments and behaviors that invalidate the vegan's experience. These triggers may include, for example, disparaging remarks about veganism (e.g., referring to veganism as a cult) or about the vegan (e.g., calling the vegan a "picky eater" or "high maintenance"). Trauma specialists have found that people are more likely to develop a traumatic response if others minimize, dismiss, or celebrate the very thing that traumatized them.[7]

The less a vegan feels understood in their experience, the more unsafe they will feel, because if others don't understand their triggers, it will be impossible to avoid setting the triggers off. And if the other *does* know what triggers the vegan but insists on exposing them anyway, the vegan will feel even less safe—not only do they fear the triggering behavior, but they also lose trust in the other to care about and protect their safety. Of course, this dynamic only reinforces the vegan's view of the other as perpetrator, since now the vegan actually feels victimized by the other's behavior. For example, someone who grew up in a family where alcoholism was present may be extremely sensitive to being around alcohol. If close friends don't understand this sensitivity, they can easily say and do things that expose the alcohol-sensitive individual to the trigger of alcohol. And if the friends know of the sensitivity but simply don't think it's valid or don't care and become intoxicated frequently, the other will feel even more unsafe, as well as betrayed.

Triggers essentially bypass the brain's prefrontal cortex—the rational part of the brain—and activate our amygdala—the instinctive, fight-flight-or-freeze part of the brain. They throw us into a state of hyperarousal, or high alert: our heart races, our breathing gets faster, and we feel threatened and unsafe. When people feel unsafe, their only concern is escaping the threat so they can get back to a place of safety. Being triggered is a normal reaction of people who have been exposed to an atrocity or trauma. It doesn't mean they're weak or mentally ill. And triggers don't have to be connected to trauma; they can be the result of other factors, such as our emotional sensitivities, an issue we will discuss in Chapter 7. Whatever the cause, when we are triggered, our primary drive is to re-establish a sense of safety.

While some events are likely to traumatize just about anyone—such as war, rape, or witnessing an atrocity—everyone is unique and what trauma-tizes one person will not necessarily traumatize another. One of the most

---

7 See Judith Herman, *Trauma and Recovery: The Aftermath of Violence—from Domestic Abuse to Political Terror* (New York: Basic Books, 1992).

damaging assumptions we can make in our relationships is that the other should not feel the way they do because we assume *we* wouldn't feel that way if roles were reversed. Not only can we never know how we would be impacted by a situation until we're in it, but invalidating another—telling them their experience is wrong, or that they should not be feeling or thinking as they are—is toxic to relationships. Invalidation undermines our sense of security and unravels our connection.

VEGAN TRIGGERS AND DISCONNECTION

The traumatic dynamic between a vegan and a non-vegan often unfolds in a predictable manner. Consider the following anecdote about Elizabeth, a vegan, and Joanna, her non-vegan wife.

Elizabeth gets triggered by seeing meat, eggs, or dairy, and particularly by seeing her wife, with whom she is emotionally close, eat such products. But Elizabeth doesn't feel she has the right to ask Joanna not to eat these foods in front of her. Intuitively sensing that Joanna will feel controlled and get defensive, and having bought into the carnistic myth that her needs as a vegan are less important than Joanna's needs as a non-vegan, Elizabeth bites her tongue.

Elizabeth feels unsafe and disconnected in this situation. Although she feels a need to re-establish safety and connection, she isn't aware of these deeper needs. All she knows is that she feels sad, angry, and anxious as a result of Joanna's behaviors. What Elizabeth does know is that in order to feel better, she needs to reduce her exposure to traumatic triggers, which in her case are animal products. On top of this, though she may not be fully conscious of it, Elizabeth needs to stop seeing Joanna as a perpetrator.

Elizabeth realizes that because of carnism, Joanna has distorted perceptions of veganism and is probably automatically defensive around the issue of eating animals. Direct communication therefore feels impossible. So Elizabeth communicates indirectly, trying to get her needs for safety and connection met through roundabout means. For example, she may maneuver the foods on the table or avert her eyes in order to avoid having to see them. Or she may casually mention statistics about the impact of animal agriculture on the environment ("By the way, did you see the recent UN report saying that we should all be vegan?"), comment on Joanna's health ("Didn't you say you made a New Year's resolution to eat more healthfully?"), or share a story that reflects her disappointment about the lack of connection she is feeling ("Mary and Fred [a vegan couple] seem so happy together; it must be nice for them to share their life passion").

Joanna, picking up on the emotional charge of Elizabeth's commentary, starts to feel triggered (when one person is triggered, it often triggers the other). Joanna also feels distrustful, sensing that what's being said and what Elizabeth is actually feeling or wanting do not match. And Joanna feels controlled, partly because Elizabeth *is* trying to control the situation and partly because carnism causes non-vegans to perceive vegans as controlling even when they're not.

COMPASSIONATE WITNESSING: THE ANTIDOTE TO TRAUMA

The key to managing this complicated dynamic is for both parties to practice compassionate witnessing and to explicitly commit to ensuring the safety of the other. It is essential, though, to recognize that the playing field is not level: both carnism and trauma create a significant imbalance of power between the individuals. As mentioned above, carnism causes both non-vegans and vegans to see vegans' needs as less important than those of non-vegans.[8] And unless the non-vegan is actually triggered by some dynamic in the interaction—for example, if they have an emotional sensitivity to conflict or to disappointing others that's causing them to feel unsafe—the vegan is likely the one whose safety feels most at risk.

In order for a productive dialogue to unfold, both parties need to feel that there is a safe container for it. For the vegan who is traumatized, this is especially important: the vegan needs to feel understood and not judged for their emotional reactions. Telling a triggered person that the problem they are upset about is not that bad, or that they're just too sensitive, or that they'll have to learn to live with a triggering behavior is a recipe for disaster:

---

8 Of course, other factors, such as gender and race, play a role in how we value one another's needs, and these must also be taken into account.

it is practically guaranteed to trigger them further and to seriously damage their trust in the other. And the non-vegan needs to know that they won't be judged for who they are, that they won't be seen as "less than" or as a bad person if they are not ready to become vegan. We all need to trust that the people in our lives are committed to our safety, especially in our vulnerable moments. These are the sensitive moments when we collapse more deeply into our pain, and they are also the sacred moments when, with the right response, true healing and transformation can take place.

Compassionate witnessing is the antidote to trauma. No matter how triggered people are, when they feel genuinely seen and understood and cared about, their reactivity can deflate like a balloon whose air has been released. And once this has occurred and the conversation has been brought to a deeper level where both people can talk about what they need in order to feel secure and connected, then practical problem-solving can take place. But there must be a total commitment to a solution in which each person feels fully safe and a willingness to dialogue until that point is reached.

It is also important to examine ourselves as much as possible during our negotiation. We should not encourage others to extend the boundaries of their comfort zone to meet our needs unless those needs are truly about our safety. For instance, if the non-vegan tells the vegan that their own sense of safety depends on having the freedom to eat what they want, it may be worthwhile to consider whether this request is truly about safety or if it's actually about control. In upcoming chapters, we will discuss specific ways in which vegans can discuss their needs with non-vegans so that the potential for conflict is minimized.

TRAUMA IS CONTAGIOUS

When we are around traumatized people, we can start to experience trauma ourselves.[9] One reason trauma is contagious is because our trauma narrative guides how we think, feel, and behave toward others. So if, for example, we experience the other as a perpetrator, we treat them accordingly and

9 Judith Herman, *Trauma and Recovery: The Aftermath of Violence—from Domestic Abuse to Political Terror* (New York: Basic Books, 1992).

their thoughts, feelings, and behaviors emerge in reaction to ours. If they feel attacked or judged by us, they will feel victimized by us and perceive *us* as a perpetrator. Or they may buy into our narrative (especially if ours is the dominant narrative) and feel guilty and ashamed—or throw up their hands and give up trying to do the right thing, and just embrace their role as perpetrator. Either way, they can end up sharing our trauma narrative and feeling and acting accordingly.

Trauma is also contagious because traumatized people (or people who are not traumatized but who are unaware of how easy it is to "catch" trauma) often spread traumatic material without thinking about its impact on others. For example, while it's important for members of the general public to become aware of the suffering of farmed animals, many non-vegans are exposed to such imagery in a way that traumatizes them, which can cause more problems than it solves. Well-intentioned vegans, knowing that people tend to turn away from animal suffering in order to avoid feeling distress, often use shock tactics by presenting people with graphic imagery they weren't prepared to witness. Feeling caught off guard and not having given consent to witness the suffering, non-vegans can feel traumatized by the material and victimized by the vegan. And rather than direct their anger where it belongs—toward the industries that are exploiting animals—they may direct it at the vegan, whom they perceive as a perpetrator. A simple way to avoid this problem is to get another's consent before presenting them with traumatic material.

Vegans also traumatize one another, such as when one vegan launches into a horror story about something they witnessed, which shocks and horrifies the other vegan. Again, a simple solution is to not make others unintentional witnesses of violence—and if someone starts to do this to you, to ask them to stop.

Finally, vegans often traumatize themselves by choosing to witness animal suffering when they don't need to—when it won't directly help the cause. If you're already vegan, there's rarely a good reason to witness more trauma; doing so may only reduce your resilience and add to the epidemic traumatization among vegans.

Whether relating to themselves, other vegans, or non-vegans, it is important for vegans to respect boundaries. For all of us, healthy boundaries are essential for protecting ourselves from traumatization and for enabling us to have healthy relationships with others.

PROTECTING AND RESPECTING BOUNDARIES

Our boundaries are the lines we draw around ourselves to protect our personal space—physically, psychologically, and emotionally. Think of relationships as being made up of drivers on a road; our boundaries are like the surface markings designating lanes. Any behavior that invades our space is often experienced as a boundary violation. Consider, for example, how you feel when someone is standing too close to you and invading your physical space.

People often cross each other's boundaries unintentionally, because different people have different boundaries and we don't always intuitively know where the invisible lines of others are. When it comes to being exposed to meat, eggs, and dairy, many non-vegans don't automatically pick up on vegans' boundaries, because non-vegans don't have the same boundaries. So the non-vegan may not understand why simply eating meat in front of the vegan can feel like a boundary violation. It is therefore up to those of us whose boundaries are being crossed to identify and articulate what we need for our boundaries to be respected.

To determine what your boundaries are, you can ask yourself the following questions: What behaviors cause me to feel disconnected from the other? What behaviors cause me to feel unsafe? Certain behaviors are always a violation of boundaries, such as teasing that we don't find funny, or judgments. But plenty of behaviors may not be boundary violations to others, even though they are to us. It's our responsibility to identify and articulate our boundaries, to protect ourselves and to give others the opportunity to respect our needs.

BEYOND TRAUMA: DEVELOPING PERSONAL RESILIENCE

We are resilient—able to withstand and bounce back from stress—when we have a strong *psycho-emotional immune system*. When our relationship is resilient, it is secure and connected, and when we are personally resilient, we are more connected with ourselves—psychologically and emotionally—and secure in our lives. For vegans, developing personal resilience is central to being able to withstand the traumatic stressors they will encounter and to heal from trauma they may have already experienced.

Developing resilience is especially important for those who may have a personal history of trauma. We are more prone to becoming traumatized when we have experienced trauma in the past, especially if our past trauma has not been adequately processed. Witnessing atrocities can open up old wounds that need attending to. When we commit to developing resilience, we commit to taking care of ourselves, which may require that we attend to past traumas that need healing. It can be helpful to understand that those who are drawn to the transformation of atrocities often do have a personal trauma history; the empathy that comes from having been victimized is often what drives them to work toward protecting other victims of violence.

The first step to increasing resilience is to commit to making it a priority. And a priority is not just an idea; it is an idea that is acted upon.

Attending to Our Needs

We are resilient when we take into ourselves as much or more than we give out. Think of yourself as having an energetic bank account, with a finite amount of energy in each area of your life—physical/practical, emotional, social, and spiritual. If you continue to deplete your energy, you will eventually become bankrupt. Every time your energetic bank account is not balanced, your resilience—your psycho-emotional immune system—is compromised, and you are at risk of being traumatized or at least of being negatively impacted by the challenges you will inevitably face in life. Consider how your risk of illness increases whenever your physical immune system is compromised.

Just as we develop relationship resilience by creating security and connection through being tuned in to and responsive to one another's needs, we develop personal resilience by being tuned in to and responsive to our own needs, by taking care of ourselves. For example, we keep our body healthy by sleeping and eating well and exercising, we make sure we feel secure in the practical areas of our life (e.g., our home and finances), we feed our mind in a way that feels engaging rather than draining, we honor our feelings, we maintain healthy connections with others, and we feed our spiritual needs (however we choose to define "spiritual").

Attending to our needs requires self-awareness, the ability to know what we need and what will help us fulfill our needs. It also requires that we compassionately witness ourselves, so we don't judge or minimize our needs. Attending to our needs does not make us selfish; it makes us more resilient individuals who will be far better able to impact our relationships and the world the way we wish to.

Resilience is important not only for vegans' personal well-being and for the well-being of their relationships; it is also vital for creating an impactful vegan movement. But most vegan activists don't prioritize resilience. One reason for this neglect is that resilience is simply not a cultural value; in many cultures, people are encouraged to ignore their needs—to overwork, self-medicate, and neglect themselves. Another reason is that STS causes us to devalue resilience. For example, the more survivor guilt we have, the more we feel we should work harder and the less deserving we feel of slowing down—and the harder we work, the worse our STS becomes, in a feedback loop. STS is both a cause and a consequence of self-neglect.

In addition, many vegan activists fear that if they slow down, they'll stop. This fear is often a traumatic distortion that emerges when activism is driven by trauma. Vegans may fear that if they stop engaging in the compulsive behaviors that are driven by feeling triggered, they won't care enough to keep fighting the good fight. On the contrary, however, when we come to our activism from a place of self-connection and presence, we are more effective and more likely to be active for the long haul. Trauma-driven behaviors are inherently unsustainable; activists driven by trauma eventually burn out, and they often drag others down with them in the process. Giving ourselves permission to let go of our trauma is a gift to ourselves and to the movement.

Letting Go of Perfectionism

Perfectionism, as we discussed, can be a symptom of STS, but it can also be a *cause* of STS, since a perfectionistic attitude reduces resilience. Perfectionism causes us to think, feel, and behave in ways that make us less secure and connected, with others and with ourselves.

Perfectionism causes us to have either-or thinking: either we're successful (perfect) or a failure; either we're good (perfect) or bad. The perfectionistic mindset causes us to have impossible standards that we're always chasing but can never quite reach, since perfectionism is not about the *goal* but rather the *process*. When we are perfectionistic, we are addicted to a way of being, a way of relating to ourselves, others, and the world. We are driven less by our goals than by the process of obsessively striving to reach those goals—the goals are just an excuse for us to have something to be perfectionistic about. Our perfectionistic pursuits keep us perpetually focused on future aims or stuck in past regrets: they take us out of the present, which is where we need to be in order to create resilient lives and relationships.

Vegans can easily get caught up in perfectionism because they are frequently exposed to unhealthy, perfectionistic messaging around veganism, such as angry, judgmental commentaries denouncing celebrity vegans who've deviated from an all-vegan, all-the-time lifestyle. This messaging not only reinforces perfectionism, but it also reflects a fundamentalism that can create divisions among vegans and turn off non-vegans. It can therefore be helpful for vegans to strive not to be "perfectly vegan" but rather to be "sustainably vegan"—as vegan as possible without becoming perfectionistic and compromising their resilience needs. Many vegans have the privilege of being able to be vegan all the time, but some vegans do not. It is no doubt better for not only vegans and their relationships, but also for the world, if vegans relieve themselves of the irrational and judgmental perfectionism that can diminish their resilience and lead to burnout.

Avoiding perfectionism toward non-vegans is also important, and one way to do this is to think of carnism and veganism on a spectrum: what is important is not simply where we are on the spectrum, but where we are heading. Most people do not become vegan overnight, and while many people are resistant to the notion of being vegan, most people do support core vegan values and see the benefit of becoming *more* vegan. Encouraging others to be as vegan as possible is often a more realistic, respectful, and effective way to advocate veganism. Furthermore, social movements succeed not when everyone in society is a core supporter but when enough people are supportive enough. This is not to say we should discourage those who are open to becoming vegan; rather, we need to appreciate that approaching ideology as though it is devoid of psychology—that is, promoting a belief system and way of life that doesn't take into account the psychological position and needs of those we are reaching out to—is both ineffective and counterproductive.

Vegans can also become perfectionistic because the type of person who is drawn to social causes likely has a high level of conscientiousness, a personality trait that can increase perfectionistic tendencies. And finally, vegans may become perfectionistic because of how carnism causes vegans to feel like "tokens" of the vegan movement—representatives who cannot get sick or be morally inconsistent (which, of course, all human beings do and are), lest they be seen as letting down the cause.

One way to offset perfectionism is to appreciate that we have inherited a messy world. For the most part, we didn't create the mess we find ourselves in; it was handed down to us. So we have to make choices that are quite different than the choices we would make if the world were ideal. When we relate to reality as it is rather than as we wish it were, we relieve ourselves of a heavy burden. And we give ourselves permission to be our imperfect human selves, which enables us to embrace ourselves in the fullness of who we are, messed-up parts and all. Then we care less about being perfect and more about being authentic and present. We can also learn to say "I don't know" and not feel like we must always have all the answers to the questions posed to us—which we do not, and cannot, have.

Educating Ourselves

While it's important to accept that we don't have to have all the answers pertaining to veganism and carnism, it's also helpful to have *some* answers—in particular, to have information that can support our resilience. Knowledge is power, and understanding the following can help us feel more empowered and less likely to get triggered:

- the symptoms and causes of STS
- the impacts of carnism on non-vegans and vegans
- the principles of creating secure, connected relationships
- the basics of effective communication
- the fundamentals of veganism—including a handful of vegan "sound bites"

This book provides information on the first four points. In terms of the final point, if we learn the basic philosophy of veganism and the impacts of veganism on human health, animal welfare, and the environment, as well as the essential points of vegan nutrition and eating, we will articulate our beliefs and opinions more clearly and be less likely to feel frustrated and tongue-tied when the issue comes up. And when we learn vegan "sound bites," short answers to the most common questions and challenges posed to vegans, we can avoid ending up in lengthy and often pointless debates about eating animals.

Creating Connections with Like-Minded Others

Studies have shown that social connections are a central component of resilience.[10] Trauma, however, causes us to disconnect from others and also from ourselves. Preventing and healing trauma, then, depends on creating and maintaining social connections.

For vegans, it is vital to have a community of like-minded others, no matter how small. Even one or two people who share your view can make a tremendous difference to your resilience. Living in a carnistic culture, where you may feel chronically misunderstood and offended, takes a psychological and emotional toll and can leave you feeling isolated and alone. Knowing that others understand and share your beliefs can be extremely empowering. Many communities now have vegan organizations or meet-ups for this very purpose. If yours does not, consider connecting with others online.

---

10 See, for example, Daniel P Aldrich and Yasuyuki Sawada. "The Physical and Social Determinants of Mortality in the 3.11 Tsunami," *Social Science and Medicine* 124 (2015): 66–75.

Appreciating Individuality

The vegan paradigm shift can cause vegans to forget that they were ever *not* vegan. A vegan may see someone eating a hamburger and wonder how on earth that person can do such a thing, when just several months or years ago that may well have been the vegan themselves. So one of the reasons vegans may feel alienated from non-vegans is because vegans tend to forget their own carnism. This "vegan amnesia," as author Tobias Leenaert calls it,[11] gets in the way of vegans' ability to feel connected with others and to communicate about the issue. Vegans are bilingual, understanding both carnism and veganism, and acknowledging this fact can help vegans relate and communicate much more effectively with non-vegans.

Conversely, rather than see the non-vegans in their lives as fundamentally different, sometimes vegans don't see them as different *enough*. This attitude is not unique to vegans; it's normal and inevitable among all people in relationships. We all have a tendency to see those we are in a relationship with—particularly those we are closest to, such as our romantic partner—as extensions of ourselves, as we do with other things we identify with, such as our cars and homes.

When we see the other as an extension of ourselves, we experience their behaviors as a reflection on us. So when they do things that are not in alignment with our values, we feel like *we* have somehow acted against our values. For example, if you value stylish dressing and social courtesies and your partner goes out wearing old, ripped clothing and is socially awkward, you may feel embarrassed, as though their behavior says something about your own values. Of course, in some way, your partner's behavior does reflect on you; after all, you chose this person to be in a relationship with. But usually this reflection is far less powerful than we perceive it to be, and part of developing secure, connected relationships is learning to accept the other as they are without judging them or buying into the judgments of others. (If the difference between you and the other is so significant that you simply cannot feel

---

11 See veganstrategist.org.

comfortable with it, then you can explore ways to navigate it, issues we'll discuss in upcoming chapters.)

The more we can limit this tendency to view the other as an extension of ourselves, the better. What is normal is not always healthful. When we base our identity on how the people and things in our lives are perceived by others, we limit our own and the other's well-being. Consider the narcissistic parent who forces their child to be exactly what the parent needs them to be in order to feel like a success. Both parent and child ultimately lose in this arrangement.

When we don't recognize our tendency to see the other as a reflection on ourselves, we can end up feeling unnecessarily frustrated and triggered. Vegans may, for example, feel like they are compromising their own values by being in a relationship with someone who isn't also vegan. The vegan can feel almost like a sell-out, like they are somehow betraying their principles by "sleeping with the enemy." They may feel ashamed when the other eats animals, as if they themselves were eating animals. Or they may worry that they look like a "failure" to other vegans for not having been able to get the people closest to them to understand and adopt veganism. It's important to recognize when this kind of projection is occurring and to avoid letting our perceptions of what others may think get in the way of respecting and feeling connected with the non-vegans in our lives. Remember: people are more than just their ideology, and relationships are based on more than just shared ideals.

Practicing Gratitude

Studies have shown that practicing gratitude has a direct and significant impact on our mood and overall psychological well-being. Shifting to an attitude of gratitude can be an important part of developing resilience. Practicing gratitude can be as simple as stating aloud one thing a day you are grateful for or keeping a gratitude journal.[12]

---

12 An excellent resource for practicing gratitude as well as for improving your overall mood and resilience is Sonja Lyubomirsky's *The How of Happiness: A Scientific Approach to Getting the Life You Want* (New York: Penguin, 2008).

Cultivating Self-Awareness and Mindfulness

Perhaps the most important practices to help keep ourselves and our relationships resilient are self-awareness and mindfulness. The more self-aware we are—the more we know what we think, feel, and need—the less self-neglectful we will be. And the more mindful we are—the more present, or in-the-moment we are—the less we are at risk of being hijacked by the destructive ways of thinking and relating that reflect and reinforce STS. Of course, self-awareness and mindfulness are not unconnected: the more self-aware we are, the more mindful we will tend to be, and vice-versa.

Creating space in our lives is an important way to become more self-aware and mindful. If we are constantly racing from one task to the next, jumping from one thought to another, our minds are cluttered and we cannot hear the deeper voice within us. It's like trying to hear the birdsong outside the window when you're talking on the phone and have the television and radio on in the background. You can create space by removing some of the things that take up your time and attention, by creating uncluttered time every day. Use this time to do whatever you feel will help you decompress and relax: go for a run, read a novel, cook for your family, and so on. In other words, pause and take a break, daily.

It's also important that vegans take a break from advocating or talking about veganism. Often, vegans feel compelled to advocate veganism at every opportunity. And while it's important to raise awareness when possible, it's also important to know when not to advocate. Sometimes, you may need to just enjoy a social event and not have to be The Vegan. It's exhausting to always be "on," and it can prevent you from connecting with others as the individual you are rather than as the advocate you feel you should (always) be.

We can also make a practice of noticing and attending to our inner dialogue, the self-talk we engage in, an issue we'll discuss in Chapter 8. Studies have shown that the way we talk to ourselves impacts our self-concept, mood, performance, and overall psychological well-being.[13] And

---

13 See, for example, A. Hatzigeorgiadis, N. Zourbanos, E. Galanis, and Y. Theodorakis, "The Effects of Self-Talk on Performance in Sport: A Meta-analysis," *Perspectives on Psychological Science* 6, 4 (2011): 348–56, and Ethan Kross and Emma Bruehlman-Senecal, "Self-Talk as a Regulatory Mechanism: How You Do It Matters," *Journal of Personality and Social Psychology* 106, 2 (2014): 304–24.

most of us talk to ourselves in a way we would never tolerate from others, continuously criticizing and shaming ourselves. Recognizing and altering our self-talk can transform our lives and make a tremendous difference in our resilience.

Mindfulness is both a practice and a state of being. Practicing mindfulness helps us become more mindful, more present.[14] There are different ways to practice mindfulness, but by far the most common one is meditation.[15] Many studies have investigated the benefits of mindfulness meditation, and the correlation between mindfulness meditation and improvements in both psychological and physical well-being are significant.[16] You don't have to meditate for long periods of time to reap the benefits of this practice—even 10 minutes a day can make a difference.

Holding on to Hope

Vegans need to know there is reason to hope. Despair, which is the opposite of hope, is often the Achilles heel of those who are working to end an atrocity such as carnism. The problem can seem so vast, so overwhelming, and so hopeless. And mainstream media, steeped in carnism and often beholden to carnistic industries, certainly don't report otherwise. So we rarely, if ever, hear of vegan successes. Despair is toxic to resilience, sapping our energy and our belief in the possibility of a better future.

Hope is the antidote to despair. And when it comes to veganism, there is much to be hopeful for. The vegan movement is one of the fastest-growing social justice movements in the world today, and there is no indication that its growth will slow down. When we look back at social change over the course of history, we can see that carnism is following precisely the path of the other "isms" that have begun to topple.

---

14 I highly recommend *The Mindful Vegan: A 30-Day Plan for Finding Health, Balance, Peace, and Happiness*, by Lani Muelrath (BenBella Books, 2017).

15 I recommend checking out headspace.com, where you can download an app that helps those who are not experienced with meditation understand mindfulness and begin to practice mindfulness meditation.

16 See, for example, Daphne M. Davis and Jeffrey A. Hayes, "What Are the Benefits of Mindfulness? A Practice Review of Psychotherapy-Related Research," *Psychotherapy* 48, 2 (2011): 198–208.

When a behavior becomes a choice, it takes on an ethical dimension that it didn't have in the same way before. Oppressive systems depend on convincing people that participating in a practice that is against their values is necessary—necessary, for example, for the survival of the country, the race, or the species. Such practices are therefore seen as a matter of self-defense: if we don't harm others, we will be harmed ourselves. In many places in the world today, people can no longer fall back on the "eating animals is necessary" argument, so more and more people are beginning to feel increasingly ethically uncomfortable with animal agriculture. Consciousness is shifting, and the world is becoming increasingly pro-vegan. All the indicators point to a future in which veganism will have replaced carnism as the dominant ideology.

When vegans and non-vegans alike don't understand the experience of being vegan, particularly the experience of STS, they can undermine the security and connection in their relationships. Perhaps you had secure, connected relationships before you became vegan, or perhaps you were already struggling and the veganism simply added another layer to your struggle. Either way, once you recognize how STS can block your path to security and connection, you can more readily establish healthy ways of relating. You can also improve your own well-being and resilience so that you feel more sustainably vegan and more personally empowered.

Often, trauma brings beauty and depth, authenticity and strength, to our lives. Being willing to bear witness to the darkness that many turn away from comes with a price, but it also carries a gift—not only to those whose suffering we are working to alleviate, but to ourselves and to our relationships. As Ernest Hemingway wrote in *A Farewell to Arms*, "The world breaks everyone, and afterward many are strong at the broken places."

Chapter 7

UNRAVELING CONFLICT: PRINCIPLES AND TOOLS FOR CONFLICT PREVENTION AND MANAGEMENT

Conflict management is one of the most essential skills for all people to learn, and it is especially so for those in veg/non-veg relationships. Yet very few of us ever receive the instruction necessary to manage our conflicts skillfully.

Imagine driving a car with as little training as most of us are given to manage conflict. When you're old enough to get behind the wheel, you're simply told to figure out what to do. You're never even taught the rules of the road. So you fumble and grope and draw on your memories of watching others drive—others who also learned entirely without instruction and who developed bad habits in the process. Finally, you get your car on the road. But during your drive, and the drives that follow, you have many mishaps. At best, you have minor collisions in which you (and those you hit) are only temporarily injured; at worst, you have major crashes that cause permanent damage. And your bad habits, such as not wearing a seatbelt and passing in no-passing zones, become more ingrained as you repeat them over and over. Because you don't understand the rules of the road, you blame others for your violations, or you blame yourself for theirs. And fear is your constant companion: fear because of past crashes that haunt you and fear because you lack the skills to keep yourself safe. You may never venture into high-risk situations, such as freeways, because you're too afraid of being hurt again.

Conflict, or interpersonal conflict, is the struggle between people that emerges when one or both are unable to get their needs met, especially their needs for security and connection. In more secure relationships, conflict is generally managed skillfully and with integrity, and it strengthens security and connection. In less secure relationships, conflict tends to decrease each individual's sense of security and connection. And although conflict is usually less frequent in secure relationships, it is normal and inevitable in all relationships. What matters is not *whether* we experience conflict in our relationships but *how* we experience it—how we think of it and how we manage it.

When we don't understand the nature of conflict and we fail to appreciate its value, and when we have not learned how to manage conflict effectively, we can cause great pain to ourselves and others. But with an awareness of the nature of conflict and an appreciation of its importance, we can head off all but the most necessary of conflicts. What's more, we can appreciate that each conflict we have is an opportunity: when we respond to conflict with integrity, our mutual trust deepens, as do the security and connection of our relationship.

CHRONIC CONFLICTS: KILLERS OF CONNECTION

In general, the conflicts that cause problems in our relationships are not one-time or short-term events; they are chronic conflicts. *Chronic conflicts* are ongoing conflicts that often result from our failure to manage or resolve the shorter, or simpler, conflicts, which can then grow into something more complicated and problematic. For many people in veg/non-veg relationships, their ideological differences have led to the development of chronic conflicts.

Chronic conflicts reflect painful patterns that may have been repeated so often that resolving them feels impossible. With each repetition, the conflict becomes increasingly confusing, as new layers of misunderstanding and hurt are added that both complicate and obscure the original problem. For example, what began as a simple difference between your desire to bring a vegan dish to your in-laws' holiday gathering and your partner's desire to honor the family tradition by bringing the usual carnistic dish can become a minefield of offenses—arguments about whether you or his family are his priority; different memories about how many times you've given in to each other's demands; debates about whether it's more important to honor your vegan values or the family's traditional values.

Over time, as offenses pile up and we are unable to find resolution, we become increasingly hurt, angry, and hypersensitive, so we are more easily provoked and our reactions to the provocations are more intense. We can also begin to lose faith in the other's willingness to respond to us with compassion, so we feel increasingly unsafe and distrustful. We therefore share fewer of our thoughts and feelings and, as a result, become increasingly disconnected and insecure.

So many failed attempts to resolve a conflict can leave us feeling mentally and emotionally exhausted, as well as hopeless. Our fatigue and despair may lead us to simply avoid saying or doing anything that could spark the conflict, as we resign ourselves to an icy truce in which we skate around the fringes of our relationship rather than engage in the midst of our connection.

Most close relationships, particularly romantic partnerships, tend to have one or several chronic conflicts that keep re-emerging. Chronic conflicts are normal, and they aren't necessarily a sign of doom. And when we develop basic conflict management skills, these patterns can be interrupted no matter how long they've been going on. Chronic conflicts are like messy balls of yarn; they appear to be composed of many threads all twisted together, but often they are just one long strand that got so wound up that it feels impossible to unravel. Once we identify the specific attitudes and behaviors that keep us stuck in our patterns, we can disentangle them and create new, more empowering ones.

CAUSES OF CONFLICT

The cause of a conflict can often be traced to one of four factors:

- competing needs
- behaviors that may or may not be inherently problematic
- primary emotions and physical emotional states
- narratives—stories that we tell ourselves about behaviors or emotions or about a situation

Regardless of the cause of conflict, beneath the surface of most conflicts in our relationships is a struggle for one or both parties to feel secure and connected, to feel that each person is tuned in to and responsive to the other's needs. In other words, despite what we may seem to be in conflict about, often, on a deeper level, we are struggling to feel that we matter to the other—that we are valued and protected.

Competing Needs

When our needs get in the way of the other's needs being met, and vice versa, we have competing needs. Competing needs often lead to conflict, not because they are problematic in and of themselves but because we have problematic beliefs about them.

If we believe that when needs compete, only one person can ultimately get their needs met, or that getting our own needs met is more important than meeting the needs of the relationship (finding a win-win solution), we will fight until we get what we want, likely at the expense of the other and certainly at a cost to our relationship. Or if we believe that the other's needs are "wrong"— if we see their difference as a deficiency and judge them accordingly—our attitude will probably cause them to feel ashamed, angry, and defensive. (In addition, if we believe that the other's needs are more important than our own, we will likely fail to honor our needs or hold the other accountable for respecting them, and we will feel increasingly resentful and disconnected.)

On the other hand, if we believe that we won't be happy unless we are both happy, we automatically seek solutions that are win-win—or that are win-win enough. For example, perhaps your non-vegan partner has a need to "keep the peace" in their family and doesn't want to insist that the holiday dinner you both are hosting be vegan, but it's important to you not to have animal products in the house. You can honor your partner's needs without judging them as "wrong" and you can, together, consider alternatives, such as having the dinner at someone else's home rather than yours.

Behaviors

Behaviors that lead to conflict can be active or passive—they can be something we do, or something we fail to do. And they can be benign, with no negative intention and nothing inherently problematic about them, or they can be non-relational.

Benign behaviors include innocent miscommunications and

misinterpretations. For example, if the non-vegan you're dating shows up for your dinner date with a bottle of wine that's not certified vegan, you could interpret that as disrespectful, even though the non-vegan may not have realized that not all wines are vegan.

Non-relational behaviors are those that are inherently disrespectful, and they include criticism, making unfair demands, projection, stonewalling (refusing to engage in an interaction that's important to the other), and essentially anything that does not reflect empathy and compassion.

Primary Emotions and Physical Emotional States

Primary emotions are emotions that are automatic and instinctive. For example, when we're faced with a dangerous assailant, we instinctively feel fear, a primary emotion. Primary emotions can cause conflict simply because they can cause us to take action automatically, without pausing to think about whether our actions are rational.

Primary emotions should not be confused with *secondary emotions*, which are a part of the chain of conflict (discussed below) but come after primary emotions. Secondary emotions may be a reaction to a primary emotion, as when our fear of the assailant turns to anger. Anger, in this case, is a secondary emotion that empowers us to protect ourselves. A secondary emotion may also be the result of an interpretation of a primary emotion or a situation. For example, if you encounter a stranger who gives slight indications that they could be a dangerous assailant, but you're not sure that they actually are dangerous, you may judge yourself for feeling afraid and then feel the secondary emotion of shame. Or if you give your non-vegan mother a gift basket of vegan foods for Christmas, she can feel angry if she assumes you're trying to push your lifestyle on her, or grateful if she assumes you're trying to share a positive culinary experience with her.

Physical emotional states are emotional states that result from physiological influences. For example, due to a chemical imbalance, you may feel depressed, anxious, or euphoric ("manic"). Or if you have secondary traumatic stress (STS) because of animal suffering you've seen, you may be instantly triggered into a strong emotional reaction by something that reminds you of the trauma, such as seeing a truck of animals being driven to slaughter. These states can spark conflict because they can cause us to engage in behaviors and to create narratives—stories about our situation—that cause conflict. For example, if you're depressed, you may have difficulty listening, be hypersensitive to criticism, and lose interest in sex. And you may interpret your lack of interest in listening or sex to mean that you're no longer in love with your partner.

Narratives

We are powerfully influenced by our narratives, the stories we make up about an experience or situation based on our interpretation of it. For example, if you share a documentary that includes graphic footage of animal slaughter with your non-vegan parents, who then continue to eat meat, you can interpret the situation in any number of ways. You can assume that your parents don't care about farmed animals enough to change their diet and you can judge them as selfish. Or you can assume that they do care but they don't have the moral fiber to stand up for what they believe in and you can judge them as weak. Or you can consider that they've been eating a traditional diet for so long that such a change may feel overwhelming and impossible to them and you can accept their choice, even if you don't like it. Whichever interpretation you believe will determine how you feel about your parents and the situation.

Narratives are sometimes the original cause of conflict: sometimes, everything is fine but we create a story in our minds that distresses us and we react to it. For example, you might be on your way home from work and you pass a cozy, candlelit restaurant, which makes you think regretfully that you can't share romantic dining experiences with your partner because of the tension around your veg/non-veg difference. You start to feel angry with your partner and disappointed in your relationship, so that by the time you get home, you're conflict-ready. Even when narratives are not the original cause of conflict, they are usually a key factor that drives, maintains, and increases the intensity of a conflict. Narratives always show up somewhere along the chain of conflict.

Our narratives get us into trouble largely because we don't see them for what they are; we simply assume that what we're thinking is a fact rather than a story we made up in our head. It is particularly dangerous not to question our narratives when we're dealing with an emotionally sensitive issue, because when we're in a heightened emotional state or are feeling vulnerable, we often have less access to the rational parts of our brain, so we are less likely to think objectively. But the good news is that narratives are largely within our control, once we learn how to recognize them.

Our *conflict narrative* is the story we tell ourselves about our conflict.[1] For example, perhaps you're an organized, punctual planner and your partner is a spontaneous free spirit who is frequently tardy and often loses things. How you, as a couple, structure your time and day-to-day living will require a good deal of negotiating—and if you aren't successful, you can easily develop a chronic conflict that reflects a power struggle about how things should be done. And you will likely create a narrative about the conflict, such as "We're incompatible" and perhaps "I'm right and my partner is wrong, and if my partner doesn't become more like I am, we can't stay together."

As with all narratives, our conflict narrative may be more or less accurate. Also, it may be our narrative alone or it may be shared by both of us. Our conflict narrative will also determine how each of us feels about the conflict and how we try to solve it. How we define a problem determines how we define the solution.

SCHEMAS: THE LENSES WE WEAR

Schemas are mental frameworks. They are like a pair of tinted glasses that colors everything we see. Schemas include beliefs, assumptions, and images about a particular person, group, or situation. We automatically and naturally create schemas in order to create categories in our minds that simplify our mental processing. For example, when you think of a nurse, an image probably immediately comes to your mind, most likely of a medically minded, caregiving female wearing a uniform. All this information is

---

1 For an excellent resource on understanding and managing conflict narratives, see Andrew Christensen, Brian D. Doss, and Neil S. Jacobson, *Reconcilable Differences: Rebuild Your Relationship by Rediscovering the Partner You Love—Without Losing Yourself*, 2nd ed. (New York: Guilford Press, 2014).

automatically available to you at once because you have a schema for "nurse."

When it comes to our relationships, our schemas of ourselves and the other play an important role in determining how we relate. Although most of us are not even aware that we have schemas, these mental constructs drive many of our thoughts, feelings, and behaviors.

Self-Schemas

Our *self-schema* is the schema we have about ourselves, and it is made up of a set of beliefs that create our narratives and our feelings. We often have several self-schemas for the different roles we play, such as professional, parent, and advocate.

A new form of psychotherapy, called *schema therapy*, examines the specific self-schemas that have a negative impact on our relationships.[2] Sometimes, these problematic schemas can cause and/or intensify the conflicts we are experiencing around our veg/non-veg difference. The problematic schemas are based on a set of destructive and inaccurate beliefs about ourselves, others, and our relationships. The destructive beliefs create *core fears*, which drive many of our distorted narratives, intense emotional reactions, and defensive behaviors—sometimes referred to as *defensive strategies*. And our defensive strategies, which are designed to prevent our fears from coming to pass, often cause what we fear to actually happen.

For example, if we have an "abandonment schema," we have a belief that we are unlovable and that others will eventually abandon us. We have a core fear that we will be abandoned. So when our partner doesn't return our phone calls right away or is inattentive, we create a narrative that such behaviors mean our partner is abandoning us. And this narrative can lead to intense emotions, such as fear and anger. We then engage in defensive strategies to reduce our distress, such as withdrawing and rejecting our partner before we can get rejected, or intensely pursuing them to force them into closer contact with us. Of course, such strategies often bring about the very fear we are trying to avoid: feeling controlled or attacked, our partner may pull away from us. This just

---

2 See Jeffrey E. Young and Janet S. Klosko, *Reinventing Your Life: The Breakthrough Program to End Negative Behavior . . . and Feel Great Again* (New York: Penguin, 1993).

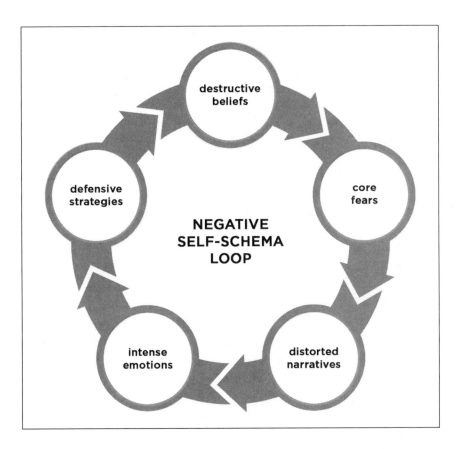

confirms our destructive beliefs that we are unlovable and will be abandoned.

Not all conflict is driven by negative self-schemas, and not all negative self-schemas are the result of past conditioning; they can also be caused by psychological problems, such as depression or anxiety. In addition, not all problematic self-schemas are necessarily based on so-called negative beliefs. Sometimes, for example, we may have a self-schema that positions us as superior to the other: we may have a self-schema that we are more principled and more self-disciplined than they are. We may not recognize that we simply have different principles and are able to be disciplined in different areas of our lives.

Other-Schemas

We also have a schema about the other, although this schema is rarely as deep-seated as our self-schema.[3] Our *other-schema* is the set of beliefs and narratives we hold about who the other is and why they do the things they do. As with our self-schema, we may have several schemas about the other. And we usually have one or two specific schemas that describe the other in relation to a conflict, as they have for us. For example, a vegan's schema of their non-vegan sibling may be that the non-vegan is selfish, lazy, or weak-willed. The sibling may have a schema of the vegan as moralistic, judgmental, and rigid.

Confirmation Bias

Schemas create *confirmation bias*—the tendency to notice and remember only those things that confirm the assumptions of our schema and to give these things more value than those that contradict our schema. For example, your confirmation bias of your non-vegan partner may, for example, cause you to overlook your partner's significant reduction in consuming animal products and only notice the times they don't eat vegan foods.

Confirmation bias also affects our conflict narrative and our self-schema. With each repetition of our chronic conflict, our narrative and our schemas of ourselves and each other become exaggerated and solidified. We can start to see each other almost as caricatures.

One helpful method for diminishing the negative impact of our conflict narratives and our schemas is to actively look for evidence that disproves them. If, for example, you look for instances of when your partner *does* eat vegan foods, or you seek alternative explanations for why your partner sometimes chooses not to eat vegan, you can disrupt the pattern you are in and think more flexibly and objectively.

---

3 For an excellent resource on identifying schemas about yourself and the other and shifting your conflict patterns, see Matthew McKay, Patrick Fanning, and Kim Paleg, *Couple Skills: Making Your Relationship Work* (Oakland, CA: New Harbinger, 2006).

HIDDEN EXPECTATIONS AND GROWING FRUSTRATIONS

We bring to our relationships countless expectations, many of which we aren't aware of and most of which we don't articulate. These implicit expectations are assumed ways of being, usually resulting from our own past experiences and our own beliefs about how relationships and the people in them are supposed to operate. For example, if, in your family of origin, dinners were always sit-down meals with everyone at the table, you probably expect to do the same with your partner and children. We rarely talk about these expectations, simply because we assume that they are shared by the other— we usually don't even recognize that we have certain expectations until they are not met and conflict has emerged.

While some expectations are healthful and necessary, such as expecting to be treated with respect, we can get into trouble when we project unrealistic or unfair expectations on the relationship or when we "should" the other into conforming to our expectations, which may not even be in their best interest. For example, if you expect that your partner will mingle alongside you at social gatherings, but they spend most of their time off to the side talking to one person or sometimes even reading, you can get frustrated with what you interpret as anti-social and rude behavior.

It's important to recognize expectations for what they are so they don't lead to chronic frustration, disappointment, and conflict. Our frustration and disappointment are in direct proportion to our (positive) expectations: we become disappointed and frustrated when our expectations are not met. When we expect sun and it rains, when we expect a smooth ride and we hit traffic, or when we expect our best friend to become vegan after learning about animal agriculture and she doesn't, our reaction is usually one of frustration and disappointment. If we had expected any of these outcomes, we might still not like them but we wouldn't feel the same distress. In relationships, when our expectations are chronically frustrated, *we* can become chronically frustrated, so that something as trivial as whether to put the forks facing up or down in the dishwasher can turn into an all-out power struggle.

When you find yourself frustrated or disappointed in your relationship, stop and ask yourself what expectation you have that is not being met. You can then check your expectation: Is it trivial, such as in which direction the toilet paper roll should hang? Or is it important, such as whether your family takes your veganism seriously? Is your expectation in the best interest of yourself and your relationship? Does it reflect a core need you have in order to feel secure and connected in your relationship?

Once you have some clarity around your expectation, you can have a conversation with the other about it. Putting our expectations on the table, examining them objectively, and discussing them openly is essential for maintaining security and connection in our relationships.

THE GIFT OF THE "HIGH-MAINTENANCE" PARTNER

Many of us fail to attend to the health of our relationships because we have learned to believe the myth that a (good) relationship should be easy—that if we have to put effort into making our relationship work, then it's probably not the relationship for us. This assumption can exist in all relationships, but it's especially common when it comes to romantic relationships, and it is kept alive by romance novels, Hollywood, and the fact that most of us receive no education whatsoever on what healthy relationships actually require. Secure, connected relationships take time and effort, as well as the willingness to address misunderstandings, hurt feelings, and any conflicts as they arise.

Usually in relationships, one partner is more "relational" than the other, meaning they are more tuned in to and responsive to the needs of the relationship, and they are therefore often the one to do more relationship maintenance, to do the work of keeping the relationship healthy. For example, they would be the first to raise the flag when a symptom of relationship distress pops up; perhaps there has been a lack of emotional connection, or maybe an in-law is starting to triangulate the relationship.

It's normal for labor to be divided in relationships: we tend to do more of what we are naturally good at and let the other do more of what they are naturally good at. A more securely attached partner, for example, will carry the burden of keeping a couple optimistic in difficult times, and a more handy partner will fix more problems around the house. Relationships are more connected and secure when we see and value the strengths each person brings and acknowledge the effort they put forth.

It's especially important to value those strengths that keep our relationships sustainable and healthy, and yet, because of the widespread assumption that relationships should not take effort, we often disparage, rather than appreciate, the more relational person. For example, when they try to talk about problems, their concerns may be dismissed, and they may even be perceived as the cause of the problems in the first place: "Everything was just fine until you had to go and start digging up that argument we had from a week ago. Can't you just let it go already?" or "I'm happy; the relationship is fine. Why do you have to go creating problems where there are none? Why do you always have to find something to complain about?" Of course, when one party has a problem, the relationship has a problem.

Imagine a risk analyst at a company of sales executives. The analyst is responsible for noticing risks and suggesting ways to avoid them. What if, whenever the analyst raised the alarm, the others told them that they were "making a big deal out of nothing," or called them "high maintenance"?

The truth is, it's far less likely that an individual is high maintenance than that the relationship itself has become high maintenance. Relationships—like homes or cars—that are not properly maintained will indeed require much more effort.

HIJACKED BY TRIGGERS

One factor that can both cause and intensify conflict is being triggered. When we're triggered, we're hijacked by an intense negative emotion. We end up looking at the world through the lens of the emotion.

We can tell we're triggered when we have a stronger-than-called-for reaction to a situation, when there is a "charge" around our emotional response. When we get triggered, we can go from zero to 60 in an instant. Our emotions flare up, as though a short fuse has been lit that quickly triggers an explosion. We all know what it feels like to be triggered, and we typically know what at least some of our triggers are. When we say that someone or something "pushes our buttons," we are often referring to a trigger.

Being triggered causes some of our most intense conflicts and can add an extra layer of complexity to the already complicated dynamics of veg/non-veg interactions. Being triggered is also a major obstacle to resolving conflict. When we're triggered, we're less able to think, feel, and act rationally or compassionately. The rational and calming part of our brain literally starts to shut down. And if we don't recognize that we're triggered, we can just keep pushing forward in a conflict, saying and doing things that are hurtful and that harm our relationship.

Because being triggered is such an uncomfortable experience, many of us go to great lengths to avoid it, which can end up causing more problems than it solves. For example, if we get triggered by not being listened to—interpreting this response to mean that we're not interesting or important—we may talk excessively, which can cause the other to tune us out and bring about the very behavior we fear.

Our triggered reactions are deep-seated patterns that become more ingrained every time they are repeated, like deepening grooves on a record. If we aren't aware of these patterns, we can remain on autopilot and reinforce rather than reduce them. For instance, each time we talk too much to avoid not being listened to and we end up tuned out by the other, our belief that we aren't interesting or important is reinforced and the vicious cycle of reacting to and reinforcing triggers continues.

Being triggered is contagious. When one of us is triggered, we can easily trigger the other. And when we trigger each other, we can confirm each other's fears and reinforce our extreme reactions. For example, take Anaya, a vegan, and her partner Jon, a non-vegan. One of Anaya's triggers is feeling intellectually inferior, and during a discussion about veganism, Jon says something that she interprets as dismissive of her opinion. Anaya feels ashamed and angry, and she attacks Jon, calling him an opinionated intellectual bully. Jon, whose parents used to call him self-centered because he wasn't very tuned in to and sensitive to others' experiences, gets triggered, feeling judged as selfish and therefore as morally inferior. Ashamed and angry, he lashes out at Anaya, telling her she's overreacting and being irrational, which confirms her fear that she's not smart enough (she's not "rational") and triggers her further. So of course, she reacts by telling Jon that he's insensitive, further triggering him.

The Spectrum of Triggeredness

When we're triggered, we're in a state of *heightened arousal*, meaning we are emotionally and physically agitated and insecure. We can be mildly aroused or completely hijacked. Triggeredness exists on a spectrum.

Often, when we are in a state of low-grade, or mild, triggeredness, we don't even realize we're triggered. We may just feel hypersensitive, or raw, and can go on like that for hours, days, and even years. Vegans can live in a chronic state of low-grade triggeredness when the people closest to them are not allies. The constant threat of being exposed to traumatic triggers can keep the vegan on high alert, ever-ready to defend against more distress. Non-vegans, too, can become chronically triggered, anxious about saying or doing the wrong thing that will set the vegan off. Whenever a major conflict has not been fully resolved, both parties can remain triggered for extended periods of time.

The problem with being in a state of low-grade triggeredness—apart from the fact that it feels bad, drains our energy, and negatively impacts our relationships—is that the drizzle of mild arousal can easily turn into a full-scale emotional deluge. Minor infractions can erupt into major blowouts.

By the time we're fully triggered, we're in a state of *flooding*.[4] Our nervous system is literally flooded with adrenaline and other hormones. We are in fight-flight-or-freeze mode, and our only concern is getting out of the situation that is causing us such distress. When we're flooded, we are unable to think rationally and our creativity and empathy are seriously compromised. Our thinking is black-and-white, our emotions are all-consuming, and our bodies are on high alert. Asking someone who's flooded to consider other perspectives on a situation is like asking a drowning person to contemplate politics. Our words would fall on deaf ears, because the only thing that matters to the other is staying alive, getting back to safety.

And flooding doesn't resolve simply when the triggering stimulus stops. Even if we resolve the conflict that caused the flooding, once our body has

---

4 John Gottman, *What Makes Love Last? How to Build Trust and Avoid Betrayal* (New York: Simon and Schuster, 2012).

been in such an intense state of arousal, it stays that way until our system has been able to recalibrate. It takes time for all the hormones and other chemicals that have inundated us to subside and for the painful emotions to wane. Most people need at least 20 minutes to calm down after being flooded; some people need longer and some situations can be so triggering that even those whose systems normally calibrate quickly will need more time to settle down.

When we're aware of our level of arousal, we're in a better position to make healthy choices. For example, when you recognize that you're even mildly triggered, you can appreciate that your emotions are exaggerated and your perceptions are distorted, so you don't take your feelings and thoughts too seriously and you don't make decisions based on your current experience. And when we're aware of the level of arousal of the other, we can better respond to their needs. For example, if the other is flooded, you can honor their need for time to calm down and not push for resolution during or right after the conflict.

The Recipe for Triggering

Couples therapists Christensen, Doss, and Jacobson explain that the typical recipe for triggering has either two or three ingredients—an emotional allergy (they use the phrase "psychological allergy"), a provocation, and sometimes a stressful environment.[5] We get triggered when at least the first two of these ingredients come together.

Emotional allergies are our pre-existing sensitivities or vulnerabilities. For example, you may be extremely sensitive to the idea of being incompetent or to feeling out of control. We all have a handful of emotional allergies that we bring into our relationships, and identifying our and the other's allergies so that we can protect these sensitive areas can truly be transformative.

Sometimes protecting the other's emotional allergies requires us to do things that don't seem fair, like being inordinately reassuring if they have

---

5 For an excellent explanation of this recipe for triggering, and for ways to manage conflict, see Andrew Christensen, Brian D. Doss, and Neil S. Jacobson, *Reconcilable Differences: Rebuild Your Relationship by Rediscovering the Partner You Love—Without Losing Yourself*, 2nd ed. (New York: Guilford Press, 2014). The term *emotional allergy* was coined by Lori H. Gordon. See her article "Intimacy: The Art of Relationships," *Psychology Today*, December 31, 1969.

an abandonment allergy or letting them have access to our phone if they're allergic to betrayal. Often the behaviors that protect the other don't seem rational, but that's because emotional allergies are not rational. Even if our own allergies clash with the other's—perhaps we are allergic to feeling controlled while the other, who is allergic to betrayal, needs to know our whereabouts and dealings—we can still maintain a commitment to the other's safety while we remain in dialogue about how we can find a solution so we both feel secure.

Provocations are behaviors that cause our allergy to flare up. For example, if your non-vegan partner is allergic to feeling like she's not a good person, she may get triggered when you hint at the fact that the free-range eggs she's eating are not cruelty-free. Your comment is the provocation. Provocations can also be our own thoughts. If, for instance, you have an allergy to betrayal, you can get triggered just imagining an employee of yours doing something deceptive. And a provocation can be a completely innocent act that simply provokes a reaction in us. For instance, perhaps your parents offer you money to help out while you're between jobs, but your allergy to being needy gets triggered because you assume they're suggesting you aren't independent enough.

Our *environment* is anything external to our allergies and provocations that impacts our reaction. When our environment is stressful, we're at increased risk of being triggered. For example, if you're sleep deprived or you've had a stressful day at work, or if you're dealing with a personal crisis, you will be more susceptible to provocations. Conversely, the less stressful our environment is, the less susceptible to provocations we will be.

As with physical allergies, emotional allergies exist along a spectrum of severe to mild. Provocations, too, can be severe or mild. So the degree to which we are triggered depends on the degree of our allergy and the severity of the provocation. For instance, if you're only mildly allergic to pollen and there isn't much pollen in the air, you'll have a very different reaction than if you have a severe allergy and pollen levels are high. And your allergic reaction will be intensified if your immune system has been weakened, perhaps by an illness or stress.

Our emotional allergies and reactions can cause us a good deal of shame, because we feel so vulnerable and can feel so out of control when we're triggered, and also because we often end up doing things to others that we later regret. So it can be helpful to realize that *everyone* gets triggered and reacts to provocations in less-than-optimal ways. Even the most relationally savvy of us is not immune to being triggered, and even the most secure and connected relationships have their share of triggered interactions.

Soothing Triggeredness

Certain behaviors can help us calm down after we've been triggered. *Self-regulating behaviors* (such as deep breathing or counting to 10) help us calm ourselves, and *co-regulating behaviors* help us reassure and calm each other.[6]

While we can use our rational minds to provide each other with reassurance and develop insights, relationship experts Susan Campbell and John Grey suggest we use at least some co-regulating behaviors that bypass our rational mind, since when we're triggered, it's the non-rational part of the brain that is activated.[7] We can, for example, use touch, eye contact, soothing tones, and short, reassuring phrases. And neuropsychologist Stan Tatkin suggests that we make a habit of employing co-regulating behaviors on a regular basis, especially during times of separation and reconnection, such as when we leave for work or arrive home, and when we fall asleep and awaken.[8] Goodbyes and hellos that include hugs, eye contact, and welcoming voice tones can do wonders to maintain our sense of security and connection.

EMOTIONAL AWARENESS: DEFENSIVE AND VULNERABLE EMOTIONS

When examining our emotional reactions in our conflicts, it can be helpful to ask the following question: What deeper, more vulnerable emotions may be underneath the obvious ones?

---

6 For a more detailed explanation of managing triggers, see Susan Campbell and John Grey, *Five-Minute Relationship Repair: Quickly Heal Upsets, Deepen Intimacy, and Use Differences to Strengthen Love* (Novato, CA: New World Library, 2015).

7 Ibid.

8 Stan Tatkin, *Wired for Love: How Understanding Your Partner's Brain and Attachment Style Can Help You Defuse Conflict and Build a Secure Relationship* (Oakland, CA: New Harbinger, 2011).

As we become aware of our emotional reactions, we may notice that we have two types of emotions—vulnerable ones and defensive/protective ones. Often, we start out feeling vulnerable but we quickly become defensive. We end up losing touch with our original feelings and only feel those emotions that are designed to protect us against further hurt.

When we are unaware of the deeper, vulnerable emotions that triggered the protective ones, we don't know what we actually need in order to feel better and we therefore can't communicate our needs with the other. For example, perhaps you feel sad and ashamed when someone at dinner makes a joke about your veganism and your partner doesn't stand up for you. What you need is to feel witnessed by your partner and to feel that they have your back—that they are your ally. You need to feel like your experience matters to them and to trust that they will be there for you when you're hurting. If you aren't aware of your vulnerable feelings and your needs, you can't articulate them to your partner. So instead of turning toward your partner and sharing your thoughts and feelings, you become angry and cold toward them, emotionally withdrawing.

Another problem is that our protective emotions tend to trigger protective emotions and behaviors in others. For example, anger, which is usually a protective emotion, is often met with anger or with a defensive strategy such as withdrawal.

When we speak from the vulnerable parts of ourselves, we are much more likely to be met with empathy and compassion. Just as our protective emotions tend to bring out the protective emotions in others, our vulnerable emotions help others connect with their vulnerability.

THE CHAIN OF CONFLICT

The majority of conflicts, particularly chronic conflicts, are caused not by a single factor but by a chain reaction of factors, each one sparking the next. Most conflict is the result not of actual problems, but of how we *react* to certain factors. We cause conflict when we react to a factor in an unproductive way, which then often sparks the other to react to us in an unproductive way, which then causes us to react in an unproductive way, and so on. And each time this cycle is repeated, the conflict is reinforced, becoming chronic and more complex.

Defensive Strategies

Our unproductive reactions are defensive strategies, methods of managing our distress that are designed to defend us against further pain and give us a sense of control. Defensive strategies are often coping mechanisms that we developed when we were young and had to find a way to cope with painful situations. For example, if you had an angry and abusive parent, you may have learned to cope with others' anger by becoming passive and disconnecting from your feelings and disengaging from the interaction. This coping mechanism may have served you when you were too young to know any other way to manage your distress, but it ultimately works against you in your adult interactions. But because we have used our coping mechanisms for so long, they are deeply ingrained in us; they are automatic, unthinking reactions that we don't even recognize as the unproductive strategies they are.

Our defensive strategies can end up creating new problems that are often worse than the issue we were originally dealing with. Imagine, for example, that you're feeling depressed, and rather than seek help, you turn to alcohol. In an attempt to manage the pain of the depression, you end up with another, more complicated condition—alcoholism. So now you have to deal with the depression *and* the alcoholism and try to sort out what's what.

Breaking the Chain of Conflict

It takes time, commitment, and trial and error to break the chain of conflict. It is far easier to continue our defensive strategies, even if they don't serve us in the long run. When we stop using them, we are faced with the fears they were designed to relieve—and facing these fears takes courage. For example, when you speak honestly and directly about your fear of being triggered by being exposed to meat, or your fear of not being able to maintain connection with the other across your ideological differences, you relinquish control and expose your vulnerability. This kind of change in a pattern of relating is difficult and comes with a learning curve. So we need to be patient and compassionate with ourselves, and not reinforce our negative schemas every time we act in a way we're not especially proud of.

Awareness is the first step in interrupting the chain of conflict: we must try to become aware of each of the factors in the chain (and understand that we can interrupt the chain at any point in the process). It can be very helpful to write out your conflicts as they arise. When you've experienced a conflict, try to write down what you remember of it as it unfolded, word for word. Then go back and try to understand the specific factors driving your conflict. The more you write out your conflicts, the easier it will be to unravel them and prevent them from reoccurring. Once you have clarity about your chain of conflict, you can consider alternatives to each of the factors in it, ways of interrupting the chain. Changing patterns is not just about stopping the ones that don't work; it's also about replacing them with ones that do work.[9]

Appendices 3, 4, and 5 provide a sample conflict, a chart for you to fill out, and a set of guiding questions to help you complete the chart.

It can also be helpful to talk with others who can help you sort out your thoughts and perhaps see your blind spots. But remember, only discuss your problems with someone whose integrity you trust and who never disparages the other or your relationship—even if they believe the relationship is problematic—or it can make matters worse.

It's often best to communicate with the other after you have developed clarity around your own actions and reactions. You can set a time to sit down and discuss what you were both thinking and feeling, and what you need in order to feel secure and connected again. In order to do this effectively, it's important to understand the principles of effective communication, which we will discuss in the next chapter.

EFFECTIVE CONFLICT MANAGEMENT

Effective conflict management requires that we relate to conflict and everyone involved with as much compassion and clarity as possible. To the best of our ability, we bring integrity and awareness to our painful interactions, in order to help transform them. Ideally, both parties are committed to this process. But even if the other is unwilling to engage in the process, as long as they are not

---

9 Andrew Christensen, Brian D. Doss, and Neil S. Jacobson, *Reconcilable Differences: Rebuild Your Relationship by Rediscovering the Partner You Love—Without Losing Yourself*, 2nd ed. (New York: Guilford Press, 2014).

being abusive, *you* can stay engaged and change your own way of relating, which itself can help shift the cycle of conflict. And after you practice the principles and tools discussed in this section, if the other is still unable or unwilling to do so, you have important information about your relationship and can consider if the relationship is in fact something you want to continue to invest in.

Prioritizing Safety

In order to manage conflict with compassion, we must make the other's safety and security a priority. People who feel unsafe are often unable to be rational and empathetic. To this end, it's essential to avoid threatening abandonment or shaming the other. Threats to leave the relationship, even if you truly mean them in the moment, are often experienced as cruelty, and they can be devastating to the trust you may have worked to build. Even indirect threats can have this effect. Similarly, suggestions that the other is not good enough, especially if you compare them negatively with others, can be heartbreaking and can leave wounds that never fully heal. Behaviors that undermine security drive a wedge between us and the other and can cause serious damage.

Developing Awareness

In order to manage conflict effectively, we must be committed to developing awareness, of ourselves and the other. We cannot break the cycle of attack-counterattack if we remain on autopilot. We need to learn to be self-observers, to take a step back from our thoughts and feelings and witness them as objectively and compassionately as possible. When we witness ourselves in such a way, our thoughts and feelings lose some of the charge they had, and we develop insight and self-restraint.

We can also bring our awareness to our reactions, pausing before engaging in a behavior to ask if it's really going to serve us, if it reflects our values and the kind of person we want to be. We may still feel distress, but we don't have to be controlled by the distress. We can witness our distress, try to understand its source, wait it out, and decide not to react in a defensive manner. This act of creating space—between ourselves and our thoughts and feelings—is profound. It is an act of mindfulness, an empirically validated practice to reduce stress, improve relationships, and enhance our overall quality of life. Mindfulness helps us shift from having automatic reactions to practicing intentional responses.

Delivering Effective Apologies

Many of us do not apologize in a way that truly helps offset the hurt we may have caused. An effective apology is an important part of the process of managing and repairing conflict. An effective apology reassures the other that

- we understand the hurt we have caused,
- we feel remorse about what we did,
- we take responsibility for our actions, and
- we will do our best to prevent the same thing from happening again.

These components are necessary for the other to feel reassured that we genuinely care about their well-being and that they won't get hurt in the same way again. Generally, when someone asks for an apology after we've already given them one, it's because the original apology was insufficient to reassure them. Telling them, "I said I'm sorry. What more do you want?" will likely only make things worse, as this communicates a lack of concern for the fact that the other feels unseen and/or unsafe. It also reflects a lack of awareness on our part that our apology may not have been delivered effectively. In addition, if we respond to a request for reassurance in such a way, the other may withdraw and stop reaching out for an apology that they genuinely need in order to trust and reconnect with us again. Saying "I'm sorry" is rarely enough to help the other feel witnessed, connected, and reassured.

Effective apologies include the following:

- Saying, directly, that you apologize: using the words "I'm sorry," or "I apologize."
- Showing that you take responsibility for your actions and that you're aware of what actions caused the hurt: "I'm sorry I yelled at you" rather than "I'm sorry I hurt your feelings." Saying "I'm sorry you feel hurt" is expressing sympathy for the hurt (as in, "I'm sorry your fish died") rather than acknowledging your responsibility in the hurt.

- Empathizing and verbally expressing that you understand the pain your actions caused. Your apology should be on a similar level of emotional intensity as the pain the other experienced. If you said words that you know would be devastating for the other to hear, simply saying "Sorry about that" in a casual tone of voice won't cut it. And, repeating the apology multiple times may be necessary. Many people resist repeating apologies, but that resistance is often more a matter of ego than anything else. If simply repeating our words of apology can make another feel safe, why wouldn't we do it?
- Offering to make amends, to make it up to the other. You can ask what would help the other to feel better, and if their request is acceptable to you, do it.
- Accepting that forgiveness may take time. Just because you apologized doesn't mean the other will automatically feel trusting and forgiving.

Principles and Tools for Effective Conflict Management

The following guidelines can help reduce the amount of conflict you experience and can change destructive conflicts into constructive ones.

- Become "conflict allies." Change your conflict narrative so that instead of you each being opponents against each other, you see yourselves as allies against a problem that is threatening the security and connection of your relationship.
- Pause before reacting. Take five deep breaths. If reacting to what just occurred is not truly time-sensitive, leave it until you've had time to cool down. For example, you can make a practice of not sending off an emotional email until you've had at least one night to sleep on it. Most of our regrets about how we behaved during a conflict are about reacting too quickly, not waiting too long.
- Maintain goodwill toward each other, to the best of your ability. Give each other the benefit of the doubt.
- Remember that most conflicts can be repaired; rarely is damage

irreparable. We can, at any moment during our conflict, change the way we relate to the conflict and shift our dynamic toward repair.

- Allow emotions to cool before pursuing discussion. If you feel triggered, or if you feel you are being disrespected, call for a time-out. Agree to check back in with each other after a specific period of time, ideally between 30 minutes and a couple of hours, and to revisit the conversation if you both feel calm enough to do so at that point. Some people need more recovery time than others, so respect each individual's needs.

- Aim for full understanding of each other's narrative, feelings, and behaviors. Understanding helps offset distorted narratives, and it helps us reconnect with our empathy. As you explain yourself, be sure to point out that you are offering an explanation, not an excuse, for any behaviors that may have hurt the other.

- Use humor, when appropriate. Compassionate humor cuts through defenses and helps remind us that often what we are in conflict about is not necessarily as threatening as it seems.

- Stay on your side of the street. Remember: you can only know for sure what *you* think and feel. While it's important to try to empathize, you cannot truly know what is going on in another's heart and mind unless they tell you.

- Stick to one topic at a time. It may be tempting to start dredging up old hurts, but conflicts can easily become confusing and overwhelming when we discuss too many topics at once. There is a hub at the center of most, if not all, chronic conflicts. Try to identify the hub and to see how seemingly different conflicts may be spokes on that wheel. For example, rather than discuss the fact that your always-busy partner didn't let you know she changed weekend plans until the last minute, and that she often leaves home in a rush, so her dirty dishes stay in the sink until you wash them, you can identify the root problem—that she doesn't seem to value your time as much as she does her own.

- Avoid the disconnecting attitudes and behaviors we discussed in Chapter 1, such as criticism, judgment, and put-downs.

- Avoid what psychologist Mira Kirshenbaum calls "off-the-table-itis," taking a topic off the table for discussion over and over so it never gets addressed.[10]
- Engage in the emotionally connecting behaviors we discussed in Chapter 1, such as compassionate witnessing and turning toward each other.
- Appreciate that how you recover from conflict—what you do to repair hurt feelings and what actions you take based on what you learned from the conflict—may have more of an impact on the security and connection of your relationship than does the conflict itself.
- Commit to forgiveness, an issue we will discuss in Chapter 9.
- Schedule regular meetings once a week, for about 30 minutes, to discuss your relationship and to ensure you don't let problems fester.[11]
- If you haven't been able to find a solution to meeting each person's needs adequately, rate the importance of each of your needs on a scale of 1 to 5. Then give priority to the highest-ranked needs for each person.
- Learn effective communication. Effective communication is a skill that in itself can transform relationships, and we will discuss it in the next chapter.

When we learn to manage conflict effectively, conflicts can become opportunities to increase our integrity and deepen the security and connection of our relationships. Effective conflict management requires us to develop the self-awareness necessary for clarity and insight and the courage to be vulnerable and authentic. It requires us to prioritize compassion and fairness over control and defensiveness.

Over time, we can come to trust that we will remain secure and connected even in the midst of conflict—so we can be more fully ourselves, no longer fearing disconnection and openly sharing our thoughts, feelings, and needs in our veg/non-veg relationship, and allowing the other to do so as well. Effective conflict management can help our lives, and our relationships, grow toward their fullest potential.

---

10 Mira Kirshenbaum, *Too Good to Leave, Too Bad to Stay: A Step-by-Step Guide to Help You Decide Whether to Stay In or Get Out of Your Relationship* (New York: Penguin, 1996).
11 An excellent resource is Marcia Naomi Berger's *Marriage Meetings for Lasting Love: 30 Minutes a Week to the Relationship You've Always Wanted* (Novato, CA: New World Library, 2014).

Chapter 8

EFFECTIVE COMMUNICATION: PRACTICAL SKILLS FOR SUCCESSFUL CONVERSATIONS

For many vegans, communicating with non-vegans can be confusing, frustrating, and demoralizing. Vegans *know* that their choice not to consume animals is based on the principles of compassion and justice shared by most humans and that veganism is not only rational and ethical, but also feasible for many people today. And yet vegans can find themselves tongue-tied and despairing because of the defensiveness they encounter from many non-vegans, who may cross-examine vegan beliefs and practices, looking for signs of hypocrisy or holes in the argument, and who may make wildly inaccurate statements about veganism, presenting them as hard facts. What's more, non-vegans, who are often simply expressing the convictions and conditioning of the belief system they grew up in, are rarely aware of such defensiveness; most non-vegans have no idea that, to a greater or lesser degree, they are speaking the language of carnism.

Effective communication may be the single most important skill any of us can learn, and its benefits go well beyond helping bridge the veg/non-veg communication gap. Effective communication can literally transform our lives and relationships and make all our interactions healthier and more productive. To communicate effectively, we must be aware of and able to express, with compassion and clarity, our thoughts and feelings, and to help others do the same. So effective communication is much more than stringing the right words together; it is a way of life. Effective communication is a way of relating to ourselves and others that helps build understanding, empathy, and integrity and leads to greater connection and security in our relationships.

We are constantly communicating, because we are constantly interacting. Whether verbally or non-verbally, our interactions are always sending a message. Often, though, we're on autopilot when we communicate, and we're not aware of the message we're sending. For example, if your brother emails you a recipe you'd been asking for and in your busyness you don't reply with a "thank you," you're communicating that you either don't appreciate his efforts or don't care enough to take the time to share your appreciation. Either way, he gets the message that his experience doesn't matter to you, and, to a greater or lesser degree, he will feel resentful and less connected to you. When we learn effective communication, we become more conscious of ourselves and others, resulting in interactions that are intentional rather than automatic and increasing rather than decreasing the security and connection in our relationships.

Ineffective communication is one of the key causes of conflict between vegans and non-vegans. It is also a key cause of the epidemic of arguments and chronic frustrations in many people's lives and relationships. When we don't know how to communicate effectively, we can become exhausted, resentful, and despairing from countless misunderstandings, from our ongoing attempts to revise and rephrase our message in an attempt to be understood, and from our sense of "loose ends"—issues that we can never seem to resolve and that never go away. We can also start to feel worn down from the many toxic commentaries we are exposed to throughout the day on social media and elsewhere that are poisoning our consciousness, because we don't recognize the ways in which these forms of communication are harmful. When we communicate effectively, we free up a tremendous amount of energy. Not only can we largely avoid draining and toxic interactions, but we no longer carry the burden of feeling silenced, unable to articulate what we need to say.

Effective communication is available to all of us. It is a method and a set of skills that enable us to understand and be understood by one another. It's based on a set of principles and tools that take effort and practice but can be learned by anyone who is truly committed.

A HEALTHY PROCESS: THE FOUNDATION OF EFFECTIVE COMMUNICATION

Every communication has two parts: the content and the process. The *content* is what we are communicating about, and the *process* is how we are communicating. People tend to remember far more of the process than the content; once a conversation has ended, we often don't recall much of what it was about, but we do remember how we felt during the interaction.

Keeping Agendas Healthy

Effective communication is built on a healthy process. And a healthy process is the same regardless of what we are communicating about. For example, whether we are discussing if we should stay in or go out on a Saturday night, or if we should have dairy products in our home, the same principles of a healthy process apply. When we have a healthy process, our goal, or agenda, is mutual understanding. Our goal is not to win, or to be right, but rather to understand and be understood—to share the truth of our experience. In this way, a healthy process is connecting; it is always a win-win endeavor.

Often, we are unaware of our own agenda when we enter a communication; we may be driven by the desire to get our way or prove our point without even realizing it. It's important for us to self-reflect so we can be sure that a hidden agenda doesn't sabotage our attempts to have a productive conversation. We can, of course, disagree with one another and want a certain outcome from our conversation. Perhaps, for example, you hope that you won't be expected to attend your cousin's meaty barbecue. But this goal should be secondary to mutual understanding. Only when we are at the point where we genuinely understand one another can we create mutually acceptable solutions to any disagreement we may be having.

A process is often not fully healthy or unhealthy; rather, it can be *more* or *less* healthy. The healthier our process, the more validating and compassionate it is to both ourselves and the other. And the less healthy our process, the more invalidating and shaming it is. When our process is healthy enough, no matter what the content of our conversation, no matter how different our opinions and needs may be, we can discuss just about anything openly and honestly—and we can deepen the security and connection of our relationship.

Discussing Rather than Debating

Generally, when our process is healthy, we discuss rather than debate. Debating is rarely productive. The debate model works only in a small handful of situations, such as during a courtroom battle or a political campaign. When we debate, our goal is to win, to be right, and therefore to make the other lose, to be wrong. Debating is a counterproductive form of communication in the vast majority of circumstances.

When we are dealing with differences of opinion, such as those surrounding veganism and carnism, we tend to focus primarily or entirely on the content without paying attention to the process, and we can easily fall into debate mode, trying to convince one another of the rightness of our position. Debating under such circumstances can only lead to problems. Not only does debating tend to create defensiveness—nobody wants to be shown to be wrong—but when it comes to talking about the ethics of eating animals, the facts rarely sell the ideology. Carnistic defenses distort perceptions, so it's difficult to have a straightforward, objective conversation about veganism.

Debating is especially unproductive with those we are closest to. It's challenging to talk about points of disagreement in any circumstances, but with individuals in a close relationship, power struggles and long-standing grievances may have already been established, so the tendency to resist being wrong can be even stronger.

For example, consider Jeannette and Reggie, a veg/non-veg couple. Over the years, Jeannette has been increasingly frustrated with Reggie for what she sees as him not standing up for himself or for the things he believes in. Jeannette believes that Reggie is always giving in to his family's unfair demands because he doesn't want to cause conflict. She also feels that Reggie doesn't address important ethical issues. For instance, even though Reggie has three siblings, he's always the one to bail out his troubled cousin, and he avoids confronting his cousin on what seem to be her shady and illegal dealings.

For his part, Reggie has been frustrated with Jeannette's criticism of him and what he believes are her unrealistic expectations of him. For instance, he believes that Jeannette doesn't appreciate that he's been the family caretaker for most of his life and he can't just drop the ball on the people he's closest to. If Jeannette and Reggie start talking about the ethics of eating animals, Reggie's sensitivity to feeling criticized and Jeannette's sensitivity to Reggie's seeming refusal to take a stand on important issues will likely make the conversation far more emotionally charged than it might otherwise be. When we don't recognize the deeper issues in our relationship and work to create a healthy communicative process, our conversation can easily spiral into a heated debate that has less to do with eating or not eating animals than it does with who gets to be right and assert their power.

Focusing on the process takes the conversation out of the realm of ideas and brings it to the deeper level of how people relate to one another—about ideas, but also about everything else, including needs, feelings, and experiences. When we discuss rather than debate, we can talk about even the most difficult issues more productively.

PRACTICING CONVERSATIONAL INTEGRITY

Every communication has two sides—transmitting and receiving. We play the role of transmitter when we are the speaker (or performer of an action). We play the role of the receiver when we are the listener (or witness to an action). Effective communication requires that we practice integrity in each of these roles.

Effective communication is validating rather than invalidating. Each party helps the other feel that what they think, feel, and need is valid—that they matter—and they don't suggest that the other's experience is "wrong." Because it is based on the principles of integrity, effective communication increases our sense of self-worth.

When we practice *conversational integrity*, we do our best to bring the values of compassion, curiosity, justice, honesty, and courage to our communication. When we practice compassion, we try to look at the world through the other's eyes and not judge them. When we practice curiosity, we are genuinely interested in learning about the experience of the other rather than jumping to conclusions or simply waiting for our turn to speak and make our own point. When we practice justice, we treat the other as we would want to be treated; we try, for example, to neither talk too much nor too little. Honesty is saying what's true (with compassion) rather than what's easy. And courage is the willingness to be vulnerable, to say and hear the truth even when it's hard.

In order to practice conversational integrity, we need to slow down our communication process. We need to interrupt our automatic process to break old habits and replace them with new ones. When we spend a lifetime communicating on autopilot, we get used to cruising through our communications passively. Stepping up and taking the wheel takes effort: it takes the willingness to be awake and present. It also takes the willingness to pull our weight and not expect others to do more than their fair share. When we pull our weight, we don't, for example, make others work to understand what we're saying, interrupt us in order to get a word in, or struggle to hold our attention when we are the listener. One simple way to make sure you are practicing conversational integrity is to pause every few minutes during a conversation and ask yourself questions such as the following:

- How does the other seem to be feeling right now?
- Have I been talking more than listening?
- Have I asked about the other—how they are feeling, what they are thinking?
- Have I been listening too much, not sharing enough?

Our guiding question in all communications can be: "How will my behavior (what I say or don't say, my tone of voice, etc.) impact the other?"

To practice conversational integrity, we need to develop self-awareness. If we are not aware of what we are thinking, feeling, and needing, we can end up "acting out" and communicating in a way that disconnects rather than connects us to each other. When we act out, we communicate an unconscious feeling or need through a behavior. For example, perhaps you're angry that your sister forgot, again, to make the minestrone soup that she brought to the family potluck with veggie stock instead of chicken stock, even though you've told her that you can't eat it otherwise. Rather than acknowledge your anger and address the issue directly with your sister, you end up, a few weeks later, "not feeling well" and canceling, at the last minute, your attendance at the elaborate dinner party she's been planning for months.

Finally, practicing conversational integrity means that we accept that the only thing we can know with certainty are our own thoughts, feelings, and needs. It means allowing the other to be the expert on their own experience. In other words, we don't define the other's reality. In Chapter 2, we discussed how defining reality—communicating that the other's thoughts, feelings, or needs are wrong—is fundamentally disrespectful and is the foundation of psychological abuse. When we define another's reality we invalidate their experience, and this behavior is almost guaranteed to trigger defensiveness. Mind reading is simply not possible, and attempts to do so only lead to problems.

Consider the following examples of defining reality:

Non-vegan: "I love animals."

Vegan: "No, you don't. You eat them."

The non-vegan is talking about their feeling of love. The vegan, however, somehow believes they know what the non-vegan is feeling better than the non-vegan does. Is it not possible to *feel* love for animals and still eat them? Did the vegan not love animals when they used to eat them?

Vegan: "I can't believe Dad called me a 'plant murderer'—and worse, everyone was laughing along with him!"

Non-vegan: "Settle down, it was just a joke. Why do you always have to be so serious?"

How, then, do you disagree without invalidating the other? How do you share the truth of your experience when the other may be defensive? How do you increase the chances that when you talk about something sensitive and potentially loaded, such as veganism, your message is heard as you intend it to be? Beyond the principles of effective communication, we need to learn the specific tools with which to practice them: we need to learn to express ourselves and listen effectively.

EFFECTIVE EXPRESSING

When we express ourselves effectively, we reduce misunderstandings, we avoid resentment because we say what needs to be said in a timely fashion, and we build trust. Essentially, we create a safe environment for the listener so they can be more receptive and less defensive and we can have an open and compassionate exchange. We speak directly and honestly rather than give confusing or mixed messages that require the listener to figure out what we "really" mean and to read between the lines. We pay attention to the listener's needs so they don't have to strategize to keep us on track, slow us down, or pull information out of us. Our message is complete, so the listener isn't made anxious by having to fill in the blanks, and our message is as compassionate and unbiased as possible, so the listener is less defensive and more receptive. We stay connected with our empathy and keep the lines of connection open between ourselves and the other. The listener feels that they are seen and that they matter. And we can learn from the insights we may gain when we are communicating honestly and openly. Often, some of our most important learnings come from hearing ourselves talk.

Discussing Versus Advocating

In order to practice effective expressing, vegans need to appreciate the difference between discussing and advocating. The main difference is the goal of the communication. The goal of discussing is to reach mutual understanding. And the goal of advocating is the same—with the additional objective of increasing the chances that the other will allow themselves to be influenced by the information being shared.

An advocate speaks out on behalf of others in order to bring about positive change for those others. Many people become vegan because they care deeply about the cause and they therefore feel compelled to speak out to raise awareness of the plight of animals. So they are automatically advocates. This natural advocacy component of veganism can cause two problems for vegans communicating with non-vegans. First, advocates—vegan or non-vegan—are often perceived as moralistic, even when they are not, and people are generally defensive against the message of those they see as moralistic. In addition, vegans tend to blur the line between discussing and advocating, which can cause misunderstandings and defensiveness when what is needed is mutual understanding without any attempt to influence the other.

Debunking the Moralistic Vegan Stereotype

Advocates speak out against injustice—but they are not direct victims of injustice themselves. So advocates tend to have less freedom to raise awareness of an injustice without being labeled as "moralistic" than would a direct victim. Consider, for example, how differently we perceive a veteran who speaks out against war and a student who is an anti-war activist.

Advocates are often seen as taking the moral high road, as representing a moral choice that others perhaps could have made but didn't. So non-advocates can feel "less moral" by comparison. When people feel they are in a position of moral inferiority, they tend to do one or both of two things. They project onto the other that the other feels morally superior (even if the other doesn't feel this way), and they offset their discomfort by trying to prove that the person they are comparing themselves to is in fact less moral—to rebalance the moral scales. And when it comes to veganism, vegans also have to contend with the fact that carnistic culture actively promotes the stereotype of the "holier-than-thou," or moralistic, vegan.

Vegans frequently report that simply stating that they are vegan leads to them being told all the ways in which veganism isn't morally superior to eating animals: "What about all the plants that have to die for you to eat them?" "The only reason animals are even alive is because we eat them. So you'd rather they not even be born?" "All that packaged vegan food that's shipped long distances is terrible for the environment, worse than the chicken that's processed down the street." And so on.

Some vegans do, however, see themselves as morally superior to non-vegans, and this stance is both arguably inaccurate and otherwise problematic. The choice to be vegan is an act of integrity and reflects an important ethical stand. But the idea that one individual is morally superior to another is, in all probability, an illusion, and is a counterproductive way to think about issues. How can we possibly determine who is, in fact, morally "better"? Is it the humanitarian who eats animals or the vegan who verbally bullies those who don't agree with her point of view? Would the celebrated philanthropist from Europe be as morally commendable if he'd been born into poverty and sold into child sex slavery in India? What if he'd been born with a genetic predisposition for bipolar disorder? Most of us, perhaps all of us, do the best we can with the cards we have been dealt. And regardless of whether you believe there is a hierarchy of moral worth, framing a conversation about individuals' moral superiority and inferiority is pretty much guaranteed to sabotage any productive outcome. So it's good practice not to use this frame at all.

Separating Discussing from Advocating

Because many vegans are also advocates, the boundary between discussing and advocating can be blurred. A conversation that starts out about whether to make the family dinner with soy cheese or cow's cheese can easily turn into a conversation about veganism in general, with the vegan playing the advocate. The tendency to cross from discussing to advocating is one reason why simple conversations between vegans and non-vegans turn into arguments.

The impulse to shift from discussing to advocating doesn't mean that vegans shouldn't advocate; anyone who cares about an issue will naturally feel the need to communicate in a way that opens hearts and minds and increases the chances that others will be sympathetic to and supportive of the issue. But both vegans and non-vegans would do well to understand the natural tendency of vegans to advocate and not take offense when it happens. Furthermore, vegans should be especially careful not to advocate when a different conversation is really what needs to happen. For example, the aforementioned conversation about soy cheese versus cow's cheese was originally about each person's needs and wants. If that original issue—understanding and negotiating needs, which is essential to emotional connection—is not attended to, discussing vegan ethics can seem like it's sabotaging connection. And as long as needs remain unattended to, the original conversation will feel unresolved. So, after the original issue has been addressed, veganism can be discussed further if both parties are interested in doing so.

Sometimes discussing needs and advocating veganism naturally overlap. For example, the vegan may need to explain what happens in the production of cow's cheese to help the listener understand why the vegan feels so offended by it and unable to serve it. But even in this situation, the goal should not be advocacy but mutual understanding in order to arrive at a mutually satisfying agreement about how each person's needs can be met. In general, a relationship should not be a forum for advocacy, since advocacy in that context can easily initiate a power struggle.

Using Whole Messages

In their excellent book *Messages*, authors Matthew McKay, Martha Davis, and Patrick Fanning present an essential tool for effective expressing—"whole messages."[1] Whole messages are based on the principles of nonviolent communication, and they are designed to prevent us from defining reality and to create an atmosphere of objectivity, respect, and trust.

Whole messages contain four parts: observations, thoughts, feelings, and needs. Not all messages will require the expression of all four parts, of course, but this formula can be applied in any situation where we want to ensure that we communicate clearly.

When we express our observations, we share what we have observed with our senses—what we have seen, heard, and so on. Observations are reports of objective facts, not speculations, interpretations, or conclusions. For example, an observation may be "It's 90 degrees Fahrenheit," or "I left my phone at home today," or "Vegans don't consume animal products."

When we express our thoughts, we are sharing our conclusions or perceptions based on our observations. Our thoughts are our subjective interpretations of what we have observed, and they may include our value judgments, beliefs, or opinions. For example, a thought might be "Relationships take work," or "Denmark has an interesting history of progressive social change."

When we express our feelings, we share our emotional experience. You might say, for example, "I felt embarrassed, angry, and hurt when Brian made that comment about vegans having an eating disorder," or "I feel ashamed

---

1 Matthew McKay, Martha Davis, and Patrick Fanning, *Messages: The Communication Skills Book*, 3rd ed. (Oakland, CA: New Harbinger, 2009).

of what I said to you yesterday," or "I'm so happy and grateful that you're coming to the lecture on veganism with me; it really means a lot to me to be able to share this part of my life with you." Often we say "I feel" when we really mean "I think." For example, you might say, "I feel like a lot of people are starting to care more about their carbon footprint," when you are actually expressing a thought.

When we express our needs, we communicate what we want or hope for. As we discussed in Chapter 2, many of us are ashamed of having needs and have never learned how to articulate them, so we try to get our needs met through indirect means. However, expecting others to meet our needs without having clearly communicated them is unfair, and it's a recipe for disappointment and conflict. The more we practice expressing our needs, the better. When you express a need, you might say, "Could you stop by the grocery store on your way home? I'd really love to make pasta for dinner tonight and we're all out." Or "When you said that you won't go to the veggie festival with me and the kids on my birthday, I felt like you made a unilateral decision that affects the whole family. Can we put aside some time this evening to talk about this?" Like our observations, thoughts, and feelings, our needs reflect *our* experience, so expressing our needs should not include blaming or judging the other. In addition, expressed needs should be concrete, direct, and doable.

Relationship expert Terrence Real suggests that it's sometimes helpful to add a fifth part to our message, the question "How can I help you give me what I need?"[2] This can be a useful addition that shows understanding and support and that increases the chances of getting our needs met.

Consider the following scenario, in which a whole message is not, and then is, employed:

> Susan, a vegan, has just returned home from her company's Christmas party and she's talking with her non-vegan wife, Ellen.

---

2 Terrence Real, *The New Rules of Marriage: What You Need to Know to Make Love Work* (New York: Ballantine Books, 2007).

Ellen: So how'd the party go?

Susan: It was good, but Joe gave me a wool scarf. I didn't say anything when he gave it to me; I've told him I'm vegan but he's almost 80 years old and he just doesn't get what veganism means. I didn't want to hurt his feelings so I just accepted his gift and figured I'd give it away.

Ellen (rolling her eyes): Seriously? You're always complaining you don't have enough clothes and now you won't wear a perfectly fine scarf because it's wool? It's better for the sheep to get rid of all that hair once in a while, and anyway, the scarf was already bought and paid for so it's not like you're even supporting the wool industry. If you ask me, you're really becoming extreme.

Susan: Well I *didn't* ask you, did I. You have no clue about wool production but suddenly you're such an expert on how the industry's good for sheep. Do you have any idea what those animals go through? And if *you* ask *me*, what's "extreme" is paying someone to exploit innocent animals just so you can have a piece of material to wrap around your neck!

Here's Susan's response to Ellen's comments, using a whole message:

What you just said was really hard for me to hear.

Observations: I told you I got a wool scarf I don't feel comfortable wearing, and you rolled your eyes. Not only that, but you told me—a vegan who you *know* is informed about how animal products are manufactured—that wool production is good for sheep. And regardless of how the wool industry works, I'd made it clear I wasn't ethically comfortable wearing the scarf, but you said I should do it anyway, and you even told me I was becoming "extreme."

Thoughts: I can't help but interpret your reaction to mean that you don't take my values seriously, that you don't understand what it means to me to be vegan—which is a central part of who I am. I think if you really understood what veganism means to me, you wouldn't have suggested that I act against my values. In fact, it seems like you actually look down on my veganism, and—when you said I'm extreme—like you're judging me for holding to my values.

Feelings: I feel offended, and, honestly, I feel hurt because I feel like you don't really see me for who I am, like one of the most important parts of me is invisible to you. When I feel judged and invisible like that, I just pull back, and so I end up feeling less connected with you.

Needs: I wish you'd learn more about veganism, so you could better understand me. I'd really appreciate being able to share some information about veganism with you so you can get a sense of what the world looks like through my eyes, and so ultimately, we can both feel more connected. What can I do to help you do this for me?

Whole messages can immediately and powerfully reduce defensiveness. With the simple act of owning our experience—being clear that our thoughts and feelings are our interpretations of reality, not the definition of reality—and allowing others to own their experience, we create an atmosphere of mutual empowerment and validation and we are much better able to work toward a solution.

Using whole messages can transform our communication. It takes practice, but if we stick with it, it can become second nature. Communicating with whole messages is a bit like learning a new language. At first we have to put effort into thinking through what we're going to say and we may stumble through our conversations, but over time, we become fluent and start to think in our new language. And when we think in whole messages, we're more objective, compassionate, and unassuming. We're better able to stay on our side of the street and to recognize when others are not staying on theirs.

A good way to learn to become more proficient in using whole messages—and also to gain clarity about conflicts or problems—is to write out your whole message before sharing it. You can do this exercise on its own or while filling in the Chain of Conflict Guiding Questions and Chart. You may want to share your whole message in writing with the other before discussing it, or you can even read it aloud to them.

Keeping Messages Direct and Clear

Effective expressing requires that messages be direct. Many people are not good at reading between the lines, and it's unfair and counterproductive to assume that others will know what we're implying if we're indirect. So, for example, rather than saying "Helen's lucky her husband doesn't have to travel for work," you could say, "I miss you since you've been so busy lately. I could really use a whole weekend for just the two of us, to reconnect." Or instead of saying, "Sometimes I feel like nobody wants to talk about anything but themselves," you might say, "I would really love to talk to you about some things going on in my life."

Effective expressing also requires that messages be clear. So, for example, it's clearer to say "I'm hurt and angry" than "I don't feel well." Clarity also means keeping our body language congruent with our words. Our bodies are always communicating, and when their message contradicts that of our words, the listener will not know which message to believe. For example, don't say "I'm great!" with a sad face, "I'm so sorry" with a smile, or "I'm interested in your point" as you yawn. Many people's bodies tell a different story than their words, and the listener can feel distrustful and misled by this kind of mixed messaging.

Keeping Difficult Conversations Simple and Short

When you're communicating about a problem or a conflict, it's best to focus on only one topic at a time. As noted in Chapter 7, conflicts are often like wheels, with multiple spokes but one common hub. In addition, try to keep difficult conversations as short as possible, ideally to a half hour or so. Conversations that continue beyond an hour are rarely productive; they often last so long because communication has not been clear and effective, and the longer they last, the more confusing and problematic they can become.

One way to make sure difficult conversations stay on topic and don't run overtime is to sort out the problem for ourselves first, to the best of our ability. Often, we enter into difficult conversations feeling upset and wanting resolution but without having taken the time to really get clear about what we've experienced and what we need. We can end up using the other as a processing bag like a boxer uses a punching bag, processing our experience with them in order to sort it out for ourselves. This can get us into a lot of trouble. When we have not sorted out our thoughts and feelings and we use the other to help us get clarity, our brainstorming process can hurt them. As we express whatever comes to our mind, we can state our concerns in a way that's not well thought out and that may be simply a reflection of our own fears and emotional allergies. We can say things we regret and exhaust the other in the process.

Responding to Disparaging Humor

Disparaging humor is humor that puts others down. Often, those others are members of non-dominant social groups. Such humor has been used throughout history to maintain prejudice and power imbalances. Making light of the suffering of those with less power both hides the fact that there's a problem—that there's an oppressive system—and minimizes the problem when it is recognized. Racist humor, for example, trivializes racism and its impact on people of color. Disparaging humor also invalidates the message of those who advocate change, either by mocking them so they are too embarrassed to speak out or by creating degrading stereotypes of them so they aren't taken seriously. Consider the many offensive jokes there are about feminists. Disparaging humor is so effective because it's difficult to see it for what it is or to respond to it appropriately.

Disparaging humor toward vegans is extremely common, but the phenomenon is largely invisible. Otherwise well-mannered people often make unkind jokes about vegans—usually right in front of the vegan—even though they would consider similar jokes about members of other non-dominant groups, such as Muslims or African Americans, totally inappropriate. And the vegan is left with the choice of laughing along with the others, thereby participating in their own oppression, or not—at the risk of being told they have no sense of humor and can't take a joke.

The first step to responding to disparaging humor is recognizing it for what it is. Any disparaging comment directed toward a person because of their membership in a social group—ethnic, gender, religious, ideological, and so on—is by its very nature prejudicial. And any comment whose intention is to make fun at the expense of another is disrespectful and, when that other is a member of a non-dominant group, discriminatory.

How to best respond to disparaging humor depends on the situation. Depending on who makes the comment (your boss, your mother, a stranger at a dinner party, and so forth), you may choose different ways to respond. You can choose whether to respond at all, whether to respond in private or public, and whether to do so directly or indirectly. With all situations, you should start with goodwill, with an assumption that the person who made the comment didn't realize how offensive it would be. Many people truly don't realize that anti-vegan humor is as disparaging and hurtful as it actually is.

With those close to us, it's important to communicate honestly and directly about our experience. You may wish to speak to close family or friends in private so you don't "call them out" on their disrespectful behavior in a way that embarrasses them. However, if you can speak from a place of compassion, you may consider saying something in front of others, to raise awareness among those who have just witnessed the event. (Only do this if you truly feel secure doing so; for many people, such public commentary can be very uncomfortable.) To highlight the fact that their "joke" is about a social group, you might say something like "Would you call a Muslim a picky eater for not eating pork?" Or you could ask for more information, putting the other in the position of having to explain a statement that was designed to put you down: "Why do you say vegans are hippies?" or "That's interesting. I never considered Albert Einstein [who was vegetarian] a hippie." Or you can simply ask "What did you mean by that statement?" or say

"I think I'm missing something here. I don't get the joke. Can you explain what you meant?" You may simply want to say, "Wow—I never expected to hear socially offensive humor from someone as conscientious as you."

You can also make a joke to turn the situation around so the non-vegan better understands your experience: "I'll eat veggie soup with chicken stock if you'll eat potato soup with kitten stock." When used wisely, humor can be a tool for raising awareness. Humor has historically been used not only to maintain, but also to transform oppressive systems. For example, comedians such as Margaret Cho have used humor to open people's minds to new ideas and demonstrate the absurdity of supporting prejudice: "Because I wasn't 'Asian enough,' they decided to hire an Asian consultant!"

In some situations, you may want to take the person aside and simply tell them what it felt like for you to hear their joke. You can use a whole message:

> When you said that vegans are radical weirdos, I couldn't help but think you were getting a laugh at my expense, using humor to put me down and belittle what I care most about in the world. I mean, you know I'm a vegan, and you also know veganism is central to who I am, an incredibly important part of my life. So I felt really offended. I was thinking that if I said the same thing about Christians, knowing how much your religion matters to you, you would have felt pretty insulted. I also felt really embarrassed—people were laughing at me, or at least they were laughing at my values, which are a major part of me—and I felt tongue-tied, not knowing how to respond to save face. I really need to know that you understand what this experience was like for me, and to know that in the future you won't put veganism down in front of me like that.

In some situations, it may simply be the lesser of evils to say nothing. You may not be able to confront your boss, for example, for her occasional anti-vegan comments without risking your job. Or you may simply not want to put forth the effort to call out a stranger on their joke when the timing doesn't seem right.

Appendix 8 provides an example of how to request that you be treated respectfully, and you can use part or all of that text to respond to hostile humor.

Tips for Effective Expressing

Following are some guidelines for effective expressing:

- Use "I" rather than "you" statements. This shows you're speaking for yourself and taking ownership of your experience. It's also more accurate. And it helps prevent blaming, which is not productive. For example, say "I feel angry" rather than "You make me angry." Nobody can make us feel a certain way; our feelings are simply our reactions to events.

- Avoid using "should" whenever possible. "Should" is often interpreted as judgmental, scolding, and controlling. Rather than say, "You should eat more healthfully," you could say, "You might want to consider ... ," "It may be worthwhile to look into ... ," "You may want to try ... ," or even, "If I were in your situation, I imagine I might want to ... "

- Use "and" rather than "but" whenever possible. When we say "but," we erase or invalidate everything that came before it. For example, rather than say, "Your potato salad was delicious, but I'd love to try it next time without so much pepper," you could say, "Your potato salad was delicious, and I'd love to try it next time with less pepper."

- Be solutionary. Often, when we're talking about things that matter to us, such as our relationship issues or veganism, we can get stuck focusing on the problem and spending more time talking about what's wrong than what's right, discussing what we shouldn't do rather than what we could be doing. Our focus on the problem makes sense: we are often all too aware of what's causing us (or others) to suffer. But when we are problem focused, we can get stuck in a despairing mindset and cause others to feel that way as well. Many people are more motivated by positive possibilities than by negative realities, so it's a good idea to focus more on the former than the latter.

- Focus on what you want to grow. There is a Buddhist teaching that we all have within us the seeds of greed, hatred, and desire as well as the seeds of love, compassion, and empathy. Our job is to water the right seeds. If we want to cultivate compassion, we need to water the seeds of compassion in others. For example, when your colleague tells you that she used to be vegan, your leading question can be to ask why she became vegan in the first place—rather than why she stopped being vegan.

- Don't overinform. Many people tend to give too much information, especially when they're talking about a far-reaching cause such as veganism. Effective communication requires a balanced exchange of ideas (as opposed to a monologue), and when it comes to veganism, the facts rarely sell the ideology. Whether you're talking about your relationship or your ideology, share only as much information as needed to help the other understand your perspective. Beyond that, you can offer them a leaflet about veganism (it's a good idea to carry such leaflets around for just this purpose), and the Internet can provide everything else.

- If you're talking about being vegan, do so from the perspective of your personal experience. Share your own story. This keeps others from feeling "shoulded" and it helps keep the focus on developing mutual understanding rather than on advocating veganism. For example, if someone asks you why you're vegan, you can say, "I'm vegan because one day I learned about what happens to the animals, and I was shocked and horrified. I never knew how bad it was. And once I saw those images of animals suffering, I couldn't eat animals again." You can also share your story of having used carnistic defenses: "I used to believe that eating animals was normal, natural, and necessary. I didn't realize these were actually myths, because I grew up believing they were proven facts." It's also a good idea to include some of the benefits of being vegan: "I'm thrilled that my health has improved so much," or "I didn't expect that vegan foods would be so delicious and easy to make."

- Be careful not to use triggering concepts or phrases. Many vegans believe that accuracy is preferable to diplomacy, but referring to meat as a "corpse" or "dead flesh," or to animal agriculture as "state-sanctioned murder" or "rape" is more likely to lose friends than to win supporters. Triggering words cause the listener to immediately shut down to a message and to feel resentful and distrustful.

- Avoid comparing different kinds of exploitation. This can be deeply offensive to many people. Vegans who argue that animals suffer more than humans or that animals and humans have similar experiences of exploitation are opening up dialogue that is unlikely to end well. The way to compare exploitations is to focus on the cause, rather than the consequences, of the exploitation—on the mentality of violence that underlies all forms of exploitation. You could say, for example, "Although the experience of each set of victims of violence and exploitation will always be unique, the *mentality* that enables the violence is the same. The same psychological mechanisms, such as denial, empathic numbing, and distorted ways of thinking enable all violent systems." You could also explain that this is a key reason for being aware of and sensitive to different systems of oppression, such as sexism, classism, and carnism. Creating a better world is not simply about changing one behavior at a time but about shifting consciousness so that all our behaviors are based on integrity.
- Develop emotional literacy. Emotional literacy is the ability to identify and articulate our emotions, and it is essential for effective expressing. (There are plenty of resources available on the Internet for learning this skill.)

EFFECTIVE LISTENING

There is truth to the maxim that a great conversationalist is a good listener. When we are in the presence of a good listener, we feel truly heard, valued, and attended to. We feel that we matter, and we feel encouraged to explore and share our truth, so we often develop greater self-insight and new perspectives on the situation we are in. We don't feel rushed to make our point, and we feel safe knowing that we won't be judged. We feel we can be our authentic selves, and this feeling alone can be liberating.

Good listeners are, unfortunately, few and far between. Most of us are starved for the kind of attention we get from someone who knows how to listen, so when we find a sympathetic ear, it can feel intoxicating. We may find ourselves sharing personal information we never intended to disclose or talking so much we end up apologizing for monopolizing the conversation. Effective listening is so powerful because the listener helps us see ourselves through compassionate eyes, so we feel validated and empowered. Often, when we are experiencing a problem or conflict, the simple act of being listened to can melt our defenses and allay our fears. Many problems are solved simply through having them heard.

When we are an effective listener, we are present. We are not thinking about the future or the past; we are not wishing we were anywhere other than right where we are. We are here, now, practicing the "three Cs" of effective listening: compassion, curiosity, and courage. And in so doing, we help the other to be more present as well.

When we don't listen effectively, we pay a high price, and so do those with whom we communicate. We can be seen as boring and narcissistic, interested only in our own life and unable or unwilling to focus on others. We can get caught off-guard by problems we didn't see coming because we weren't paying attention. Many relationships, for example, have ended with one person shocked and devastated because they hadn't taken the time to listen when the other was trying to communicate their unhappiness and needs. And when we don't listen effectively, we lose connection and intimacy, because others feel like they don't matter enough for us to pay attention to them. People stop sharing themselves when they get the message that the listener isn't interested in what they have to say—and perhaps the best way to communicate disinterest is to not listen well.

Effective listening has two components—compassionate witnessing and active listening. Compassionate witnessing, as we have discussed, is paying attention with our eyes and minds as well as with our hearts. It is listening with compassion, empathy, and without judgment, and with the goal of understanding.

Active listening includes the following:

- using engaged body language
- clarifying
- paraphrasing
- giving feedback

Engaged body language includes keeping our arms unfolded, not yawning or hiding our faces behind our hands, pointing our body toward the speaker and leaning slightly forward, and, when possible, making eye contact. Some people are not able to focus when they make eye contact, and in some cultures, eye contact is seen as rude. If you are communicating with someone from a culture where eye contact is a sign of listening, it's best to let them know if you prefer not to make eye contact so they don't misinterpret your body language as communicating disinterest.

Clarifying is asking for more information when we need clarity, which helps ensure we understand the other and shows we are listening. For example, you might say, "So was it your mother, or your stepfather, who made the comment about you being impossible to cook for?"

Paraphrasing is summarizing in our own words what the speaker said, and then we can check with them to be sure we understood correctly. Paraphrasing, like clarifying, helps both speaker and listener. For example, you could say, "So it sounds like you were surprised and hurt to hear that your parents are so intolerant of your dietary needs. You hadn't realized they were feeling that way, since they'd always acted so accommodating."

Giving feedback means sharing our reaction to what was said—sharing our thoughts, feelings, and possibly advice (if the speaker wants it). All of this should happen only after we've been a compassionate witness; people are rarely open to feedback if they don't first feel fully listened to and understood. For example, you could say, "Thank you for sharing all that with me. I'm glad you trust me enough to be so open with me. To be honest, it's a little hard for me to hear that you feel judged by me when you eat eggs. I'm not sure how to change that, but I want to, and I want to discuss this further. I'll need some time to think more about what you said, so let's set aside time to talk this evening."

Active listening is an essential component of effective listening. It's not enough simply to be quiet when another is talking. If we don't respond, we communicate that we either didn't listen or that we don't care enough to share our feedback. Either way, the other will feel ignored, hurt, and resentful and will be less likely to communicate with us openly again.

Although not all situations require that we employ all four components of active listening, if someone has spoken to us, it's our responsibility to show them that we've heard them. They have no other way of knowing whether we paid attention. Expecting others to be mind readers—whether they are our partner, employee, or a stranger on a bus—is neither fair nor feasible. It's our job as the listener to communicate that we have listened, even if the expresser's statement didn't require a full response. At the very least, we need to make the right noises to let them know we've heard them: "Oh, okay" or "Aha." Total silence after any communication will almost inevitably be interpreted as dismissive, disinterested, and simply rude. And ideally, we respond in a tone that matches the tone of the situation. So if your partner excitedly shares with you that they finally reached their weight-training goal, and you say in a flat tone, "Yeah, that's great," they will likely not feel heard. Or if your colleague tells you of a painful breakup and you say, "Huh, sorry about that," they'll feel you're not empathizing with them.

It can also be helpful to become aware of our blocks to listening,[3] the situations that make it more difficult for us to listen effectively. Perhaps you are less able to listen effectively at a certain time of day, in certain environments (e.g., where there are loud noises or distractions), with certain people, or around certain topics. When we know our personal blocks to listening, as well as those of the other, we can plan our conversations accordingly and reduce the risk of our communications being unproductive or harmful.

COMMUNICATING WHEN EMOTIONS ARE HIGH

When emotions are high, it's especially challenging to communicate effectively. And of course, those are often the times when we most need to communicate effectively. Learning a few principles can help us manage our communication in challenging emotional circumstances.

First, it's best to catch ourselves before we're at the point where our emotions are preventing us from communicating well. With practice and attention, we can learn to monitor our internal experience, to regularly check in with ourselves, so we're less likely to be caught off-guard by strong emotions. And as we make effective communication a practice, we minimize the likelihood of getting emotionally hijacked, since we aren't letting issues

---

3 Matthew McKay, Martha Davis, and Patrick Fanning, *Messages: The Communication Skills Book*, 3rd ed. (Oakland, CA: New Harbinger, 2009).

build up and we feel empowered to speak our truth when we need to.

If you notice you're starting to feel triggered, you can share that fact with the other. Psychologists Susan Campbell and John Grey suggest saying something like "I notice I'm having a strong reaction to what you just said," or "I notice I'm starting to feel triggered."[4] When we share that we're feeling triggered, we show self-awareness and help ourselves stay connected to our inner observer. We also give the other important information: when they know a vulnerable part of us has been activated, they can be more careful not to tread on our sensitivities.

Similarly, we can use the language of parts. Saying, for example, "A part of me is feeling angry about what you just said" shows that we are not "blended" with that part, that not all of us is angry (which is generally the case; no matter how angry we get, there is always a deeper part of ourselves that remains present). Saying "A part of me is feeling angry" is much less threatening than saying "I am feeling angry," or worse, "I am angry." The final statement suggests a total merging of us and our anger.

If you notice that the other seems triggered, especially if they tell you as much, do your best to reassure them. Remember, when we're triggered, we're feeling unsafe. We are less rational and our only objective is to return to a place of safety. All of us have vulnerable and young parts of our personality that need compassion and understanding. Reassuring the other that we're on their side and stating directly that we care about their safety and that we're committed to ensuring that they feel secure can help bring them back onto safe ground. We can also ask what we can do to help them feel safer. They may not know what they need to feel safer, but showing them we're committed to their well-being can in itself make a difference.

Finally, know when to stop a communication. It's best to stop a communication if we feel it's impossible to maintain empathy for the other or if we notice that we can't feel curious and compassionate. It's also best to stop a conversation if we feel disrespected and the other is not responding to our requests to communicate in a way that feels respectful to us. If that

---

4 Susan Campbell and John Grey, *Five-Minute Relationship Repair: Quickly Heal Upsets, Deepen Intimacy, and Use Differences to Strengthen Love* (Novato, CA: New World Library, 2015).

happens, take a time-out for an agreed-upon period, with a promise to return to the conversation. It's important to make clear that the pause you're requesting is temporary and that you intend to return to the conversation within a reasonably short period of time, as we discussed in Chapter 7. Otherwise, the other will feel abandoned, which can cause them to feel unsafe and distrustful. If, when you revisit the conversation, you find you are still too upset to communicate effectively, ask for another time-out. Just be sure nobody uses time-outs to avoid discussing an important issue that ends up never getting resolved.

COMMUNICATING WITH OURSELVES

The principles and practices of effective communication also apply to how we communicate with ourselves. For better or worse, we are always communicating with ourselves, and most of us do so in a way that we would not tolerate were it to come from anyone else. One simple and powerful way to both improve our communication and enhance our self-worth is to become aware of our internal dialogue, or self-talk (as mentioned in Chapter 6), and restructure it so that it's empowering rather than shaming.[5] It can be useful to set an alarm to go off several times during the day. When it does, pause and ask yourself questions such as "What am I saying to myself? Am I talking to myself the way I would talk to someone I cared about? Does my internal dialogue reflect compassion and curiosity, or is it judgmental and shaming? Am I defining my own reality, telling myself I'm wrong for what I think and how I feel?"

Learning effective communication can significantly improve our ability to communicate across our ideological differences. But the benefits of effective communication go well beyond helping us discuss issues related to veganism. When we practice effective communication in our relationships, we validate and empower one another and strengthen our security and connection. When we practice effective communication toward ourselves,

---

5 For an excellent resource on identifying and restructuring your self-talk, see David D. Burns, *Feeling Good: The New Mood Therapy* (New York: Avon Books, 1980).

we learn to think more objectively and feel more compassionately about our own experience. So effective communication can help us transform our relationships and our lives.

Chapter 9

CHANGE: STRATEGIES FOR ACCEPTANCE AND TOOLS FOR TRANSFORMATION

The million-dollar question for many vegans in relationships with non-vegans is what kind of change, if any, they have the right to ask for. In fact, this is often a critical question for anyone in a relationship where some kind of difference is getting in the way of them feeling secure and connected. Especially when it comes to a key difference in our attitudes and lifestyles, we may wonder how much we can expect the other to actually change. What is realistic? What is fair? And how can we request change in a way that doesn't compromise the security and connection of our relationship?

Let's assume you've been putting into practice the principles outlined in this book. And yet there's a difference between you and the other that's preventing you from feeling secure and connected enough in your relationship. The difference may well be that the other is not vegan and you are, but maybe that's not it. Maybe the other is vegan, but you're an activist and they're not. Or maybe the other is not vegan, and that's okay with you, but a personality difference between you is causing problems.

Whatever the difference you're dealing with, if you don't want to end your relationship, you have two options. You can accept the difference and let go of your need for the other to change. Or you can accept the fact that the difference exists, accept the other for who they are, and still request that they change. In either case, acceptance must come first. The only question is whether acceptance alone is enough or whether, after accepting the difference, you still need change in order to choose to remain in the relationship.

Understanding the principles of acceptance and the tools to effectively request and work toward change is the final step in creating a secure, connected relationship, a relationship of integrity. With this awareness, you can put into practice the insight expressed in the Serenity Prayer: "God, grant me the serenity to accept the things I cannot change, the courage to change the things I can, and the wisdom to know the difference."[1]

ACCEPTANCE OF WHAT IS

A new psychological model used for personal and relationship growth is called acceptance and commitment therapy, or ACT.[2] ACT is based largely on the Buddhist precept that *acceptance of what is* is essential to growth and well-being. In the ACT model, people struggling with a difference in their relationship that's causing disconnection are encouraged to work toward the acceptance of that difference before moving into the change process.

Acceptance is the opposite of resistance. We are in a state of resistance when we judge experiences as "wrong," assuming that things should be different than they are and wishing for change. Acceptance is an attitude, a state of mind in which we accept that "what is happening is happening," and we then decide what we want to do about it. For example, if you're feeling fear, you can resist the fear, judging it as "bad" or "wrong" so that you fight it down or try to avoid it—tactics that generally don't work. Or you can notice that you're feeling fear, without judgment, and accept that fear is simply a feeling you're having. You can compassionately witness your fear, which not only makes you less fearful in the moment but also gives you a better ability to work toward reducing the fear in your life.

Accepting what is does not mean that we accept disrespectful behavior or that we are passive in our life and the world. It simply means we're not judging reality for being what it is, even as we work toward transforming reality. And acceptance is not the same as tolerance, which is a form of resistance where we simply decide to live with something that we continue

---

1 The Serenity Prayer is often attributed to the American theologian Reinhold Niebuhr.
2 For an excellent resource on ACT, see Matthew McKay, Patrick Fanning, Avigail Lev, and Michelle Skeen, *The Interpersonal Problems Workbook* (Oakland, CA: New Harbinger, 2013).

to judge. Acceptance is a choice, a conscious decision not to judge or wish things were different.

Accepting rather than resisting what is—whether we're accepting the fact that it's raining outside or that our parent was just diagnosed with a serious illness—can increase the well-being of ourselves and our relationships and helps us take the action necessary to bring about constructive change. It may seem paradoxical, but it's when we stop resisting that we're in a position to make healthy choices and take positive action. When we resist, we feel like a victim of circumstances, and we create new problems, such as depression and interpersonal conflicts.

ACCEPTANCE AS A PREREQUISITE FOR CHANGE

Acceptance is a necessary first step toward change for several reasons. First, when we are in a state of acceptance, we become more clear about what we actually need to change. Sometimes, when we stop resisting whatever it is that's bothering us, we find that we don't actually need it to change after all. You can experiment with this in your relationship by giving yourself permission to accept the difference you've wanted to change. Envision yourself living, perhaps not ideally, but comfortably—well enough to feel secure and connected—with the difference. For example, imagine knowing that your non-vegan partner is dining with friends and eating meat. Imagine your partner coming home and greeting you. Really try to imagine both of you smiling, hugging hello, and feeling happy to reconnect after you've been apart. Imagine feeling proud of both of you for working through this challenge in your relationship, and imagine feeling a spaciousness inside yourself that allows you to accept something that used to be so hard for you. Perhaps living with the difference is more possible than you thought.

Another reason acceptance must precede change is because people resist changing when they don't first feel accepted. Sometimes people cling to behaviors they might otherwise be willing to change simply as a form of rebellion against not feeling accepted. This can be especially true when the change we're asking for has a moral component, as with veganism. Whether they say so aloud or not, the other may claim, "I won't change, just because you've made me feel guilty." Guilting people into changing is neither respectful nor productive and it will only increase their defensiveness and decrease their openness to the issue. Everyone needs and deserves to be accepted for who they are, and we must appreciate this even if we choose not to stay in a relationship with someone whose difference from us makes it impossible for us to feel secure and connected with them.

We must also accept before asking for change simply because it's the ethical approach. If we accept the fact that the difference exists and we accept the other for who they are—even if we know the difference is not something we want to continue to live with—when we do request change, we're not bringing judgment into the request. We're saying, "I accept that this is how things are and who you are, even though it's not a way of life that I can be comfortable with." Acceptance allows us to bring greater integrity to the change process.

Finally, acceptance should precede requests for change because sometimes acceptance alone is enough to bring about the change we would ask for. When people stop feeling judged, they are generally much more open to making changes.

FORGIVENESS

Forgiveness is an act of acceptance; it is accepting that what happened in the past happened in the past. Forgiveness does not mean condoning what happened, nor does it mean we no longer feel hurt: we can forgive without excusing, and we can forgive even if we're still in pain. We can also appreciate that forgiving does not mean forgetting. Forgiveness is the conscious decision to let go of resentment, which is a form of anger. Before asking for change, it's helpful to try to forgive past hurts. The less resentment we have, the more open and less defensive to our requests for change the other will be.

In addition, it's sometimes hard to know what we need another to change if we're carrying around resentment. With resentment often comes a desire for retribution, and a request for change can be an excuse to enact a punishment. For example, imagine that you ask your non-vegan mother to stop cooking for you because she keeps forgetting to keep animal ingredients out of your food. Even though she promises to take more care from now on, you may still resist her offers to cook, simply because you feel resentful. Knowing how important cooking for you is to her, you may resist giving her other opportunities to provide for you because you want her to feel bad, since she made you feel bad.

RESISTANCE TO CHANGE[3]

Before asking for change, it's helpful to be aware of some of the ways in which people resist change. With this awareness, resistance is less likely to be an obstacle to the change you're hoping for. Resistance to change is normal, in both the individual who's being asked to change and the one who's requesting the change.

One reason people may resist change is because they don't feel that the person asking for the change truly understands and respects their position. We need to understand why the change we are asking for is something the other person has not chosen to do on their own. What obstacles do they see to such a change? What would be hard for them, if they did try to make the change? And what will they need in order to change in a way that's doable for them? In other words, we need to do our best to understand their struggle and not assume that just because *we* live a certain way or have made a particular change, it should be just as desirable or easy for them do so.

Sometimes vegans gloss over the challenges that moving toward veganism may pose to another. Many vegans understandably perceive the situation as a matter of life and death—because technically, it is. But saying things like "When it's a matter of an animal's life and your taste buds, there's no excuse not to be vegan" comes across as invalidating and is, frankly, counterproductive. And such an attitude can be perceived not only as minimizing the other's struggle but as offensive: comparing an animal's life with, for example, the other's need for family connection is unlikely to create trust and goodwill.

What most people need in order to be more open to change is to be

---

3 For a more comprehensive explanation of resistance to change and the change process, see Andrew Christensen, Brian D. Doss, and Neil S. Jacobson, *Reconcilable Differences: Rebuild Your Relationship by Rediscovering the Partner You Love—Without Losing Yourself,* 2nd ed. (New York: Guilford Press, 2014).

understood and empathized with, to be witnessed in their experience. If you truly try to understand the other, such conversations about change will be less charged. What, for example, would they have to give up that might feel like too much? If you have difficulty empathizing with those who struggle to become vegan, it can be helpful to consider areas in your own life where you draw the line. What, for example, do you do that's not vegan-friendly but that you feel you're not ready or able to live without? For some vegans, it's taking certain medications; for others, it may be working for a company that sells non-vegan products. We live in a world where it's simply not possible to be 100 percent vegan, 100 percent of the time. When we can appreciate our own lines, we are more likely to appreciate the lines of others. It can also be helpful to remember our own carnism, what it was like for us before we changed.

People also tend to resist change when they feel that the change would ultimately not be in their own best interest, that they would be changing for the wrong reasons. If, for example, someone is changing simply to avoid conflict and to keep the peace or because they feel pressured and judged, they are unlikely to be open-minded and open-hearted enough to truly embrace and therefore maintain the change.

Relationships Are Not Business Contracts

One reason many of us resist change is that we have misguided beliefs about the nature of change and of relationships. We often assume that relationships, and the individuals in them, should not change in any significant way. We treat relationships like business contracts, assuming that any modification to the way we started out is a breach of our agreement: "You weren't like this when we first got together; this isn't what I signed on for." Yet just as healthy individuals change and grow, so do healthy relationships. Most of us intuitively understand this; after all, we wouldn't want our partner to be the same as they were 20 years ago when we were college kids.

In secure, connected relationships, asking for change is a constant part of interacting: "Can you please stop leaving your clothes around the living room? I really don't want to have to pick up after you all the time," or "I get distracted and have trouble refocusing every time you interrupt me when I'm at work, so please don't call me during the day unless it's important, okay?" or "I need to be able to plan my week in advance, so can we make a schedule on Sundays so I know what to expect?" When people expect that needs will differ and that asking for change is a normal part of a relationship, they are less reactive to such requests. Negotiations like these can then happen as parts of casual conversations that never lead to anything more than "Oh, okay, sure," or "I really don't like to plan so far in advance. Can't we just plan a few days at a time?" Of course, asking for more significant changes is more complicated, but negotiating around change is nevertheless a normal part of healthy interacting.

"Love Me or Leave Me; Don't Try to Change Me"

The belief that we and our relationships should not change is reinforced by the myth that relationships—especially romantic relationships—are based on unconditional acceptance of each other's behaviors, that we should never expect, let alone ask, another to change. While it's true that we must accept who each other *is*, it is far from accurate to assume that we should accept all each other *does*. People are unique, with different ways of being and often very different needs. It's impossible to have a harmonious relationship with another without making many modifications to how we might normally behave, and it's unrealistic to think otherwise. When we're in a relationship with another human being, we each have to communicate what does and does not work for us, so that we can make the necessary adjustments to keep each other safe and happy. Too often, when one person even hints that they may want the other to change, they're confronted with the age-old response, "This is just who I am. Love me or leave me!" Many of us fail to realize that loving us means, sometimes, asking us to change.

The Unfair Burden of Bridging the Gap

A related assumption is that if one person changes, it's that person's responsibility to accept and manage the new difference in the relationship: "*You're the one who's changed, not me, so it's not fair of you to expect me to do things differently.*" And while both individuals do need to discuss what kinds of adaptations they each need to make in order to maintain their connection, it's neither fair nor feasible for one person to be told they have to bridge the new gap alone. Relationships are partnerships and whenever one person expresses a need, new or not, the other has a responsibility to hear that need and do their best to meet it (as long as it doesn't require them to compromise their integrity).

The times when we generally don't expect the changed partner to bridge the gap are when they have more social power (they are a member of a dominant social group that the other does not belong to) and/or when the change itself reflects the position of the dominant social group. How much power we have in our relationship has a major influence on what we expect from ourselves and the other, in large part because it determines how open we are to being influenced by one another.

For example, if two partners are vegan and one changes to become a non-vegan, the expectation will likely be that the vegan—the unchanged partner—will bridge the gap. But if two partners are not vegan and one changes to become a vegan (all other power roles, such as gender and class, being equal) the expectation will likely still be that the vegan—this time the changed partner—will bridge the gap. The non-vegan, who is a member of the dominant social group and whose ideology is backed by society, will not be expected to change in order to accommodate the vegan. Even the most compassionate of non-vegan partners is likely to take this stance, simply because of the widespread, incorrect assumption that it's not appropriate for a vegan to expect their partner—or anyone, for that matter—to accommodate them.

My Will Versus Your Influence

Another related belief that causes us to resist change is that any changes we make must be the result of our own independent decision-making process. In other words, we learn that we should not be influenced by others, especially by our romantic partner. How often do we hear people speak judgmentally about one member of a couple, saying, for example, "Well, he's only doing it because of her"? Clearly, changing negative habits, such as quitting smoking, rarely draw such criticism. But neutral and even positive changes, such as adopting a healthful diet, are often met with such responses. So we may resist change simply because we fear being perceived as weak, as lacking our own opinion and will. This fear is particularly common among males, who, unfortunately, have been taught to resist the influence of the females in their lives, to the detriment of themselves and their relationships. But research in this area has shown that males who allow their female partners to influence them have more fulfilling and resilient relationships.[4]

Change and Control

Sometimes people resist changing because they equate being asked to change with being controlled. If we demand, rather than request, change, then the other's experience of feeling controlled makes sense, since demands *are* controlling. But some people feel controlled even by simple requests.

One reason some people easily feel controlled is that they have an allergy to being controlled, so they are hypersensitive in this area. If that's the case, it's important to have a conversation about how to communicate needs so that they can be heard and responded to, because control allergy or not, if we don't have the ability to influence each other, we won't be able to maintain a secure, connected relationship.

People may also feel easily controlled because of how their perceptions have been shaped by society. As we discussed, members of dominant social groups (e.g., non-vegans) have learned to interpret requests from members of non-dominant groups (e.g., vegans) as demands, even when they're not, and to experience any challenge to their own control as controlling, even when it's not.

The Discomfort of Change

Change is often challenging on both a practical and emotional level, because it forces us to stretch our comfort zone. Breaking habits takes effort, as we reprogram ourselves to think, act, and often feel differently. For example, even if you know it's good for you to stop eating sugary foods, once you commit to eliminating these products from your diet, you will have to face

---

4   Thomas H. Maugh II, "Study's Advice to Husbands: Accept Wife's Influence," *Los Angeles Times*, February 21, 1998.

mental and physical cravings, as well as disappointment when others are enjoying such foods and you cannot.

People typically resist change until it becomes more uncomfortable to maintain their current way of being than to adopt a new one. For example, if someone's gambling is negatively impacting their financial stability, relationships, and career, they would obviously want to change that behavior. Yet most people who compulsively gamble are unable to stop the behavior when they want to, in large part because the comfort that gambling brings them outweighs the losses they face as a consequence of it.[5] It's only when the scales tip—when they're losing more than they're gaining, when the pain of continuing the behavior is greater than the pain of stopping it—that they are able to begin the process of change.

Fears about Change

Much of what we do, we do to feel safe. Sometimes, we resist change because we have fears about what the change may bring. To be ready for change, we must feel safe enough to make such change in our lives.

One reason we may fear change is because we fear we will fail, that we don't have enough know-how or willpower to follow through with our decision. It can therefore be helpful to make sure the change we request is realistic. For example, if you are asking your partner to become vegan, you could suggest that they do so slowly, through a process of learning about veganism and replacing animal products with vegan foods over a period of time and at their own rate.

We may also fear changing because we fear a loss of identity or a loss of connection in some of our relationships. For example, someone may worry that becoming vegan would change the way others see or relate to them: Would they be stereotyped as weak, weird, or elitist? Would they no longer feel included in their friends' annual cookout? Again, these fears can be easily alleviated by suggesting that the other move toward veganism over time rather than diving right into it.

---

5 This statement is not meant to minimize the biological component of addiction. On the contrary, the biology of addiction is one reason for the comfort the addictive behavior brings.

Another reason we may fear change is because we're afraid of the "slippery slope." We may wonder, "If I start on this path, how far will it take me? What if I find that I'm being expected—by the other, or by myself once I start thinking differently—to change beyond what I'm comfortable with, to give up too much?" Unsustainable change, change that doesn't feel safe or doable, is not in the best interest of anyone. But as long as the person changing is committed to maintaining self-awareness and self-sustainability, this fear need not be an obstacle.

CREATING A PRO-CHANGE ENVIRONMENT

We don't change until we're ready to, and we cannot force anyone, including ourselves, to be ready to change. Forcing the readiness to change is like trying to make a body heal. But just as we can do things that speed up a body's recovery, such as taking vitamins and ensuring adequate rest, we can act in ways that create an environment where change can more easily occur. The first steps to creating a pro-change environment are to ask for the right kind of change and to ask for such change in the right way.

Asking for the Right Kind of Change

When it comes to asking for significant changes, such as lifestyle changes, we should only ask for them when it's necessary for our own well-being and for our ability to maintain the security and connection of our relationship. And such requests must be both *respectful* and *reasonable*: they must respect the other's well-being and be reasonable for the other to fulfill.

What we can respectfully ask for is a change of behavior—as long as the change we are requesting does not require that the other violate their integrity. The change must also be understood by the other to be in their own best interest, to be something they truly see as valuable for themselves. For some people, meeting the needs of someone they are close to and supporting the security and connection of their relationship is a good enough reason to change. But for the change to be sustainable, the person changing should see at least some benefit for themselves in it.

It's not respectful (or reasonable, for the most part) to request that the other change their values, personality, or attitude. These qualities are core to who we are, and our values and personality are largely unchangeable. Included in our personality are our emotional allergies, our deeply embedded sensitivities that are often hardwired. And while it's possible to change our attitude—and wanting another's attitude to change is understandable— it's not respectful or reasonable to ask for attitudinal change, because our attitude is a highly personal aspect of who we are. Saying, for example, "I want you to care more about animals" is asking the other to change their beliefs and feelings.

Instead, we can ask for behavioral change that might lead to attitudinal change. For example, you can ask your non-vegan parent to read and watch specific materials, to learn about what happens to the animals who become food and about how carnism shapes attitudes regarding eating animals. But it's important to accept that the other has a right to their attitude and that they may or may not choose to change it based on what they've learned.

Requesting Veganism

Only you know what you need from the other in order to feel secure and connected enough with them. Perhaps you believe that you simply cannot feel connected to someone who is not fully vegan.

Before requesting that the other become vegan, though, it's important to determine whether this is something you actually need. Perhaps you can feel connected enough with the other as long as they are vegan enough and/ or as long as they are an ally to you. Or perhaps you can accept that the other eats animals as long as it's not around you. You can start out by seeing if some less dramatic changes will suffice, with the understanding that if they don't, you will both revisit the conversation. Sometimes we don't know what we need until we experience it.

If you determine that you need the other to become vegan, is this something you can reasonably and respectfully request? It depends. If your request is for strictly behavioral change—not asking the other to change their values or attitude but simply to change what they consume—then it may be possible to make this request respectfully. Whether it's reasonable or not depends on your circumstances: if you live in Los Angeles or Berlin, then it's certainly a more reasonable request than it would be if you were living in the countryside. But ultimately, whether a request is reasonable must be determined by the person being asked to change.

If you determine that requesting vegan behavioral change seems reasonable, it's a good idea to ask the other to slowly move toward veganism, to increase the chances that the change will be sustainable. You can also explain why you need them to be vegan in order for you to feel secure and connected. People need and deserve to fully understand the basis for requests for significant change. And you may want to phrase your request in the positive rather than the negative. Ask for more of what you want rather than less of what you don't want. One useful framing is talking about "crowding out" rather than "cutting out" foods. When more plant-based foods are added, there is less room for animal-based foods.

Requesting Versus Insisting

Many vegans believe that if they don't insist that others become vegan, they are giving others "permission" to eat animals, and they aren't taking a strong enough stand against carnism. But none of us is in a position to give adults permission to make their own choices; thinking we are is both inaccurate and grandiose. Vegans who believe that they can and should dictate how others think, feel, and behave not only risk damaging their relationships; they also risk losing potential supporters of veganism. Hearts and minds do not open when people feel judged and controlled. Legislative change typically follows social change, so laws that support veganism are unlikely to be enacted if people are not open to the vegan message in the first place.[6]

Some vegans argue that the behavior of eating animals is no different from rape or domestic violence and that if we don't insist that others stop eating animals, we are not "holding them accountable" as we would a rapist or a batterer. However, such an analogy fails to appreciate basic human psychology. Rape and domestic violence are not only illegal; they are socially deplorable (at least in much of the world), and as such, they require a much

---

6 This is not meant to suggest that vegans should not work toward policy and institutional change or that they should avoid engaging in public outreach. It is simply to point out that the way in which requests for change are approached—especially in interpersonal relationships—will determine, to a large extent, how these requests are received.

more extreme and problematic mentality than does eating animals. People who actively defy social conditioning that's designed to increase empathy and decrease support for violence—simply to serve their own interests—exhibit a level of pathology that is simply not comparable to those who conform to social conditioning that's designed to decrease empathy and increase support for violence.

When it comes to interpersonal interactions, especially in the context of our close relationships, it is neither respectful nor reasonable to try to control the other. We can decide what we will and won't accept in our lives and then decide whether we wish to continue the relationship. If we want to increase the likelihood that the other will change in a way that supports veganism, and if we want to continue in our relationship, we would do well to avoid judging the other and attempting to control them. These behaviors are fundamentally non-relational and will most likely bring about the very opposite of what we hope for.

Requesting the Other Become "as Vegan as Possible"

Requesting that the other reduce their consumption of meat, eggs, and dairy will no doubt be met with less resistance than requesting they become vegan. So you could ask the other to become "as vegan as possible." This frames veganism as the goal, so reduction doesn't become an end in itself, and it honors the other as the expert on their own ability and needs. And it is not a fixed state; it can be adapted over time, so the change always feels sustainable.

If everyone were as vegan as possible, the world would be as vegan as possible—which is a far cry from where things are at now. It would likely not be long before the scales tipped and veganism became the dominant ideology.

Requesting a Vegan Ally: The Respectful, Reasonable, and Required Change

One request that you can make that is respectful and reasonable, as well as a requisite for a secure, connected relationship, is for the other to become a vegan ally, a supporter of veganism and of you as a vegan, even though they are not vegan themselves. To be an ally of any kind, it is necessary to understand the experience and needs of the person we are supporting. Otherwise, support—and therefore allyship—is impossible.

So your behavioral request might include that the other do three things: learn about veganism (within reason, and to the point where they genuinely understand why you are vegan); witness you as you share what it's like to be a vegan in a non-vegan world, what helps you feel emotionally safe, and what causes you to feel unsafe; and do things that will help you feel more supported, such as not laughing when others tease you or helping cook vegan food to bring to dinner events so you don't feel all alone.

It is simply not possible to have a secure, connected relationship if we don't truly understand what the world looks like through one another's eyes. And when one person is a member of a non-dominant group, which a vegan is, allyship with that person is even more important, since most of the world does not reflect their experience or support their needs.

It's perfectly appropriate and fully necessary to ask the non-vegan in your life to understand veganism—not so they become vegan but so they understand you. The other needs to know enough to understand why people become vegan, why you are vegan, and what it's like for you to be a vegan in the world. They need to witness you in this deeply important area in your life, and they need to appreciate the value of veganism to you even if they don't want to be vegan themselves. If they disparage or look down on veganism, they are disparaging and looking down on you, and such contempt is the Achilles heel of relationships.

In less close relationships, of course, you wouldn't necessarily expect the same level of understanding and witnessing. But expecting the other to be respectful of who you are and what matters to you is essential in any relationship. So, for example, your father may never really understand vegan philosophy, but he can nonetheless respect your lifestyle and beliefs.[7] Secure, connected relationships are based on mutual respect, and allyship is fundamental to respect. When we don't make an effort to understand what matters to the other and when we dismiss or disparage their values, we are disrespecting them.

---

7 See Appendix 8 for how to request that another respect your veganism.

Requesting that the other become a vegan ally is naturally more respect-ful than requesting that they become vegan, in part because the change you are asking for is clearly "your business"; it's about the direct impact of the other's behavior on you. Making requests about how we want to be treated is often experienced as more respectful than making requests about how we want others to be treated, since we're expected to have a say in whatever impacts us directly.[8] Appendix 6 provides an example of how you could request allyship.

When the non-vegan in your life becomes a vegan ally, it can change the dynamic between you and the other so much that you no longer need them to become fully vegan. And when they feel less pressure to stop eating animals, they may end up deciding to become vegan. Miracles happen when people who care about each other connect with compassion and feel safe together.

Asking for Change in the Right Way

When we ask for change respectfully, we request rather than demand change. A request is a statement of a need to which the other has the right to say no without being punished or judged. We may not like it if they say no, we may even choose to leave the relationship, but we will accept them for who they are and accept their decision for what it is. When we make a demand, whether we are aware of it or not, it will not be okay with us if the other refuses what we've asked for. The other doesn't feel they have a right to say no.

Requests should be specific, not vague. So, for example, you might say "Please ask your mother if she'll keep the turkey in a separate room when we visit for dinner," rather than "Please ask your mother to respect my veganism when we visit for dinner."

Requests should include an explanation of how the behavior impacts us and why we need the change. When appropriate, we can also make it clear that our goal is to feel more connected to the other. So you might say,

---

8 Andrew Christensen, Brian D. Doss, and Neil S. Jacobson, *Reconcilable Differences: Rebuild Your Relationship by Rediscovering the Partner You Love—Without Losing Yourself*, 2nd ed. (New York: Guilford Press, 2014).

something like this:

> When we're with your family and your father's describing his hunting expeditions, I get so anxious and upset. All I can think of is the suffering of those animals, and it brings back images of the bloody videos I've seen of animals being shot. And I feel like I can't say a word, because I'm the only vegan in the room. On top of this, I feel disrespected, because your family *knows* how I feel about killing animals and they still talk about it right in front of me. And worst of all, I feel totally alone, because you laugh along with them as though I wasn't even there. I can't help but feel like you don't care about how I'm feeling, and then I pull back and start to feel disconnected from you. I really need to know you're there for me, that I can lean on you. You're the most important person in my life, and your support means the world to me. I need to know you have my back, that you get how I'm feeling and you care about my feelings. It would change so much for me to know you're by my side when things feel so hard for me. So I'm asking if you could do some things that I think would really help me feel less anxious and also more connected with you.

When requesting change, we can also offer to support the other so that we are allies in the change process. We can ask, "How can I help you in this process? Is there anything that I can change that would help you make your own change?" This is not an invitation for negotiation but rather an offer of support that will help both people feel like they're in the process together—which they are.

And finally, it's critical to allow the other to be the expert on their own choices and needs. If they agree to change a behavior for reasons they feel are sufficient and that are valid to them, accept their decision and trust that they're acting in their own best interest. For example, sometimes when a vegan's partner agrees to stop eating animals, the vegan isn't satisfied, saying, "I don't want you to be vegan for *me*. I want you do it because you believe in it." It makes sense that the vegan would feel this way; after all, people who become vegan for reasons other than believing in the cause are more likely to slip back into carnism. In addition, a key reason for the vegan's feeling of disconnection is the sense that their partner doesn't share their values.

But as we discussed, asking another to change their attitude and feelings is neither reasonable nor respectful. People have a shift of consciousness only when they're ready to. If the other is genuinely willing to stop eating animals out of love and respect for you (with the assumption that they see at least some benefit in it to themselves), they are indeed exhibiting the values that are important to you—values such as compassion, fairness, and commitment. And research suggests that when people stop eating animals for any reason, they may be more likely to have a shift of consciousness and become a supporter of the cause.[9] Even if the other never embraces ethical veganism, to have someone in your life who values your well-being and relationship so much that they willingly change their lifestyle to support you is a gift.

SUPPORTING CHANGE

Once the decision to change has been made, there are things both people can do to help ensure that it sticks and that it works for each of them. Having a realistic and compassionate attitude toward the change process is an important first step. Changing behaviors is a process, not a one-time event. As with all processes, change takes time and often includes slipups. If we recognize the process of changing behaviors as two steps forward, one step back, we will release the perfectionism and frustration we might otherwise feel. When we expect so-called failures to be a normal and sometimes inevitable part of the process, we avoid the frustration and despair that result from unrealistic expectations. Be compassionate toward yourself and the other during the change process.

We can also work to identify and minimize obstacles to change. Success is often less the result of increasing our willpower than of decreasing the obstacles in our way. So when slipups happen—or ideally before they occur—we can try to determine what obstacles stand in the way of the goal

---

9 Tobias Leenaert, *How to Create a Vegan World: A Pragmatic Approach* (New York: Lantern Press, 2017).

and seek to reduce them. "Obstacle reduction" is often far more effective than simply trying harder.

POST-CHANGE RESISTANCE: AMBIVALENCE

It's also helpful to expect resistance to the change even after the change process has begun. Post-change resistance can come from the person who is changing or from the one who requested the change.

Much post-change resistance comes in the form of ambivalence, feeling conflicted about the change. It's natural to feel some ambivalence even if we were the one who requested the change.

Most significant changes involve changing roles, which can be challenging. Even those roles that ultimately don't serve us can be difficult to break free from: no matter how painful our experience, we tend to cling to what's familiar. For example, if you're the moral overfunctioner and your partner has agreed to become vegan, as much as you've craved such a change, part of you may also feel threatened by it. You may feel less in control or worthy if you're no longer in the position of moral overfunctioner. So you may start raising the moral bar—maybe you start needing the other to be not only vegan but also a vegan activist. It's possible that your need for the other to become active is valid, but it's also possible that you're resisting change to your system. When we aren't conscious of how our roles may be serving us, we can slip back into familiar patterns and pull the other back with us.

Post-change ambivalence may also result from conflicting feelings due to a power imbalance. For example, a vegan may genuinely want her non-vegan son to stop eating animals, but she may not want her son to have to go out of his way or be inconvenienced by her request. It's common for members of non-dominant social groups to feel too little entitlement when making requests that are related to their own position. So vegans can end up withdrawing requests because once they start to get the change they asked for, they feel too guilty to accept it. This phenomenon is even more pronounced when the vegan is female, since girls and women are socialized to feel too little entitlement around their needs being met. Ambivalence can cause us to give mixed messages around our requests for change, which can impede the change process. Another reason we may feel post-change ambivalence is because change often comes with pain, and many of us grew up learning to believe that when we feel pain, it means that something's wrong. But this message is often inaccurate: consider, for example, the pain you may feel the day after a hard workout. Not all pain is an indication we're on the wrong track. The anxiety, frustration, and confusion that may accompany breaking old patterns are growing pains, natural reactions to stretching our comfort zone and evolving into a more mature self.

CAN OUR RELATIONSHIP WORK?

Let's assume you've made your request for change, but things are still not where you need them to be to feel secure and connected in your relationship. Perhaps the other refused your request. Perhaps your request was ineffective because no matter how you've tried, you've been unable to consistently practice integrity in your relationship, and the underlying dynamic between you is simply not secure enough to support positive change. Or perhaps you've gotten the change you requested, but you still don't feel content in your relationship. What now?

If the other refused to change, you can revisit the change process and determine whether you can negotiate for a lesser change, or if you can accept the difference as it is. If neither of those options is viable, then you may want to consider if it's time to discuss whether your relationship is a fit for you. If the issue is either that you've been unable to consistently practice integrity or that the other changed but you're still not happy, you need to decide where the problem lies. Is it within the other, yourself, or your relationship?

Ask yourself if you're having trouble practicing the principles in this book because the other is continuing to act in ways that sabotage your attempts to do so. If so, you will need to decide how hard you want to work to maintain your relationship. Each of us deserves to be met at least close to halfway in terms of the effort we put forth in our relationship, and if we find that we're doing the work of two—that we're having the relationship for both of us—then our relationship is more a parasitic pairing than a mutual partnership. Think of your relationship as a canoe you're both in: Are you exhausted from having to keep the boat moving on your own? If you fear that if you drop your oars, your relationship will come to a standstill, then you may be pushing something forward that lacks the momentum to continue without you overburdening yourself. If you worry that if you stop doing the bulk of relating, you will feel alone, then you may already be alone. If you're unsure whether there is an imbalance in your relationship, you can try only doing your fair share of relating for a few days or weeks, and see what happens. And if you find the relationship is indeed not sustainable without such input from you but you still feel you can't let it go, you may want to examine your attachment style, to see if your fear of relationship loss is keeping you stuck in a relationship that isn't in your best interest.

But what if you genuinely harbor goodwill toward each other and neither of you is ready to end the relationship? What if the other truly wants to be the person they know you deserve, but they just don't know how to, and they can't seem to get it together? Or what if *you're* the one who is unable to bring yourself to make the changes you know you need to? In such cases, you may want to consider counseling. A good counselor can help you sort out who's bringing what issues to the table. And if the problem between you can be resolved, they will help you to do so. It's better to seek help sooner rather than later; the earlier you start getting to the bottom of the problem, the more likely you will be to manage it effectively.

For many vegans, seeing a counselor, or therapist, can feel threatening, because the therapist is unlikely to be vegan. Fortunately, there are a number of therapists available today who are identified as veg-friendly, meaning that they are at least vegan allies.[10] Even if you work with a therapist who is not known for being a vegan ally, if they are skilled, they should still be able to help.

It's also important to be aware that certain problems that are external to ourselves and our relationship can nevertheless cause disconnection and act as obstacles to our attempts at change. These obstacles include psychological problems, such as depression, anxiety, attention deficit hyperactivity disorder (ADHD), addictions, and personality disorders. These problems are inherently disconnecting, and they can remain undetected for years

---

10 In Defense of Animals has a project to support vegans, which includes a list of veg-friendly therapists. Find more information at "Sustainable Activism," *In Defense of Animals*, https://www.idausa.org/campaign/sustainable-activism/.

or even a lifetime. It's worth doing some research and perhaps checking with a professional if you feel that such issues may be impacting you or your relationship.

If the problem you're having is not because either you or the other has personal issues that are getting in the way of your connection, then it's possible that there's an incompatibility in your relationship that's causing your feeling of disconnection. You therefore need to decide whether you can accept the limits to your connection that this incompatibility creates. You may find that you can make your peace with it. If not, and the relationship is platonic, you may want to consider changing the relationship's category, an issue we discussed in Chapter 3. If the relationship is romantic and changing its category from partner to friend feels too difficult, then you may want to have a conversation with the other about the possibility of ending your partnership.

ENDING YOUR ROMANTIC RELATIONSHIP WITH INTEGRITY

We tend to die the way we've lived, and to leave the way we've loved. In other words, if we were compassionate in life, we leave behind the remains of our caring. If we were compassionate in our relationship, we are more likely to be compassionate in our separation. And even if we didn't treat each other with much compassion during our time together, there's no reason not to start now. Remember, every interaction is an opportunity to practice integrity.

Unfortunately, many of us are not on our best behavior when we are dissolving our partnership. One reason for this is that, even with the most agreeable endings, hurt feelings often get in the way of our empathy. Another reason is that we simply have not learned how to end our relationships with integrity. On the contrary, what we are taught is to actually abuse each other in what might be the most vulnerable moments of our entire relationship. Consider the way we learn to describe breakups: we "dump" someone (like a piece of trash), and we say our relationship "failed" (as though we were being tested, and as though all relationships are meant to continue forever). And we're taught to believe that it's perfectly acceptable to ignore another's phone calls or requests for connection just because we want to, since they no longer occupy the status of "partner."

So how do we end, or transition, our relationship with integrity? First, we must commit to prioritizing safety. Relationship endings cause people to feel deeply insecure, and if we make supporting the safety of the other a top priority and let them know this, fears and defensiveness can be significantly diminished. And we need to be explicit about this commitment, so the other is clear about our intentions. You can simply say, "I don't want you to feel hurt, and I'll do everything I can to help you feel safe through this process."

One way to help ensure safety is to make the ending mutual. Unless we are in a controlling or abusive relationship, it's best not to make a unilateral decision to end the relationship. When we make a unilateral decision that has a major impact on another's life, we are wielding total control over them. Such behavior can traumatize the other. Many of us come to our relationships as walking trauma survivors, having had the devastating experience of someone we cared about and were vulnerable with make a unilateral decision to end the relationship we shared, leaving us with no say and no power.

We can avoid making unilateral decisions in two ways. First, if we are truly starting to consider whether we're happy in the relationship, we can share this with our partner early on. That way, we can troubleshoot together. We give them the opportunity to be a part of the process—which they should be, since they're a part of the relationship—and prevent the shock of an unexpected breakup, which can be traumatizing. We can also take steps to try to heal the relationship. Next, if we get to the point where we're clear we want to end the relationship but our partner still doesn't want to let it go, we can dialogue and try to find a way to come to mutual agreement. This process can take weeks, but it's well worth it. People are far less likely to feel traumatized if they have some power or say in a process that impacts them and if they can see that a decision is ultimately in their best interest. And ultimately, it *is* in their best interest not to be in a partnership where they're not cherished, as we all need and deserve to be. Even if they would still choose to maintain the relationship, they can agree to let it go if they've been able to accept that continuing would be painful for us and so, in the end, not good for them either.

Once the decision to end the relationship has been reached, we can create, together, a safety agreement. The guiding question should be "What does each of us need in order to feel safe going through this process?" Each person can share their fears and decide what they can do to allay them for each other. The agreement has to feel reasonable to both, and it can be an agreement for a set period of time, to be revisited at that point. For instance, we could agree to not dating others and to being available to talk any time one of us needs to for a period of three months. Or we can agree to a trial separation for a specified period, after which we revisit the decision to break up.

Many of us might find this kind of agreement inappropriate or unfair, especially if we're the catalyst for the breakup. After all, it's no longer our responsibility to support the other once our relationship has ended. But this process is the bare minimum we can offer any human being going through a challenging emotional experience, let alone someone we may have been intimately connected with. It is only because our culture has, for so long, normalized abusive behavior that making an effort to protect the vulnerable heart of another seems counterintuitive.

Change is inevitable. Whether we wish to change or not, we, and our relationships, are never static. Our choice, then, is not *whether* we change but *how* we change. When we are open to change, we accept rather than resist life. We are intentional, compassionate, and courageous in our actions. We can spread our wings to rise toward our potential and toward the potential of our relationship. And, as Gandhi said, we can become the change we wish to see.

Appendix 1

LIST OF NEEDS

The following list presents some common needs people may have in relationships. But it is by no means exhaustive.

It can be helpful to select your top needs and compare them with the top needs of the other. You can then discuss what actions would fulfill each of your needs. For example, if you need to feel cherished, you may need the other to tell you, specifically, why they have chosen you—what makes you special and valuable to them.

acceptance
admiration
affection
appreciation
to belong
to feel challenged
to feel cherished (special and chosen)
closeness
to be able to communicate openly
companionship
compassion
to feel competent
to be able to count on the other
empathy
freedom
fun
growth
humor

intimacy
to know and be known
love
to matter
to be needed
nurturing
order
presence
respect
safety/security
sexual fulfillment (to feel attractive, attracted, and sexually satisfied)
space
spontaneity
stability
support
touch
to be able to trust the other
to feel valued
warmth

Appendix 2

SECONDARY TRAUMATIC STRESS SYMPTOM CHECKLIST[1]

Put a check next to each symptom you've experienced in the past month. It's a good idea to do this every few months, so you can monitor your experience. This is not a diagnostic test but rather a tool to help you become aware of your potential level of secondary traumatic stress.

- Feeling helpless and hopeless
- A sense that you can never do enough
- Hypervigilance (e.g., hyper-focus on work and a sense of urgency with your work)
- Diminished creativity
- Minimizing of the suffering of others (seeing others' suffering as trivial if it isn't terrible; diminished empathy; seeing suffering in a hierarchy)
- Difficulty listening
- Avoiding and feeling overwhelmed by others
- Dissociative moments (feeling disconnected from yourself/the world)
- Guilt (feeling guilty when you're not doing something to fix the problem; feeling overly responsible; seeing others as guilty)
- Self-neglect (not attending to your own needs; seeing your own needs as unimportant)
- Chronic worry or anxiety
- Increased anger and irritability

---

1 This list has been adapted for vegans and is based on the following sources: Laura van Dernoot Lipsky, with Connie Burk, *Trauma Stewardship: An Everyday Guide to Caring for Self While Caring for Others* (San Francisco: Berrett-Koehler, 2009); Karen W. Saakvitne and Laurie Anne Pearlman, *Transforming the Pain: A Workbook on Vicarious Traumatization* (New York: W. W. Norton, 1996).

- Cynicism (loss of faith in humanity and/or the world)
- Black-and-white thinking (e.g., seeing the world in terms of good/bad, right/wrong; needing to take sides; forming workplace cliques and divisions)
- Feeling numb (feeling too little so you have to use crises or stimulants in order to feel)
- Feeling hypersensitive (to noise, feelings, demands, etc.) and perhaps feeling a need to use drugs or alcohol to calm down
- Addictions (especially to work)
- Grandiosity (feeling "better than" or superior to others; feeling that you can and should fix all problems)
- Intrusive thoughts (thoughts that come into your mind suddenly, often of suffering you've witnessed)
- Nightmares
- An obsessive desire to help certain victims
- An inability to "let go" of activist-related matters, even when you need to
- A loss of enjoyment in life
- Feeling incompetent
- Depression
- Sleep disturbances (insomnia; hypersomnia)
- Seeing the world in terms of the roles played in traumas: people (and animals) are either victims, perpetrators, or heroes

Appendix 3

Hannah, a vegan, is married to Asad, a non-vegan. The couple have an agreement that the house is vegan and that Asad will only eat animal products when not in Hannah's presence. Asad is supportive of veganism but feels it's too difficult to avoid animal products all the time; he wants to be able to dine with others and not feel like an outsider. Asad has just returned home from dinner with friends.

> Hannah: "How was your evening?" (genuinely wanting to know how Asad enjoyed the evening but also feeling a little tense, worried that he ate non-vegan food)

> Asad: "Good. It was nice to see Steve and Chen again after so long."

> Hannah: "Where'd you guys go?" (trying not to sound probing, wishing it didn't matter where her husband ate, and thinking that it's probably better not to know, but also knowing that *not* knowing will gnaw at her)

> Asad: "Just to PF Chang's. We didn't want to deal with traffic, so we stayed local." (not yet picking up on Hannah's emotional charge, so not feeling defensive)

> Hannah (relieved, because PF Chang's has a separate vegan menu that Asad always enjoys choosing from when the two of them go out together): "Oh, so did you go with the Ma Pao Tofu?"

Asad (picking up on the tension, and realizing where the conversation is headed): "No, we wanted to get three dishes that we all could share." (hoping that the conversation will stop here, before he has to say the three dishes were not vegan)

Hannah: "I'm confused. So you couldn't share the Ma Pao Tofu? What's inedible about that?"

Asad: "C'mon, you know the guys would never go for vegan." (apologetic, feeling a little ashamed knowing he wasn't assertive and he let the others determine what to order, and also getting defensive because he feels blamed and judged unfairly, since the agreement that he can eat non-vegan foods when on his own is not being honored)

Hannah: "So you had to go and fund the animal-torture industry because you didn't want your buddies to be inconvenienced by ordering food that you yourself describe as delicious? Did you even *suggest* the vegan options?" (now triggered, feeling especially angry and shocked because there doesn't seem to be any valid reason for eating animals)

Asad: "That's not fair! I eat vegan 99 percent of the time! I go along with having a vegan house, I never even order cheese when we're out together. What more do you want?" (feeling hopeless, like his efforts will never be enough, and feeling unseen and unappreciated for having made such significant changes already)

Hannah: "Oh, so it's *work* for you not to eat dead animals? It's *compromise*? I thought you were eating vegan because you actually *care* and want to be a good person. Not that you were holding yourself back from animal cruelty just to keep me off your back!"

Asad: "That's not fair! Take a look in the mirror. You're standing here berating your own spouse. What kind of a 'good person' does that!"

Hannah: "I'm not 'berating' you, I'm just telling you what's true. You said you believed in veganism, you even defended it before, and you cave in every time you're around meat eaters. It's like you have no backbone, like you're only willing to do the right thing when it's easy."

Asad: "Oh, so now I'm cruel *and* lazy? You're incredible. I bend over backwards to keep you happy and it's just never enough for you! What's the point of even trying!"

Appendix 4

CHAIN OF CONFLICT CHART

CHAIN OF CONFLICT EXAMPLE

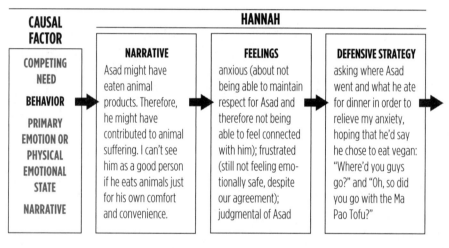

CAUSAL FACTOR	HANNAH		
COMPETING NEED BEHAVIOR PRIMARY EMOTION OR PHYSICAL EMOTIONAL STATE NARRATIVE	**NARRATIVE** Asad might have eaten animal products. Therefore, he might have contributed to animal suffering. I can't see him as a good person if he eats animals just for his own comfort and convenience.	**FEELINGS** anxious (about not being able to maintain respect for Asad and therefore not being able to feel connected with him); frustrated (still not feeling emotionally safe, despite our agreement); judgmental of Asad	**DEFENSIVE STRATEGY** asking where Asad went and what he ate for dinner in order to relieve my anxiety, hoping that he'd say he chose to eat vegan: "Where'd you guys go?" and "Oh, so did you go with the Ma Pao Tofu?"

CHAIN OF CONFLICT EXAMPLE

ASAD

NARRATIVE	**FEELINGS**	**DEFENSIVE STRATEGY**
Hannah's cross-examining me and pushing me to admit that I ate meat. She's being unfair, treating me like I'm a bad person, even though she knows we have an agreement and I didn't violate it. She's trying to control me. No matter how much I accommodate her veganism, she's never satisfied. Nothing I do will ever be enough.	defensive (feeling judged as a bad person, and feeling controlled); angry (because Hannah's not honoring our agreement); anxious (worried that if she finds out I ate meat, it's going to turn into a fight); a little guilty (even though I'm not vegan, I believe in veganism and don't like to think I've hurt animals)	shifting the focus from what I ate in order to avoid Hannah finding out that I had meat and to preemptively explain that I was just trying to keep every-one happy: "No, we wanted to get three dishes that we could all share."

(to Hannah's narrative)

CHAIN OF CONFLICT EXAMPLE WITH INTERRUPTIONS

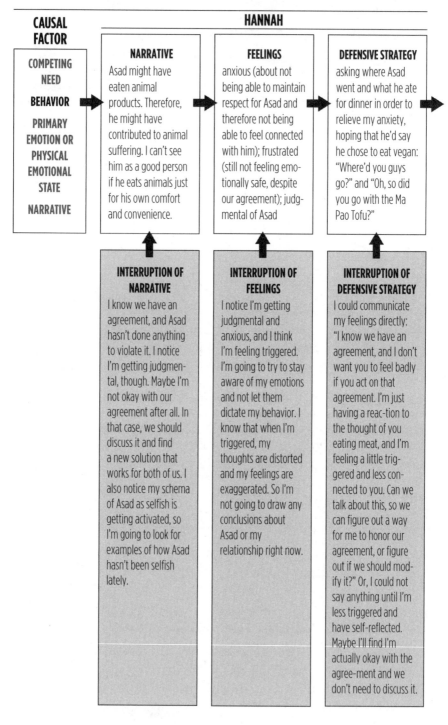

CAUSAL FACTOR	HANNAH		
COMPETING NEED **BEHAVIOR** **PRIMARY EMOTION OR PHYSICAL EMOTIONAL STATE** **NARRATIVE**	**NARRATIVE** Asad might have eaten animal products. Therefore, he might have contributed to animal suffering. I can't see him as a good person if he eats animals just for his own comfort and convenience.	**FEELINGS** anxious (about not being able to maintain respect for Asad and therefore not being able to feel connected with him); frustrated (still not feeling emotionally safe, despite our agreement); judgmental of Asad	**DEFENSIVE STRATEGY** asking where Asad went and what he ate for dinner in order to relieve my anxiety, hoping that he'd say he chose to eat vegan: "Where'd you guys go?" and "Oh, so did you go with the Ma Pao Tofu?"
	INTERRUPTION OF NARRATIVE I know we have an agreement, and Asad hasn't done anything to violate it. I notice I'm getting judgmental, though. Maybe I'm not okay with our agreement after all. In that case, we should discuss it and find a new solution that works for both of us. I also notice my schema of Asad as selfish is getting activated, so I'm going to look for examples of how Asad hasn't been selfish lately.	**INTERRUPTION OF FEELINGS** I notice I'm getting judgmental and anxious, and I think I'm feeling triggered. I'm going to try to stay aware of my emotions and not let them dictate my behavior. I know that when I'm triggered, my thoughts are distorted and my feelings are exaggerated. So I'm not going to draw any conclusions about Asad or my relationship right now.	**INTERRUPTION OF DEFENSIVE STRATEGY** I could communicate my feelings directly: "I know we have an agreement, and I don't want you to feel badly if you act on that agreement. I'm just having a reac-tion to the thought of you eating meat, and I'm feeling a little trig-gered and less con-nected to you. Can we talk about this, so we can figure out a way for me to honor our agreement, or figure out if we should mod-ify it?" Or, I could not say anything until I'm less triggered and have self-reflected. Maybe I'll find I'm actually okay with the agree-ment and we don't need to discuss it.

CHAIN OF CONFLICT EXAMPLE WITH INTERRUPTIONS

ASAD

NARRATIVE	FEELINGS	DEFENSIVE STRATEGY
Hannah's cross-examining me and pushing me to admit that I ate meat. She's being unfair, treating me like I'm a bad person, even though she knows we have an agreement and I didn't violate it. She's trying to control me. No matter how much I accommodate her veganism, she's never satisfied. Nothing I do will ever be enough.	defensive (feeling judged as a bad person, and feeling controlled); angry (because Hannah's not honoring our agreement); anxious (worried that if she finds out I ate meat, it's going to turn into a fight); a little guilty (even though I'm not vegan, I believe in veganism and don't like to think I've hurt animals)	shifting the focus from what I ate in order to avoid Hannah finding out that I had meat and to preemptively explain that I was just trying to keep every-one happy: "No, we wanted to get three dishes that we could all share."

(to Hannah's narrative)

INTERRUPTION OF NARRATIVE	INTERRUPTION OF FEELINGS	INTERRUPTION OF DEFENSIVE STRATEGY
I see that Hannah's getting agitated. I know this is a really sensitive issue for her, and I know she only gets probing like this when she's triggered. I'm not happy with the fact that our agreement doesn't seem to be working, but I'm not going to assume that Hannah's intentionally violating it. I know Hannah loves me and doesn't want me to feel controlled; that's why she went along with the agreement in the first place. We'll just have to revisit our agreement and try to figure out a new strategy.	I can tell I'm feeling defensive, and I usually get like this when I feel judged or controlled. This feeling is familiar; it always comes up when we have this argument. I know at some point Hannah and I need to talk about this conflict so we break this pattern. For now, I'm just going to try to make sure I don't act on my defensive feelings and lash out at Hannah or withdraw from her.	Instead of shifting the focus of the conversation, I could share my experience directly: "When you asked me where and what I ate, I felt like you were trying to figure out if I ate meat, so I'm feeling defensive. And you seem a little triggered—though I know I may be misreading you. In any case, I know this is a really sensitive issue for us. If you're upset about the fact that I ate meat, which I did, let's talk about our agreement and figure out if we need to modify it so we both feel okay—so you don't have to worry about what I did or didn't eat, and so I don't have to be secre-tive around you."

211

CHAIN OF CONFLICT CHART

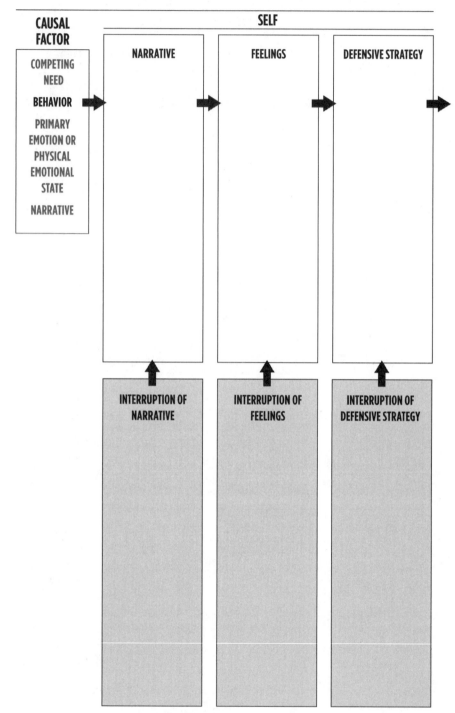

CHAIN OF CONFLICT CHART

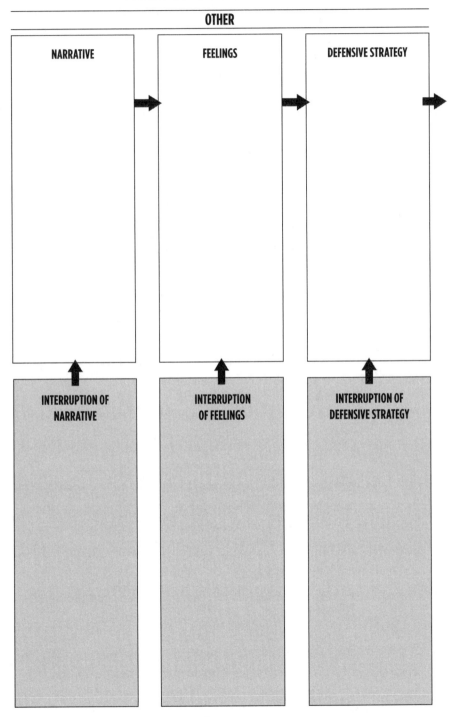

OTHER		
NARRATIVE	**FEELINGS**	**DEFENSIVE STRATEGY**
INTERRUPTION OF NARRATIVE	**INTERRUPTION OF FEELINGS**	**INTERRUPTION OF DEFENSIVE STRATEGY**

Appendix 5

CHAIN OF CONFLICT GUIDING QUESTIONS

The following questions are designed to help you gain clarity about your chain of conflict, so that you're better able to interrupt it. Try to answer as many of the questions as possible, but don't feel that you have to answer all of them. The questions are simply meant as a guide to help you reflect more deeply and objectively on your conflict.

1. What happened that sparked the conflict—what was the factor that triggered it? (For example, perhaps it was an argument you had, a thought that popped into your mind, or perhaps it was just a feeling of disconnection that you suddenly became aware of.)

2. What events came before this factor; what led to the argument, thought, feeling, etc.? (For example, maybe you were still angry from another argument you'd had in the past.)

    Try to trace your conflict back through the chain all the way to the causal factor, the original trigger: was it *competing need*, a *behavior*, a *primary emotion* or *physical emotional state*, or a *narrative*? You may not be able to identify the causal factor, but try to look as far back along your chain as possible.

3. What is your narrative of the conflict? How are you interpreting the cause or causes of the conflict?

4. Is your narrative really accurate, based on observable facts and thoughtful analysis? Or is there any other way you might be able to interpret the conflict?

5. What behaviors did you engage in as a reaction to your narrative? (Did you criticize the other? Walk away and withdraw? Reach out to try to discuss the situation with them?)

6. How did your behaviors impact the other? If you're not sure, try to imagine how the other *may* have been impacted by your behaviors.

7. What do you imagine they thought when you did what you did; what was their narrative?

8. What feelings might this narrative have brought up in them?

9. What is your schema of the other right now? In other words, think of 1–5 qualities or behaviors that describe how you are seeing the other. (Try to imagine a caricature of the other, which is often what our schemas are. What aspects of the other are exaggerated?)

10. What objective information, or facts, is your other-schema based on?

11. What facts or evidence disprove your other-schema; what are some examples of how your schema of the other may be inaccurate?

12. Is there any positive aspect of some or all of the other-schema qualities or behaviors you listed? (For example, if one quality is "unemotional," or "not empathic," perhaps the flip side of this quality is the ability to be rational and objective in situations where others may react with too much emotion or subjectivity.)

13. What deeper fear or fears might your conflict narrative and other-schema reflect? (For example, if your narrative is that the other is morally incompatible with you and your other-schema is that the other is selfish, you may fear that your relationship is unsustainable and that you'll end up alone and depressed.)

14. What is your self-schema right now? (Also consider in what ways, if any, you're seeing yourself as "better-than" or "less-than.")

15. What deeper fear or fears might your self-schema reflect? (For example, if your self-schema is that you're too demanding or never satisfied, you may fear that asserting your needs will lead to you being rejected or abandoned.)

16. What do you need in order to feel more secure and connected? (Do you need reassurance, and if so, of what? That you are loved? And what specific behaviors would you like from the other to help you feel reassured?)

Appendix 6

REQUESTING A VEGAN ALLY

When requesting that someone become a vegan ally, it's helpful to think of how they may already be an ally to you in other ways. It's always better to ask for more of something positive than to ask for less of something negative. Plus, it's easier for others to understand what it means to be a vegan ally if they already have a frame of reference for what allyship looks like.

You might also want to share your process as you make your request, which can help the other empathize with you and keep the channels of communication open. For example, if it's hard for you to share your vulnerability, or if you worry they'll judge you, you can say so. And you may or may not decide to add that you'd like to be an ally for them in their life, as well.

The following request is simply meant to be used as a guide. You can tailor it to fit your personal circumstances. Simply make whatever changes you think are necessary so that it's appropriate for the level of closeness of your relationship and so that the tone reflects your normal way of communicating. Use as much or as little of the wording below as you wish, to suit your own purposes.

I need to talk to you about something that I'm struggling with and that I'd like to ask your help with. It's hard for me to talk about this because I feel vulnerable, but it's really important, so I'm stretching my comfort zone to tell you what's going on for me.

Before I tell you how I'm hoping you can help me, I need you to understand what the problem is, so please just listen first. I need to know you understand what the world looks like through my eyes.

It's about how being vegan is affecting me, in my life.

I'm incredibly proud of being vegan, and I feel so much better in so many ways for becoming vegan. It's just that I'm dealing with a lot of pressures that are really weighing on me. Basically, because the world is still very *not* vegan, I feel misunderstood, invisible, and invalidated pretty much all the time, wherever I go, and it can be depressing and exhausting. Most of all, it's really lonely.

Wherever I am, I'm almost always the only vegan, and nobody understands what my experience is like. People make jokes about my values and beliefs, or they say things that reflect insulting vegan stereotypes, telling me I'm "overly emotional" or "radical." If I get sick I'm always told it's because of my diet, and even if I don't say a word, when someone finds out I'm vegan they immediately start telling me why my way of life is "wrong"—they try to educate me about nutrition, or they tell me why animal agriculture is necessary for the economy, or they say veganism is only for rich people, or whatever. People who have no experience with veganism suddenly become experts on it and start judging and arguing with me. It's not so much about who's right and who's wrong; it's about how people feel entitled to make comments that put down and dismiss my deepest values and beliefs. Maybe it's helpful to imagine how this would look if I were a Muslim or a Christian and people made jokes because I didn't eat pork or told me there's no such thing as God or debated the Bible with me. I know veganism isn't a religion, but it's a belief system based on values that are central to who I am, just like Islam or Christianity is for some people, so I feel disrespected in a similar way.

Plus, wherever I go, all around me are reminders of the one thing that saddens and distresses me more than anything else. I look at the world through such different eyes than people who aren't vegan. When I look at meat, eggs, and dairy, as much as I try not to, I can't help but see dead animals' bodies. I can't help but have flashbacks to the horrible videos I've seen about how those animals were raised and killed and I automatically feel horrified. I feel like I'm walking through a world filled with suffering and death but everyone around me thinks I'm crazy for feeling sad and disgusted by something *they* would probably feel sad and disgusted by if they were as aware as I am of what's happening to the animals.

Maybe one way to help you understand my experience is to imagine if normal animal products were from dogs and cats. Probably, every time you passed a billboard advertising smiling families eating burgers or whenever you sat down to a meal with people pulling apart a cheesy pizza, you'd feel the way I do.

So one thing that would reduce my stress a lot is knowing that even if the rest of the world doesn't understand veganism or me, you do. I'm not asking you to be vegan. I'm just asking you to understand my world so I don't feel so alone. I need to know you're my ally, that you of all people see me, and that you have my back, especially when things are tough. It would make such a difference for me to know I could lean on you.

You already do this for me in so many ways. For example, the only reason I can tolerate visiting my family is because I know you totally get it when they start arguing and gossiping about other people. When you look at me across the room in that way that says, "Here we go again," and then we spend the drive home talking about how difficult the visit was for me, by the time we get home I'm feeling almost normal again. You're my ally, and you help me feel like I'm not all alone.

So even though you're not vegan, I need to know you understand what veganism is, what it means to me, and what it's like for me to live as a vegan in a non-vegan world. This will also help me feel more connected with you, because I'll feel like you really see me for who I am in this hugely important area of my life.

What I think would be most helpful is to be able to share information about veganism with you—again, not to change your beliefs or your lifestyle, but just so you understand enough to understand and be an ally to me. And it would also be really helpful for me to be able to talk to you about my experience as a vegan, when I need to, just like I can talk to you about other things in my life. Would you be open to doing this? And is there anything I can do to help you help me in this way?

Appendix 7

REQUESTING COMPASSIONATE WITNESSING

Following is an example of how you can ask to be witnessed. Tailor this request however you need to in order to fit your personal circumstances; it is simply meant to be used as a guide.

As you know, being vegan is an incredibly important part of who I am. Vegan beliefs and values are central to my life. If I feel like you don't understand this major area of my life, I feel unseen and like I can't really be my authentic self with you, like I have to keep parts of myself out of our relationship. So, I end up feeling less connected with you than I want to be.

Because I want to feel more connected with you, I want to be able to share information about veganism with you—not to try to change you or make you vegan, but so you can understand *me*. Basically, I need to know that you know what the world looks like through my eyes, and that's only possible if you understand enough about veganism and what it means to me to be vegan. By "enough," I mean sufficiently for me to feel that you really get the issue, and you get me.

And I'm willing to learn about whatever is important to you, so that you can feel more seen by and connected with me (as long as the subject isn't too distressing to me, of course).

Appendix 8

REQUESTING RESPECT

Following is an example of how you can ask to be treated more respectfully. Tailor this request however you need to in order to fit your personal circumstances; it is simply meant to be used as a guide.

I know we're different in some ways, and I'm not asking you to change your beliefs or your lifestyle. I'm not asking you to become vegan. I just want us to be able to interact in a way that feels comfortable for me, and for that to happen I need to feel that you respect me, which means that you respect my choice to be vegan.

I'm not saying you don't *feel* respect for me—you're the expert on yourself and your feelings. I'm just saying that there are some things that you *do* that I don't experience as respectful. Some examples are when you made a joke about vegans being "Bambi-lovers," when you rolled your eyes when I explained to our host why I don't eat baked goods that have eggs in them, and when you debated veganism with me in front of the other guests. When you make fun of, put down, or dismiss veganism, you're making fun of, putting down, or dismissing my beliefs and values, so you're making fun of, putting down, or dismissing *me*.

Maybe it's helpful to imagine how a Muslim or Christian might have felt if you'd joked or acted annoyed that they didn't eat pork or told them there's no such thing as God and debated the Bible with them. I know veganism isn't a religion, but it's a belief system based on values that are central to who I am, just like Islam or Christianity is for some people, so I feel disrespected in a similar way.

When I feel you're not acting respectfully toward me, I end up feeling really hurt, and alone. I'm almost always the only vegan wherever I am, and I need to know that the people in my life stand by me, that they understand and respect me, even if their beliefs are different from mine.

Appendix 9

LETTER TO NON-VEGAN

Dear Non-Vegan,

Chances are you're reading this letter because there's a vegan (or vegetarian) in your life who wants to feel more connected with you.[1] Maybe you've been having trouble communicating with each other, feeling like you're speaking different languages. Maybe you've both been feeling distant and neither of you knows what to do to bridge the gap. Probably, you both want to feel understood, appreciated, and respected, and you both care enough about each other to be using this letter to become more connected. So you share the same goal.

I'm writing this letter on behalf of the vegan in your life because, for many vegans, it's difficult to put their experience into words in a way that helps someone who's not vegan understand them. The experience of being vegan is complex, and if there's been tension around veganism between the two of you, it's probably even harder for the vegan to express themselves openly and clearly.

I assume that the vegan in your life has shared this letter with you because they feel it reflects their personal experience. Still, you may be wondering who I am, and why I would be in a position to write this letter. I have a lot of experience working with vegans: I've spoken with thousands of vegans around the world, in 39 countries on six continents. And, although everybody's experience is unique, I've found that most vegans have certain experiences in common, and those are the experiences I've written about here. Also, I'm a psychologist specializing in relationships, especially relationships between vegans and non-vegans. And even though I'm a vegan

---

1 For simplicity, I've used the term "vegan" for both vegans and vegetarians.

today, I grew up eating meat, eggs, and dairy and I have many close relationships with people who are not vegan.

In all kinds of relationships—not only those between a vegan and someone who's not vegan—the key to feeling more connected (and being happier overall) is being able to "compassionately witness"[2] each other. Compassionate witnessing is listening—paying attention, with empathy, compassion, and, to the best of our ability, without judgement. When you and the vegan in your life compassionately witness each other, you gain mutual understanding and respect, and you feel safe talking about even the most challenging issues. Connection is only possible when we know and appreciate what the world looks like through each other's eyes, and when we can trust that the other will do their best to take our feelings into account when they say or do things that may impact us.

It's important for you and the vegan in your life to be compassionate witnesses to each other (as long as neither of you asks the other to witness experiences that go against your integrity or cause one of you to feel unsafe). This letter is intended to help you both start that process, by helping you witness the vegan in your life. The reason to start with you as the witness is because there's so little understanding of what it means to be vegan. For example, in the United States, there's only one vegan for every 49 meat eaters. And not only do most people have very little information about what the world of a vegan is really like, but there are a lot of misconceptions about veganism and vegans that can get in the way of non-vegans feeling connected with the vegans in their lives.

Thank you for being willing to be a witness to the vegan in your life.

To witness the vegan in your life, it's important to first understand the foundation of the vegan's experience—to understand what, exactly, veganism is. People often mistakenly believe that veganism is a trend, a religion, or a diet. It's true that in some places in the world, it's becoming trendy to be vegan, and like religions, veganism is based on values. It's also true that veganism is expressed in part through a diet. However, what veganism actually

---

2 This phrase was coined by Kaethe Weingarten in *Common Shock: Witnessing Violence Every Day* (New York: NAL Trade, Brown, 2004).

is, is a belief system that promotes compassion and respect for all beings.

And veganism is in alignment with the way most of us naturally think and feel—most of us genuinely care about animals and don't want them to suffer. But because we've grown up in a world that conditions us to eat certain types of animals (for example, depending on what culture you're from, you may have learned to eat pigs, chickens, or horses), we end up automatically thinking of these animals as food. We're taught, early on, to disconnect from the natural empathy we feel for farmed animals. Think about how you feel when you see piglets or chicks at a petting zoo or running and playing in a YouTube video. You probably naturally feel a connection with them and wouldn't want to think of them being harmed, and this feeling of connection and caring is your natural state.

The vegan values of compassion and respect for others are really human values, the values we all share, and vegans are working to create the kind of world we all want, a less violent world. So you and the vegan in your life are probably more in alignment than you might realize. Vegans aren't necessarily different from everybody else. They only seem different because the world is unfortunately set up so that most of us rarely get accurate information about veganism—and chronically misunderstood vegans, who are also frequently picked on, can start to feel, and act, like outsiders.

The main difference between vegans and non-vegans is that, at some point in their lives, vegans had an experience that caused them to realize that there's no real difference between farmed animals and other animals (when it comes to their ability to feel pleasure and pain and the fact that they have lives that matter to them). So vegans no longer see farmed animals as food. Once you have this kind of shift of perspective, your whole experience changes.

A useful way to understand the shift of perspective the vegan in your life had is to imagine the following scenario. One morning, you wake up to learn that all the meat, eggs, and dairy in the world around you are not, as you had believed, from pigs and chickens and cows but rather from dogs and cats. The person who exposed you to this truth takes you on a tour of the "real world" and shows you the factories where the animals are raised and killed. You see torment and hear yelps, hisses, and screams; you witness kittens being ground up alive, puppies being torn from their howling mother, animals being skinned and boiled while fully conscious. When you drive to work later that day, you see truckloads of these animals on their way to slaughter, their eyes and noses pushed through the slats in the sides of the vehicles, and you do everything possible to avert your eyes and harden your heart because you know you're helpless to save them.

Later, you return home to your family, who—like the rest of the world—was never exposed to the information that was shared with you and who's serving steak for dinner. When you look at the steak, you're flooded with memories of the horrors you just witnessed and feel overcome with emotion. You do your best to keep your feelings in check as you try to explain to your family what you've learned. But they didn't see what you saw, and to them you're coming across as a little deranged. Desperate to get them to see the world through your eyes, you press harder.

But they quickly become defensive and angry. The culture they were brought up in taught them to see the people who question eating dogs and cats as radicals, as overly emotional, and as caring more about animals than people. They've also been taught to believe that people like you are biased and are pushing an agenda that takes away their freedom of choice. They refuse to listen to you and tell you to stop imposing your values on others: "You make your choices, I'll make mine."

So the shift of perspective that vegans experience is a mixed bag. On one hand, becoming vegan is an incredibly empowering choice, a decision to live in alignment with the core values of compassion and justice in a world that makes it much easier to follow the path of least resistance. Many vegans say that becoming vegan has enabled them to feel a sense of pride and strength, knowing they're a part of something greater than their individual selves—a social movement that's transforming the world for the better. Vegans also say that they feel healthier and more connected with like-minded others. However, many vegans also feel chronically misunderstood, invisible, and invalidated, which can be depressing and exhausting. Perhaps most of all, it can be lonely.

A vegan is almost always the only vegan around, so they have nobody to speak with or for them, and they are frequently on the receiving end of disrespectful comments. Thousands of vegans have described, in tears, the way people commonly make jokes about their values and beliefs, often in front of others. And not only do they feel teased and humiliated, but they feel helpless to respond: either they stand up for themselves and their beliefs and are told they have no sense of humor, or they go along with the joke, which they find hurtful and offensive.

Vegans are also often on the receiving end of negative stereotyping, being told, for example, that they're overly emotional, extreme, or unhealthy. In fact, it's common for vegans who have a simple head cold to be told that they're sick because of their diet—so they feel they have to pretend to be perfectly healthy all the time, or veganism will be looked down on and they'll have let the animals down.

Countless vegans have also talked about how, as soon as they're identified as vegan, non-vegans start explaining all the ways veganism is "wrong." For example, a non-vegan may try to educate the vegan about nutrition, or about how animal agriculture is necessary for the economy, or how veganism is only accessible to rich people, and so on. People who have no experience with veganism suddenly become experts on the subject and start judging and arguing with the vegan, feeling entitled to put down or dismiss the vegan's deepest values and beliefs in a way they never would toward members of some other groups. One way to understand how vegans may feel in such circumstances is to imagine what it would seem like if non-Muslims teased a Muslim for not eating pork or if non-Christians told a Christian they'd just met that there's no such thing as God or debated the Bible with them.

Another struggle many vegans have is being constantly exposed to reminders of the very thing they find deeply distressing. After witnessing the horror of animal slaughter, vegans are continually surrounded by the aftermath of the killing—meat, eggs, and dairy. Even in their own homes, vegans often cannot find sanctuary; if those they are closest to don't understand their experience and needs, vegans can feel like nowhere is truly safe for them.

I've talked about some of the ways that vegans struggle in the world to help you better understand the experience of the vegan in your life. I know, though, that non-vegans can also struggle in certain ways. For example, a non-vegan may feel judged by the vegan in their life for continuing to eat animals, and they may feel unappreciated, that their efforts to reduce their consumption of meat, eggs, and dairy are never enough. If you're in this situation, try to understand that, while it's important that you and the vegan in your life find a way for you to feel witnessed and appreciated—everyone needs and deserves to have these needs met—the vegan probably isn't intentionally disregarding your needs. Vegans may end up acting in less-than-ideal ways because of the many frustrations they have to deal with living in a non-vegan world. They don't know what to do with the emotions that result from seeing the truth of what's happening to the animals, or from the resistance they encounter from the non-vegans around them. Once the vegan in your life feels seen and understood and respected for who they are and what they believe, they will very likely start seeing you as an ally rather than an opponent.

And ultimately, being a compassionate witness to the vegan in your life enables you to be a true ally to them. A "vegan ally" is someone who supports vegan values and the vegans in their life, even though they aren't vegan themselves. Being a vegan ally means being willing to listen to the vegan in your life, to learn about what it's like for them as a vegan in a non-vegan world, to hear what they would like from you in order to feel that you're standing beside them, supporting them in their struggle and appreciating their efforts. Try to appreciate that the vegan in your life is doing the best they can to cope with an emotionally devastating situation—a situation they have chosen to open their eyes and hearts to simply because they care, because they want to make the world a better place. And as a vegan ally, you help not only the vegan in your life; you also help the world. You become an integral part of the solution to the problem of animal suffering; allies are vitally important for bringing about positive social change.

If you can be an ally to the vegan in your life, you offer them a great gift. We should never underestimate the difference a single person can make when the other feels all alone. And in return, both of you will receive the gift of connection.